Library of
Davidson College

IBERO-AMERICANA:31

THE POPULATION OF CENTRAL MEXICO IN THE SIXTEENTH CENTURY

SHERBURNE F. COOK
AND
LESLEY BYRD SIMPSON

AMS PRESS
NEW YORK

THE POPULATION OF CENTRAL MEXICO IN THE SIXTEENTH CENTURY

BY

SHERBURNE F. COOK
AND
LESLEY BYRD SIMPSON

UNIVERSITY OF CALIFORNIA PRESS
BERKELEY AND LOS ANGELES
1948

Library of Congress Cataloging in Publication Data

Cook, Sherburne Friend, 1896-1974.
　　The population of central Mexico in the sixteenth century.

　　Reprint of the 1948 ed. published by University of California Press, Berkeley, which was issued as no. 31 of Ibero-Americana.
　　1. Mexico—Population—History. I. Simpson, Lesley Byrd, 1891-　　joint author. II. Title.
III. Series: Ibero-Americana; 31.
HB3531.C6　　1978　　　301.32′9′72　　　76-29408
ISBN 0-404-15333-X

301.32
C771p

86-7186

Reprinted from the edition of 1948, Berkeley
First AMS edition published in 1978

Manufactured in the United States of America

AMS PRESS INC.
NEW YORK, N.Y.

CONTENTS

	PAGE
INTRODUCTION	1
I. FORMULATION OF THE POPULATION DATA FOR 1565	10
II. THE POPULATION TREND, 1519–1600	17
The Population in 1519	18
The Population Trend, 1540–1570	39
The Population in 1597–1610	43
Conclusion	46
III. SUBSEQUENT POPULATION CHANGES	47
APPENDIX	
I. Tables of Population in 1565	49
II. Alphabetical List of Indian Communities	166
III. Numerical Index to Sketch Map	219
IV. Sketch Map of Sixteenth-century Indian Communities of Central Mexico . . . *following*	242

ILLUSTRATIONS

Graph of Population Decline, 1540–1570	42
Graph of Population Trend, 1519–1600	46

The Population of Central Mexico in the Sixteenth Century

Introduction

FROM HUMBOLDT'S day to the present the question of the size of Mexico's aboriginal population has challenged the ingenuity of investigators. The past two decades have been especially rich in demographic studies,[1] the most striking tendency of which is a consistent deflation of the figures given by ancient chroniclers. The authors of the present study decided to open the question again because they were singularly fortunate in having at hand a considerable body of unpublished material from the Spanish archives,[2] a careful examination of which convinced them that the estimates of sixteenth-century observers were much closer to the truth than those of modern scholars. A description of these documents will be found below in the section on sources.

Most of our population data were gathered between 1540 and 1570, thirty years of the most intense interest in the economic and demographic aspects of New Spain. The decade 1560–1570 is especially rich in statistical materials, which are drawn from sources so varied and independent that their essential agreement cannot be fortuitous. Thus we have been able to establish, so to speak, a statistical bench mark at about the year 1565, from which, with the use of supplementary data, we have been able to extrapolate reasonable population estimates for the time of the conquest, for the year

[1] C. Pérez Bustamante, "La población de Nueva España en el siglo XVI," *Boletín de la Biblioteca Menéndez y Pelayo*, Año X (1928); A. L. Kroeber, "Native American Population," *American Anthropologist*, Vol. 36 (1934); Miguel O. de Mendizábal, "Demografía colonial del Siglo XVI: 1519–1599," *Boletín de la Sociedad Mexicana de Geografía y Estadística*, tomo 48 (Mexico, 1939); George Kubler, "Population Movements in Mexico," *Hispanic American Historical Review*, Vol. 22 (1942); Angel Rosenblat, *La población indígena de América desde 1492 hasta la actualidad* (Buenos Aires, 1945); Gonzalo Aguirre Beltrán, *La población negra de México* (Mexico, 1946).

[2] Collected by Dr. Sanford A. Mosk and placed at their disposal by Dr. C. O. Sauer, both of the University of California.

1540, and for the end of the sixteenth century. Methods of calculation will be discussed more fully in the appropriate sections below.

Identification of the 1,600-odd communities concerned was necessary in order to avoid duplication, and to that end the Sketch Map was prepared. By comparing all available data we were able to identify virtually all Indian communities of importance, containing about ninety per cent of the population of the time. Although we believe that we have eliminated the danger of duplication, nevertheless there is some likelihood of omissions, owing to loss of documents or to contemporary ignorance of the more inaccessible parts of the country. Since, however, there is no way to assess such omissions, we have ignored them, in the belief that they would not materially disturb our calculations.

An examination of the Sketch Map reveals some startling lacunae: in the provinces of Coatzacoalcos, Río de Alvarado, the lower Huasteca and the Gulf Coast generally, and in the more broken sections of Michoacán, Jalisco, Guerrero, and Oaxaca. In all these places there were Indian towns in the early sixteenth century and later which cannot be identified on modern maps. The explanation of the disappearance of so many towns calls for extended study and can only be suggested here. First, it is to be noted that most of the vanished communities were in the hot country and that in the sixteenth century they were exploited principally for cacao, a crop the cultivation of which was notoriously wasteful of man power. Almost all the maize-supported communities of the plateau, on the other hand, have persisted through the centuries and still pursue the maize economy of preconquest times. Second, two of the worst spots, the lower Huasteca and Nueva Galicia, suffered the slave-catching and the senseless devastation of Nuño de Guzmán's conquest, which either destroyed or permanently dislocated the population. Third, the evidence is fairly conclusive that the coastal plains were at one time more heavily populated than they are today. It may be that certain diseases, such as dysentery, yellow fever, and European types of malaria, which became endemic there, prevented recovery. However it was, the probability remains that the population of those districts was much greater at the time of the conquest than we have allowed for, because contemporary opinion is unanimous regarding its violent diminution, even before 1530—our earliest records,—and therefore our estimates probably err on the short side.

The wayward spelling of Indian names in the Spanish documents has led us to adopt, for all identified communities, the official spelling of the 1920 Mexican census, which, incidentally, is frequently much closer to the phonetics of the originals than are the early records. One extreme example is afforded by a town which the documents call "Laustam," in the vicinity of Taxco, and which turns out to be Alahuixtlán, Guerrero. An index of such variants would be useful but would require a lengthy treatise by itself. The two indexes which we have prepared will, however, allow the reader, with a little patience, to identify all the communities here treated.

Sources.—Below are listed all the documentary sources which we have assembled in our tables. The initial letter by which they are identified refers to the column in the tables in which the material is analyzed.

A. *Suma de Visitas*, in *Papeles de Nueva España*, Vol. 1, ed. Francisco del Paso y Troncoso (Madrid, 1905).

This basic document was the first attempt at a comprehensive demographic and economic survey of New Spain, compiled at the time of the *visita* of Francisco Tello de Sandoval, as established by Kubler (*op. cit.*, p. 618). It is, however, a compilation of extant materials, and a comparison of it with the MS *Relación de las tasaciones* (q.v., "C" below) reveals that the data included in it extend over the period 1531–1544, and that there are wide differences in its treatment of the various provinces—differences in time, in methods of gathering, and in criteria of evaluation. The *Suma* is further deficient in that it omits very important sections of the country, e.g., the entire Marquesado del Valle, the province of Tlaxcala, and many of the larger Crown holdings. Therefore, in our attempt to establish the population in 1565 we have used the *Suma* data only where other data are lacking.

A statement must be included here regarding the degree of reliability of the *Suma*. George Kubler, citing an opinion of Mendieta, assumes that the population estimates of the *Suma* are too high because of the desire of the encomenderos to force more tribute and labor out of the Indians, but his assumption does not stand up under a comparison of the *Suma* with later counts. On the contrary, the estimates given in the *Suma* are demonstrably too low, because the early *visitadores* were rarely able to make an original count, but had to rely upon the figures supplied by *encomenderos* and *corregidores*, and it was their universal complaint at all times that the former, at least, concealed or depressed the number of their tributaries. It seems to have been a plain case of concealing assets from the tithe collector and of distracting the attention of the poverty-stricken Crown from the wealth of the encomiendas, which the Crown had been consistently expropriating since 1528. A notorious example of this kind of tax dodging is afforded by the Marquesado del Valle. Cortés had been granted 23,000 tributaries, along with his title of Marqués del Valle, but Crown officials repeatedly complained that although the number was really several times as great they were not allowed to make an original count.

B. *Relación de las tasaciones de los pueblos de yndios ... que están encomendados en personas particulares.* 1560. MS. Archivo General de Indias, Seville, *Indiferente general*, leg. 1529 [145-7-8], 18 ff. Also in *Epistolario de Nueva España*, ed. Francisco del Paso y Troncoso (Mexico, 1940), Vol. 9, pp. 2–48.

Relación de las tasaciones de los pueblos de yndios ... que están en la Real Corona. 1560. MS. Archivo General de Indias, Seville, *Patronato*, leg. 181 [2-2-2], ramo 38, 11 ff.

These two *relaciones* are essentially parts of the same one and are so used in our tabulation. The first is the so-called "Lista de Ybarra," and both were compiled for the purpose of assessing tithes—hence we refer to them below as the "tithing list." They afford a valuable addition to the information supplied by the *Suma*, giving data on many pueblos not listed in the latter. They were compiled after the rationalization of the tribute into "pesos de oro común" (*ca.* 1553), which was assessed at one peso a head of family, and they thus give us a direct means of calculating the population. They suffer, however, from the same tendency which was noted in the *Suma*; that is, there is throughout the tithing list a consistent depression of the figures.

The depression is well illustrated by a comparison of the values given for the Cortés estate (the Marquesado del Valle) with the inventory of that estate made in 1569 after its confiscation by the Crown, following the implication of Martín Cortés in the abortive rebellion of 1566 (Archivo General de Indias, *Audiencia de México*, leg. 256 [60-1-39], Doc. 37).

Number	Town	Value 1560	Value 1567
95	Coyoacán (D. F.)	1,890	5,271½
20	Cuilapan (Oax.)	1,400	7,464
11	Cuernavaca (Mor.)	11,840	27,300
26	Etla (Oax.)	1,000	2,439
76	Jalapa (Oax.)	750	928½
823	Matalcingo (Mich.)	270	619
30	Oaxaca (Oax.)	1,500	1,257
228	Oaxtepec (Mor.)	3,412	3,669½
95	Tacubaya (D. F.)	240	631
210	Tehuantepec (Oax.)	3,442	3,442
142	Tepoztlán (Mor.)	1,150	2,718½
45	Toluca (Méx.)	3,700	6,949
58	Tuxtla (V. C.)	1,000	1,060
142	Yautepec (Mor.)	3,050	4,973
5	Yecapistla (Mor.)	2,670	6,120
	Totals	37,314	72,139

The inventory is based upon the real assessments made prior to 1567, and the values there given may, with no great risk of overstatement, be taken as the real values of 1560. Index numbers at the left refer to the Sketch Map.

The only two discrepancies occur in Oaxaca and Tehuantepec; in the former the 1567 value is lower than the 1560 value, and in the latter it is the same. The first cannot be explained, but the Tehuantepec value is probably correct, because that territory was taken over by the Crown prior to 1560, and the value given represents the compensation allowed to the Cortés estate.

Fraud of the magnitude practiced by the Cortés interests cannot, to be sure, be taken as typical of all encomenderos. The Cortés estate, being (1) the largest holding in New Spain and (2) being held in perpetuity, occupied a privileged position. Prior to 1567 it had never been subjected to official inspection, or had successfully resisted it. The difference, however, is merely one of degree, as all encomenderos had the same motive for concealing assets.

Because of this tendency in the tithing list we have used it, as we have the *Suma*, only where other sources of information are lacking.

C. *Relación de las tasaciones que se han hecho en los pueblos que están en la Corona Real en esta Nueva España.* 1571. MS. Archivo General de Indias, Seville, *Patronato*, leg. 182 [2-2-3], ramo 40, 90 ff.

"C" contains the most complete list of Crown towns. Its great value, aside from that, lies in its giving the history of the tribute assessments of each town from 1531 to 1571. It shows, in the frequent adjustment of assessments, that the Crown consistently attempted to modify the tribute according to ability to pay.

D. *Relación del distrito y pueblos del Obispado de Tlaxcala.* Por Alonso Pérez de Andrada, Vicario General. *Ca.* 1570. In *Epistolario de Nueva España*, ed. Francisco del Paso y Troncoso (Mexico, 1940), Vol. 14, pp. 70–101.

"D" is one of the most detailed and useful of the *relaciones geográficas*.

E. *Relación de los pueblos que están en la Corona Real*. ... Ca. 1570. MS. Archivo General de Indias, *Audiencia de México*, leg. 323 [60-3-23], 6 ff.

"E" was compiled independently of "C" and confirms and supplements the latter.

F. *Relación de los tributos de los pueblos del Obispado de Tlaxcala*. 1570. MS. Archivo General de Indias, *Audiencia de México*, leg. 270 [60-2-6], 2 ff.

"F" supplements "D."

G. *Relación de todos los conventos y beneficios que ai en esta provincia de la Guasteca de Pánuco*. ... Ca. 1570. MS. Archivo General de Indias, Seville, *Audiencia de México*, leg. 1841 [92-2-1], 2 ff.

"G" is one of our few sources for the devastated province of Pánuco and is, unfortunately, extremely brief.

H. *Relaciones de los pueblos de la Nueva España cuya doctrina estaba a cargo de los padres agustinos*. 1569–1571. MS. Archivo General de Indias, Seville, *Indiferente general*, leg. 1529 [145-7-7] and [145-7-8], 60 ff.

The extraordinary care with which "H" was compiled makes it one of the most trustworthy documents in our collection. It describes each *cabecera* with its *sujetos*, giving distances between them and the number of tributaries and *confesantes* in each, and it usually states whether the information was verified or not.

I. *Relación de los pueblos de yndios que los religiosos de Sant Agustín tienen a su cargo*. ... Por Fray Juan Adrián, Provincial. 1572. MS. Archivo General de Indias, Seville, *Patronato*, leg. 182 [2-2-3], ramo 44, 6 ff.

"I" was compiled independently of "H" and includes some towns not mentioned in the latter.

J. *Cartas de religiosos*. 1565–1570. In *Relación de los obispados de Tlaxcala, Michoacán, Oaxaca y otros lugares*, ed. Luis García Pimentel (Mexico, 1904), pp. 97–153.

K. *Descripción del Arzobispado de México, hecha en 1570*, ed. Luis García Pimentel (Mexico, 1897). "K" is a companion piece to "D."

L. *Lista de los pueblos de indios encomendados en personas particulares*. 1565-1570. In same volume as "J," pp. 153-188. "L" has the disadvantage, from our standpoint, of lumping together all the towns held by each encomendero, regardless of location. Since many of the more important encomenderos held towns in widely separated districts, the difficulty of utilizing the statistics is obvious.

M. *Relación de los obispados*. ... 1565-1570. In the same volume as "J," but is a separate list from "J" and "L."

N. *Geografía y descripción universal de las Indias*. Por Juan López de Velasco. 1571. Ed. Justo Zaragoza (Madrid, 1894). A difficulty in the use of Velasco's statistics arises from his habit of including under one town a great deal of territory which in other descriptions falls under separate towns. Where such has obviously been the case we have had to ignore his figures for fear of duplication.

O. *Relaciones geográficas de la Nueva España*. 1579-1584. MS. Academia de la Historia, Madrid, 12-18-3. Published in part in *Papeles de Nueva España*, ed. Francisco del Paso y Troncoso (Madrid, 1905), Vols. 3 to 7.

This second series of *relaciones* was intended to correct and amplify the information gathered in the series of 1570, but for some reason, probably the great length of the *interrogatorio*, it lacks the precision characteristic of the first.

P. *Información ... sobre el estado en que se encontraba la sucesión de indios*. ... 1597. In *Epistolario de Nueva España*, ed. Francisco del Paso y Troncoso (Mexico, 1940), Vol. 13, pp. 3-48.

"P" is the last of many petitions to the Crown to grant the encomiendas in perpetuity. For our purpose it has the disadvantage of omitting all descriptions of towns, not even placing them in their bishoprics. In common with its kind, it sets forth at great length the pitiable state to which the encomen-

Introduction

deros have sunk because of the expropriation of their holdings and the rapid diminution of the Indian population. Since all such documents are suspect, because it was to the encomendero's interest to make out as pathetic a case as possible for himself, we have used the figures in "P" only as a collateral basis for estimating the population in 1600.[3]

---
[3] One source which, unfortunately, we were unable to use in our statistical analysis is the report of the Franciscan order, compiled about 1570 and published by J. García Icazbalceta in Volume 2 of his *Nueva Colección de Documentos para la Historia de México*, under the title of *Códice Franciscano*, pp. 1–32 (Mexico, 1888). The Franciscan report is a slapdash affair, evidently based upon hearsay and not upon original counts; e.g., "Los vecinos de Toluca serán al pie de cinco mil" (p. 9); "Ternán ambos estos pueblos [de Tenayuca] tres o cuatro mil vecinos" (p. 10); and so on throughout the report.

I. FORMULATION OF THE POPULATION DATA FOR 1565

THE NUMERICAL data derived from the documentary sources previously discussed are set forth in detail, in the tables which constitute Appendix I. The localities represented have been treated in units corresponding to the modern Mexican states, since the lack of early maps and clear-cut political boundaries make any other treatment too inexact for identification. Within each state are listed first the towns which we have been able to identify, indicated by numbers. Thereafter appear such places as clearly lie within the state boundaries but the precise location of which we have been unable to discover. It was possible to designate some of the intrastate subdivisions, in particular the Mixtec, Zapotec, and Chontal areas of Oaxaca, and the Pánuco and Coatzacoalcos regions of Vera Cruz. A moderate number of towns could be assigned only to the ancient bishoprics and are so listed. Finally, a few places could not be identified at all and were included in a separate category at the end of the tables.

Within each table certain standard information is presented. In the first column is the key number of the town, referring to the Sketch Map. Absence of such a number denotes a town the exact location of which is unknown. The second column lists the name, spelled, when known, according to the 1920 Mexican census. The next fifteen columns, lettered A through P, give the population figures for each town. The letters designate the documentary sources described in the Introduction and the columns are arranged from left to right in approximate chronological order. Thus A refers to the *Suma de Visitas* (*ca.* 1540), B to the tithing list of 1560, and so on down to the encomienda list of 1597, column P. The next column is reserved for special items derived from other sources, and the final column gives our estimate of the population in 1565.

Formulation of Data for 1565

Within each column from A to P inclusive there is a double entry. The entry on the left is the number of units derived from the original source together with a key letter indicating the type of unit involved. Thus, *p* represents pesos of tribute; *t*, tributaries; *c*, *confesantes*; and *tp*, total population. The right-hand entry is the population derived from the left-hand entry. In some of the columns, particularly A, there are figures in parentheses which denote values calculated from general ratios. The raw data almost invariably appear as (1) monetary or other units of taxation or (2) as categories of persons. The variability in terminology has been commented upon by previous investigators, frequently with the inference that to reduce the system to workable form is impossible. Nevertheless, a detailed examination of the documents has convinced us that the contrary is true.

The early taxation lists, such as those in the *Suma de Visitas* (column A), following the Aztec system, give the tribute in kind, or as commodities.[1] In or about 1553, however, the viceregal government introduced a system whereby the tribute was rationalized into money and maize, each tributary being assessed one peso and half a *fanega* (hundredweight) of maize a year. We are safe, therefore, in accepting the principle that, after 1553, one peso in tribute is the equivalent of one tributary. That such a procedure is sound, on the evidence of contemporary documents, is demonstrated by the constantly repeated identity of value between tributaries and pesos of tribute, and their free interchange of category.[2]

The early administrators of New Spain employed a varied and confusing terminology for tributaries, and the matter was further complicated by their counting bachelors, spinsters, widowers, and widows as half a tributary each. Thus we find in the records the terms *tributario, vecino, casado, vecino ca-*

---
[1] Since the preconquest tribute lists, such as that found in the *Codex Mendocino*, are not based upon any concept of head tax, their use for estimating population is probably out of the question.
[2] In a few localities the procedure was reversed, the assessment per tributary being half a peso and one *fanega* of maize a year.

sado, tributario casado, and *vecino tributante* used indiscriminately to designate a married man or head of a family. Often, particularly in Michoacán and Nueva Galicia, we find the terms *indio de carga, indio de servicio,* and *persona* also used for *tributario.* The meaning of *persona* varied with the habit of the writer: it is clear by comparison with collateral documents that many times he had in mind *tributario;* at other times, *habitante.* It has been necessary, therefore, to examine each term in its context and to determine its meaning.

The expression *personas de confesión,* or *confesantes,* employed by clerical writers is unequivocal in its meaning, since they repeatedly state that it applies to males "de catorce años arriba" and to females "de doce años arriba."

Rather infrequently the population is given as a whole "sin los niños," or "sin los niños de teta." Alternatively the expression used is "sin los niños de tres años arriba." It is clear, then, that the universal custom in population counts was to omit all infants under four years of age.

In order to convert from any of these units to total population a series of factors must be set up, the most important of which is that pertaining to tributaries. Fortunately, the material basic to an exact calculation is provided by the documentary sources themselves. For 43 representative towns we have figures showing both *tributarios* and *confesantes.* For 91 towns there are data for both *casados* and persons over three years of age. These constitute statistically adequate, unselected samples from the country at large.

One may readily estimate the total population of a town from the number of *confesantes,* for it is a reasonable and safe assumption that the *proportion* of the total population represented by children under fifteen years of age (for males) and under thirteen years of age (for females) is substantially the same today as it was in the sixteenth century. The same principle may be applied to infants under four years of age. The Mexican census of 1930 shows (1) that females over twelve, plus males over fourteen, constituted 62.6 per cent of the total population, and (2) that individuals of both sexes over four constituted 87.9 per cent. In these two categories, then, values may be directly converted into total population. We may now determine for each of the two lists of towns the ratio of *tributarios* and *casados* to population. The results are as follows:

LIST 1

A. *Tributarios* of 43 towns............... 43,562
B. Population of same.................. 168,847
C. Ratio of sums....................... 0.2579
D. Mean ratio of individual towns........ 0.2579
    For D, standard deviation............ 0.0257
    Probable error...................... 0.0173

LIST 2

A. *Casados* of 91 towns................. 97,508
B. Population of same.................. 386,053
C. Ratio of sums....................... 0.2525
D. Mean ratio of individual towns........ 0.2722
    For D, standard deviation............ 0.0443
    Probable error...................... 0.0299

It is clear, then, that since all means lie within the probable error there is no significant difference between *casados* and *tributarios* in their relationship to the total population. This is a fact of basic importance, since it permits us forthwith to neglect minor variations in terminology and to employ the same conversion factor for *tributarios, casados, vecinos,* and the rest. The factor lies very slightly above four, but we shall still be within the probable error if we employ the flat value of four. Accordingly, throughout all our calculations the total population has been derived by multiplying by four the tribute in pesos, the *tributarios, casados,* or their variants.[3]

The decade between 1560 and 1570 represents the interval of greatest stability in the population of sixteenth-century

---

[3] Ralph Roys and France Scholes, of the Carnegie Institution, arrived at the same factor of four in calculating the ratio of tributaries to population in sixteenth-century Yucatan. (Verbal note by Dr. Roys.)

Mexico. There was no epidemic of major proportions. The dislocation immediately following the conquest was over. New measures had been taken to place the economic and social status of the natives on a more reasonable and permanent basis. Fortunately, it was during this period that most of the reliable documents pertaining to population appeared, and hence our information for this decade is unusually trustworthy. We have therefore taken the middle year of 1565 as our basic datum for population.

A perusal of the tables will show that the information available varies widely from town to town. For some there exists only the *Suma de Visitas,* the *Relaciones geográficas,* or some other single source. Concerning other towns there are numerous reports. To secure a first approximation of the population in 1565 it has been necessary to adopt a consistent but somewhat empirical policy.

In treating each town in all of central Mexico except Nueva Galicia the final column (estimated population) has been filled as follows: If only the *Suma de Visitas* is used, the value from column A is transferred direct. Similarly, if only the tithing list of 1560 is used, the value from column B is transferred. If data from both sources are available, the more authoritative *Suma* only is used. If we have a figure from the *Relaciones geográficas,* column O, it is used regardless of A or B. In no circumstances is the encomienda list of 1597, column P, included among other sources to derive the final figure. If any value can be derived from columns C to N inclusive, it is used to the exclusion of all others. If, as most frequently happens, there are two or more values available in this group, their *average* is entered as the population. The result is a total figure predominantly but not exclusively derived from data obtained close to 1565. Reckoning by this method gives, for 1565, a total of 3,945,945 persons alive in the territory now included in the states of Hidalgo, México, Puebla, Tlaxcala, Morelos, Guerrero, Oaxaca, Vera Cruz, and Michoacán, together with small portions of San Luis Potosí,

Querétaro, and Guanajuato. The population of Nueva Galicia, included in the modern states of Jalisco, Nayarit, Sinaloa, and southern Zacatecas, was calculated in a somewhat different manner, as will appear below.

In order to derive a more exact value for the date chosen, an indirect method has been adopted, yielding what we may designate the *adjusted population* of 1565. For this purpose the data from the *Suma de Visitas* have served as a point of reference. It should be strongly emphasized that totals obtained directly from this source, without special qualification, are to be regarded only as means to an end and not necessarily as reflecting actual conditions at the time of the *Suma*, as pointed out in our Introduction. We employ the *Suma* in the present connection merely because it is the most complete single source of data.

There are 296 towns for which there are population estimates from the *Suma* and also from the documents of 1560–1570, the latter values being designated for convenience the C–N average. For each of the 296 towns the ratio of the C–N average to the *Suma* has been computed. The mean is 1.308. The variability is high, the standard deviation being 0.811. However, the number of population estimates is large and the standard error of the mean is only 0.047, or, roughly, 3.6 per cent of the mean. It is now possible to derive a close approximation to the values for the towns for which we have a C–N average but no *Suma* by dividing the former values by 1.308, or, more conveniently and with no serious error, by 1.3. The adjusted *Suma* values, thus derived, for 449 towns, exclusive of Nueva Galicia, have been inserted in the tables, with the use of parentheses to distinguish adjusted from original values.

There are 52 towns for which there are no data from C to N, but for which there are values from the tithing list of 1560, column B. In order to determine the relationship between B and the C–N average, the data from 282 towns were tabulated and the ratio of C–N to B was computed. The mean ratio is 1.290, almost the same as the ratio of C–N to the *Suma* values. It is therefore justifiable to make a direct transfer from column B to column A.

If all the values, original and derived, in column A are added, the total is 3,234,385 for central Mexico, exclusive of Nueva Galicia. It should again be pointed out that this is not a true figure, since it has been demonstrated that the population estimates of the *Suma* are much too low. However, if we now multiply the *Suma* total by our derived factor of 1.3, we shall arrive at the final or adjusted population for 1565, since we shall have corrected for those towns the populations of which were entered directly in the first approximation from A or B. Our adjusted total, then, is 4,204,700, without reckoning Nueva Galicia.

The estimate for Nueva Galicia had to be attacked somewhat differently, for the *Suma* figures for it are much higher than later counts. For 21 towns of Nueva Galicia the *Suma*/ C–N ratio is 1.5 (against the ratio of 0.77 for central Mexico), with the standard deviation 0.773 and the standard error of the mean 0.169. Using the same method as before, we have inserted calculated values for the *Suma* for all towns which lack such data. The total for the *Suma*, then, is 306,720. If we divide this total by our factor of 1.5, we get an adjusted value for Nueva Galicia in 1565 of 204,480, which brings our total population of central Mexico in 1565 to 4,409,180.[4]

---

[4] The reasons for the higher count for Nueva Galicia in the *Suma de Visitas* may be surmised, with a good deal of supporting testimony from contemporary witnesses. The conquest of Nueva Galicia, carried out by Nuño de Guzmán between 1530 and 1537, was the most dismal episode in the history of New Spain. Whole provinces were destroyed and the people dispersed. It seems probable that the *visitas* of Nueva Galicia included in the *Suma* were made after the removal of Nuño de Guzmán and before the devastating Mixtón War of 1541. That war and the ensuing border strife probably continued the steep decline in the population begun by Guzmán, so that the estimates of the 1560–1570 period do not reflect the relative stability achieved by the central plateau.

II. THE POPULATION TREND, 1519–1600

THE ESTIMATE of population derived for 1565 we believe to be reasonably accurate and probably the soundest that can be had for sixteenth-century Mexico. Nevertheless, from the demographic point of view it is important to obtain some notion of the magnitude of the decline in population during the first hundred years subsequent to the conquest. This can be achieved only in broad outline, since with the information now available or ever likely to be uncovered it is impossible to determine annual or even decennial fluctuations of a minor or local sort.

That the number of inhabitants was steadily diminishing is attested by a wealth of evidence. The statements of Crown and Church officials, private citizens, missionaries, and many others are unanimous with respect to the alarming and constant diminution of the native population. From 1560 onward, the documentary sources show a reduction in tribute or tributaries. We know that in the decades 1540–1550, 1570–1580, and 1590–1600 there were widespread and highly destructive epidemics. It has been demonstrated also that well into the seventeenth and eighteenth centuries there was a progressive tightening of the labor supply, accompanied by a rising wage scale.[1]

Perhaps the most conclusive piece of internal evidence is the fact that during the period 1550–1580 the family number averaged four persons. Since we are dealing actually with the social family, including relatives as well as parents and children, the natural family number was probably somewhat smaller. It is generally conceded that for an ideal population merely to maintain its numbers the natural family must be at least four, i.e., two parents and two children. But to achieve equilibrium the two children must live and reproduce. Hence in any actual population more than two children must

---

[1] L. B. Simpson, *The Repartimiento System of Native Labor in New Spain and Guatemala*, Univ. Calif. Publ., Ibero-Americana: 13 (Berkeley, 1938), *passim*.

be born if stability is to be secured. Under very good conditions a family number of five would indicate a population in equilibrium, or, perhaps, on the increase, but with the illness and poverty characteristic of sixteenth-century Mexico the number should be nearer six.

A low family number implies not only a high death rate resulting from disease and poor living conditions, but also a relatively low birth rate. One would therefore expect to find an uninterrupted downward trend in the population curve. There would perhaps be periods of rapid fall coinciding with severe epidemics or destructive wars, alternating with periods of partial stabilization. But at no time, with a family number of four, could there have been any material increase.[2] Hence any apparent-rise in the curve must be due to error in, or misinterpretation of, the documents from which the data were extracted.

In attempting to trace the course of population change in sixteenth-century Mexico, by plotting a curve or by any other method, we are forced to rely upon a very few critical dates. The most solidly established point is that corresponding to 1565. With this as a starting point, it is possible to derive two others with fair accuracy: the time of the conquest and the end of the century. In a less satisfactory manner it is possible also to get a value for approximately 1540.

The Population in 1519
Clerical Estimates

The first source of information to be considered will be the baptismal records of the missionaries who were actively engaged in conversion during the early period of Spanish colonization, immediately following the military conquest. Cortés completed the destruction of the Aztec power in 1521. The first Franciscan missionaries arrived in 1524 and began their work actively in 1525. By 1540 the initial phase of evangelization was substantially over.

[2] This principle was ignored by George Kubler, in his article cited above, with the result that he derived population curves which run counter to general experience.

Population Trend: 1519–1600 19

No actual count of baptisms has come down to us. We have, however, certain summaries or estimates of totals made by the participating friars. The numbers they reported are so large that grave doubt has been cast upon their reliability by modern historians. No competent student, we believe, has charged the friars with deliberate falsification, but their accounts have been considered grossly exaggerated. Now, extreme and uniform overestimates could have arisen from two causes only: (1) willful desire to magnify the exploits of the missionaries, and (2) slipshod bookkeeping. Of the first charge the missionaries, particularly such men as Motolinía, must be absolved. As to the second charge, we are not convinced that the missionaries' estimates of baptisms were faulty from negligence, or even that they are at complete variance with the facts. In the first place, although exact enumerations were hardly to be expected, it was definitely to the interest of the clergy to know who had been converted and who not; that is to say, the number of conversions at any particular time. Second, it was highly desirable to keep track of conversions, not only for spiritual purposes, but also for material considerations, such as the tithes collected from the encomenderos on the basis of their Indians and labor assessments. Third, the provincials and commissaries of the missionary orders were too well acquainted with their territories to tolerate gross misrepresentation in the baptismal claims. Finally, it should be pointed out that no one at the time, or since, was or is in a better position than the early missionaries to estimate the number of conversions, and to ignore their testimony would be a strange departure from historical method. Figures from ecclesiastical sources, then, may be used with a fair degree of confidence, but naturally with the reservation that the results must coincide within reasonable limits with those obtained by other methods.

In 1531 the Bishop of Mexico, Fray Juan de Zumárraga,[3] stated that by that time "more than a million persons" had

---

[3] Zumarraga to the Capítulo General de Tolosa, June 12, 1531. In Joaquín García Icazbalceta, *Don Fray Juan de Zumárraga* (Mexico, 1881), pp. 57 ff.

been baptized. Later, Motolinía[4] said that between 1521 and 1536 "more than four million souls were baptized." This figure is raised to 5,000,000 by Mendieta, who adds that by 1540 it had risen to not less than 6,000,000.[5] The analysis of baptismal figures by Motolinía is the most detailed that we possess and is worth citing *in extenso* to demonstrate the sincerity, if not the statistical competence, of this famous missionary. He uses two methods, which are summarized below.

a) By priests. In 1536 there were sixty Franciscan priests in all New Spain. (The other orders had not yet baptized many Indians, according to Motolinía.) In addition, forty others had been there, but of these twenty had returned to Spain and twenty had died. Five of those no longer present had baptized about 100,000 each, or 500,000 in all. Forty of those still present had likewise baptized about 100,000 each, or 4,000,000 in all. The total would be about 4,500,000. Torquemada, writing at a later date, supports Motolinía by citing names: according to him, Fathers Cisneros, Caro, Perpiñán, and Facuencia performed more than 100,000 baptisms each, and Father Motolinía, 300,000.[6]

b) By regions. Motolinía specifies the following towns and provinces:

1. México, Xochimilco, Tlamanalco, Chalco, Cuernavaca, Yecapixtla, Huaquechula, Chietla . . . . +1,000,000
2. Texcoco, Otumba, Tepeapulco, Tulancingo, Cuautitlán, Tula, Xilotepec . . . . +1,000,000
3. Tlaxcala, Puebla, Cholula, Huejotzingo, Calpa, Tepeaca, Zacatlán, Hueytlalpa . . . . +1,000,000
4. South Sea Coast 1,000,000
5. Converted since this calculation was made 500,000

Total 4,500,000

Motolinía thought this estimate too conservative and hazarded the opinion that the number reached 9,000,000.

---

[4] Toribio de Benevente (Motolinía), *Historia de los indios de la Nueva España*, ed. D. S. García (Barcelona, 1914), p. 105.
[5] Jerónimo de Mendieta, *Historia-eclesiástica indiana*, ed. Joaquín García Icazbalceta (4 vols., Mexico, 1945), Vol. 2, p. 124.
[6] Juan de Torquemada, *Monarquía Indiana* (Madrid, 1723), Vol. 3, p. 156.

Population Trend: 1519–1600

However, if we allow an additional 500,000 to account for regions not covered in his list, we get 5,000,000. A further million baptisms between 1536 and 1540 would yield Motolinía's figure for that date.[7]

Since the value 4,500,000 represents baptisms performed continuously from 1525 to 1536, there remains to be calculated the initial or existing population as of the end of 1524. The number of baptisms equaled the initial population, minus those persons living in 1524 who were never baptized, plus those born after 1524 who were baptized.

Of the first category, some died and some resisted conversion. Assuming, as is reasonable in the circumstances, a death rate of 100 per 1,000 and a failure of the missionaries to convert 10 per cent of the survivors, approximately 20.6 per cent of the original population must be added to the number baptized. With respect to the second group, we may assume that there was a birth rate of 40 per 1,000 and that 10 per cent of the newly born missed baptism—in which case, 32.4 per cent must be deducted from the initial population to get the number baptized.

The relationships may be formulated in a simple equation. If p represents the population in 1524, and 4,500,000 were baptized between that year and 1537, then:

$$p = 4,500,000 + 0.206\,p - 0.324\,p\,;$$

or,

$$p = \frac{4,500,000}{1.118} = 3,781,000.$$

---

[7] *Op. cit.*, pp. 107–108. There are numerous separate totals of baptisms which, taken together, lend probability to Motolinía's estimate. Torquemada (*op. cit.*, Vol. 3, p. 156) says that in 1537 there were 60,000 baptisms in Tepeaca province alone. One priest in 1539 baptized 3,600 in one day in Toluca. At the convent of Huaquechula, according to Torquemada (p. 163), for three months natives came from as far distant as twenty leagues to be baptized. In five days within this time, he says, Motolinía and two other priests baptized 40,200. In Xochimilco (p. 152) 15,000 were baptized in one day. Nicolás León, in his work, *Los Popolocas* (*Anales del Museo Nacional de México*, Ser. 2, Vol. 2, Mexico, 1905, p. 107), reports that the first apostle to Tecamachalco baptized more than 15,000 there in the year 1540. There is nothing inherently impossible or unreasonable in these claims.

To get the preconquest value it is further necessary to correct for the decline between 1519 and 1524, which was great, since these five years included the casualties of war, the famine accompanying the campaigns of Cortés, and the very bad smallpox epidemic. A 20 per cent gross mortality would not be too great to ascribe to these causes, thus yielding a preconquest value of 4,726,000, or, say, 4,700,000.

This figure, it must be borne in mind, is based upon Motolinía's baptism estimate for the Franciscan territory, which is much less extensive than that being considered in this study. A glance at Motolinía's breakdown by regions will show the absence of the Huasteca country, the coastal strip of Vera Cruz, most of Oaxaca, parts of Guerrero, and much of Michoacán and Hidalgo. And even if some of these peripheral areas were included, nevertheless the proportion of the population baptized must have been as yet very small, possibly not more than half. The initial estimate of 4,700,000 will therefore have to be increased to account for the territories not fully or even partly evangelized. For these territories values derived from our documentary sources (see tables) may be taken as follows: Huasteca and Vera Cruz, 430,000; Oaxaca and Guerrero, 2,100,000; Michoacán and Hidalgo, 1,800,000. The final total, then, of the population in 1519, according to clerical estimates, would be 9,030,000, exclusive of Nueva Galicia.

MILITARY ESTIMATES

A second indirect means of achieving a value for the population at the time of the conquest is based upon the estimates of the conquistadores themselves and subsequent narrators concerning the size of Indian armies, enemy and allied. The charge of exaggeration has also been leveled at the military men. It has been stated, with perhaps some justification, that there was a tendency among them to magnify the size of hostile armies in order to glorify the exploits of the Spaniards. Certain considerations, however, may temper the force of this criticism. In the first place, our two primary witnesses were constant participants in the events of the conquest, and both were competent and responsible. Although Cortés, in his letters to the emperor, colored his narrative to further his political ambitions, it is very doubtful that he deliberately indulged in wide distortion of material facts, such as the size of armies, or, indeed, that he had any motive for so doing. In most respects his letters give the impression of being a faithful and exact portrayal of existing conditions. Bernal Díaz' *True History*, although written forty years after the conquest, is full of firsthand observation which supplements the statements of Cortés to an extraordinary degree.[8] The testimony of two such experienced witnesses must be accepted as representing the soundest contemporary opinion and as probably coming fairly close to the truth. In the second place, it is not likely that Cortés or Bernal Díaz would overestimate the numbers of the Indian allies of the Spaniards, since, on the whole, neither of them is prone to give more credit than he must to the natives who fought on his side. If their estimate of the enemy is too large, that of the Indian allies should be too small. Nevertheless, the order of magnitude ascribed to the two groups is essentially the same.

In the third place, the size of the Indian armies and labor battalions operating in 1519 and 1520, as stated throughout the accounts of Cortés and Bernal Díaz, corresponds closely with the values given for the preceding decades by native historians in their discussions of internal warfare. The armies stated by Spanish writers to have been put in the field by Tlaxcalans, Texcocans, and Mexicans correspond very closely in size (from 100,000 to 300,000 men) with those cited by the codices and native annalists as participating in the campaigns of the tripartite alliance against the Tarascans, the Mixteca, or Tehuantepec. Such uniformity negates the assumption of serious error or deliberate falsification by any one observer.

---

[8] For an acute discussion of credibility of these two men see the two essays of Ramón Iglesia, in *El Hombre Colón y otros ensayos* (Mexico, 1944), pp. 53–115; and *Cronistas e Historiadores de la Conquista de México* (Mexico, 1942), pp. 17–69.

Accepting the Spanish figures, then, at least as a basis for argument, we may present such data as are contained in their documents. This may be done most systematically by considering certain localities or regions in detail.

a) Tlaxcala, city and province. In September, 1519, Cortés, marching from the coast, was attacked by an army of Tlaxcalans and Otomís. Cortés[9] places the number of the enemy in the first battle at 100,000 and in the second at 149,000. Bernal Díaz[10] gives 40,000 and 50,000, respectively. Andrés de Tapia,[11] who also was present, says: "... me parece que serían más de cient mil, e hay opiniones que eran muchos más de los que digo." Gómara[12] gives 80,000 and 150,000, and Herrera[13] 150,000.

For subsequent operations, the Tlaxcalans, now allies of Cortés, supplied auxiliaries. On the march to Cholula in 1519, he had with him, he says (Vol. 1, p. 216), about "a hundred thousand men well furnished for war." Gómara (pp. 127–128), following Cortés, says 100,000, but Tapia (p. 573) gives the number as "hasta cuarenta mil." After the battle of Otumba, on the flight from Mexico in 1520, the retreating Spaniards were met by a force of Tlaxcalans moving up to support them. This army, according to Herrera (Dec. III, Lib. x, p. 348), numbered 200,000 men, plus women and children. After recuperation, Cortés undertook a campaign against Tepeaca. Gómara (Vol. 1, p. 364) says he was aided by 40,000 Tlaxcalan warriors, plus carriers. Herrera (Dec. II, Lib. x, p. 351) makes it 56,000. At the beginning of the final assault on Tenochtitlán, Cortés gathered all the native

---

[9] *The Letters of Cortés to Charles V*, trans. Francis A. MacNutt (2 vols., New York, 1908), Vol. 1, pp. 200–202.
[10] Bernal Díaz del Castillo, *Verdadera y notable relación del descubrimiento y conquista de la Nueva España y Guatemala* (2 vols., Guatemala, 1933–1934), Vol. 1, pp. 117 and 120.
[11] *Relación sobre la conquista de México*, p. 573. In *Colección de Documentos para la historia de México*, ed. Joaquín García Icazbalceta (2 vols., Mexico, 1858–1866), Vol. 2, pp. 554–594.
[12] Francisco López de Gómara, *Historia de la conquista de México*, ed. Joaquín Ramírez Cabañas (2 vols., México, 1943), Vol. 1, pp. 161 and 163.
[13] Antonio de Herrera y Tordesillas, *Historia general de los hechos de los castellanos en las islas y tierra firme del mar Océano* (4 vols., Madrid, 1601), Dec. II, Lib. VI, p. 185.

Population Trend: 1519–1600

auxiliaries he could muster, including Tlaxcalans. The size of the latter contingent is given by Cortés (Vol. 1, pp. 60–61) as 25,000, under the command of Pedro de Alvarado. Gómara (Vol. 2, p. 30) makes it 60,000. Ixtlilxochitl[14] follows Cortés with 25,000, but Ixtlilxochitl was notoriously partial to Texcoco and equally contemptuous of Tlaxcala. Herrera in one place (Dec. III, Lib. I, p. 27) allows 30,000 Tlaxcalans under Alvarado, but then says (p. 28) that they amounted in all to "almost two hundred thousand" and (p. 35) that those under Alvarado were 60,000, thus agreeing with Gómara. Elsewhere Herrera (Dec. II, Lib. x, p. 363) states that, as the Tlaxcalan army passed in review before the final campaign, there were 60,000 *flecheros*, 40,000 *rodeleros*, and 10,000 *piqueros*, or 110,000 in all. It is probable that actually the number of Tlaxcalan soldiers varied from week to week and may have ranged from 25,000 to around 100,000. A fair average value might have been the 60,000 mentioned by Gómara.

If one takes these citations as a group, it appears that Tlaxcala was able to put into service an active first-line army of fully 100,000. If the emergency was really serious, the number could be increased, but probably not to the 200,000 claimed by Herrera; 125,000 would better represent the absolute maximum.

In deducing population from the size of armies we cannot proceed according to the standards of modern warfare, even when conscript armies are used. It is well recognized and has been ably set forth by Bandelier[15] that in the wholly nonindustrial states under discussion the army which embarked upon a campaign in times of grave crisis comprised the entire male population physically capable of bearing arms. There are many records of the use of twelve-year-old boys in offensive action. The older men were employed for transport and as a last-ditch reserve. Since the Spanish invasion precipi-

---
[14] Fernando de Alva Ixtlilxochitl, *Obras Históricas*, ed. Alfredo Chavero (2 vols., Mexico, 1891), Vol. 2, p. 435.
[15] A. F. Bandelier, "On the Art of War and the Mode of Warfare of the Ancient Mexicans," *Peabody Museum Reports*, Vol. 2 (Harvard University, 1877), pp. 95–161.

tated the gravest threat ever encountered by the central Mexican tribes, it is inconceivable that the last potentialities of manpower should not have been exhausted. We may assume therefore that the Tlaxcalan army included at least 90 per cent of the male population between the ages of fifteen and fifty.

The modern population of Mexico probably does not differ materially in its composition with respect to age and sex from that of 1519. According to the 1930 census,[16] out of a total population of 13,607,272 there were 3,287,750 males aged sixteen to fifty, inclusive. Nine-tenths of this number is 2,958,975, or 21.7 per cent of the entire population. If we use the factor of five, which is close enough for purposes of approximation, we get a population for Tlaxcala in 1519 of 625,000.

b) Province of México-Tenochtitlán. In the first days of the Spanish invasion, the Tenochtitlán-Texcoco-Tlacapan triple alliance was still intact and could therefore conscript soldiers from the many provinces subject to the so-called Aztec empire. Soon, however, owing to Cortés' strategy of dividing his enemy, many populous regions revolted and even went over to the Spaniards. At no time was the original full weight of Moctezuma's military power used against the invader. Hence we have no direct statement of how great an army he could have raised. In the final period, the defenders were reduced essentially to the city of Tenochtitlán itself and to the neighboring lake and valley towns, which on the whole remained faithful. Even Texcoco deserted to the Spaniards. Consequently, estimates of the size of the Aztec armies must be restricted to this limited territory.

Cortés (Vol. 2, p. 83) states that during the second march on Mexico he was opposed by 150,000 Culhuas, the name by which he always refers to the people of the island of Mexico and its immediate environs. Both Gómara (Vol. 1, p. 316) and Herrera (Dec. 11, Lib. x, p. 346) state that at the battle of

---

[16] *Quinto Censo de Población, 1930. Resumen general.* Secretaría de Economía Nacional (Mexico, 1934).

Otumba the enemy's army amounted to 200,000 men. There may have been some Texcocans present, but this army probably was composed primarily of Mexicans and Tepanecans from the northwestern part of the valley. Ixtilxochitl, in his thirteenth *Relación* (Vol. 1, p. 353), gives 300,000 as the size of the Mexican army at the siege of Tenochtitlán. It is quite probable, therefore, that the valley tribes could assemble unassisted an army of at least 200,000 men, which, multiplied by the factor of five, would yield a population of 1,000,000 for the whole province.

c) Province of Texcoco. There are more frequent references to the size of the Texcocan armies, but most of them, unfortunately, are from Ixtlilxochitl, who as a native of Texcoco was interested in magnifying the exploits of his townsmen. He says (Vol. 2, p. 416) that the city and province could put 200,000 men in the field. At the beginning of the great siege Cortés was reinforced by a contingent generally stated as numbering 50,000 (Ixtlilxochitl, Vol. 1, p. 352, gives 58,000; Gómara, Vol. 2, p. 41, 50,000; Oviedo,[17] Vol. 3, p. 387, 50,000; Herrera, Dec. III, Lib. 1, p. 40, 50,000). However, as the siege progressed and the eventual victory of the Spaniards became more certain, the estimates increased. Ixtlilxochitl (Vol. 1, p. 379) claims that 200,000 Texcocans participated and suffered 30,000 casualties.

The important estimates for the entire Valley of Mexico are, in terms of military strength, 150,000 Mexicans (Culhuas), 200,000 Mexicans plus Tepanecs, and 200,000 Texcocans. Although these estimates may overlap to some extent, since the local territorial limits are vaguely or not at all defined, the aggregate may be safely taken as 400,000 men. This would give 2,000,000 as the total population of the Valley of Mexico.

d) Cholula, Huejotzingo, Chalco. These three towns or provinces, all in contiguous territory to the southeast of the Valley of Mexico, were at first hostile, but later friendly to

---

[17] Gonzalo Fernández de Oviedo y Valdés, *Historia general y natural de las Indias*, ed. José Amador de los Ríos (4 vols., Madrid, 1851–1855), Vol. 3, p. 387.

the Spaniards. In the final year of the conquest they probably contributed their entire military strength. It is difficult to segregate their individual contributions, since they are frequently mentioned collectively. Herrera (Vol. 1, p. 23) says that the city of Cholula was able to muster 25,000 men. At the famous massacre of 1519 there is general agreement that between 3,000 and 6,000 men were killed. Herrera's estimate for Cholula's preconquest strength seems therefore not to be exaggerated. After the massacre, 20,000 would represent the probable maximum.

During the southern campaign of 1520 Cortés had a large army of auxiliaries. Gómara (Vol. 1, p. 327) puts their number at 100,000. Cortés (Vol. 1, p. 313) also gives 100,000, but later amends the figure to 120,000; about half of them were Tlaxcalans, which would leave about 50,000 for the region under consideration.

In the final operation around Tenochtitlán the allied armies numbered more than 150,000, according to Cortés (Vol. 2, pp. 109 and 124). Herrera (Dec. III, Lib. 1, p. 42) puts the number at "almost 200,000." Oviedo (Vol. 3, p. 387) allows 130,000 at the beginning of the siege, and Ixtlilxochitl (Vol. 1, p. 352), always excessive in his estimates, makes them 300,000 in all. The estimate of Cortés is probably the most accurate: 150,000. As has already been suggested, the Tlaxcalans probably accounted for 60,000 of this number and the Texcocans for 50,000, which would leave 40,000 for Cholula, Huejotzingo, and Chalco. Ixtlilxochitl (Vol. 2, pp. 435–436) shows 87,000 for Tlaxcala, Cholula, and Huejotzingo, which, if we deduct 60,000 for Tlaxcala, leaves 27,000 for the other two towns. Oviedo (Vol. 3, p. 387) assigns 80,000 men to Tlaxcala and the smaller towns, which would leave 20,000 for the latter. Herrera (Dec. III, Lib. 1, p. 27) allows 60,000 Tlaxcalans and 40,000 miscellaneous allies. Herrera probably took these figures directly from Cervantes de Salazar, who was his principal source for this part of his narrative.[18] Cortés

---

[18] Carlos Bosch García, "Las Décadas de Herrera," *Estudios de Historiografía de la Nueva España* (Colegio de México, México, D. F., 1945), pp. 143–202. Cervantes de Salazar probably got his figures from Gómara (Vol. 2, p. 30).

himself (Vol. 2, pp. 60–61) specifies for the beginning of the siege 30,000 men from the three towns of Cholula, Chalco, and Huejotzingo, but this group was probably augmented before the final capture of Tenochtitlán. A total of 40,000 for the three therefore seems appropriate for this period.

The region concerned had, however, suffered rather severely during the preceding two years, and it is likely that its original strength was considerably greater than would be indicated by the 40,000 men present at the siege. If we accept Herrera's estimate of 25,000 for Cholula alone, as seems reasonable, we may assign 20,000 each to Chalco and Huejotzingo, or 65,000 in all. Multiplied by our factor of five, the population of the three towns comes to 325,000.

e) Michoacán. There is a statement by Ixtlilxochitl (Vol. 2, p. 418) that in 1521 the cacique of Michoacán started out to help the Mexicans against the Spaniards, but reconsidered and withdrew. He had prepared an army of 200,000, evidently first-line troops, including 100,000 Tarascans and 100,000 Teochichimecs. These numbers would imply a population of 1,000,000. Although this seems large, it may actually be an underestimate. There are accounts of even larger Tarascan forces operating prior to the conquest, and it must not be forgotten that this tribe was able to administer a decisive defeat to the Aztecs in the fifteenth century. Numerically the Tarascans must have been fully as strong as the Aztecs and their immediate allies.

f) Other regions. There are a few scattered references to armies of various isolated towns and provinces, not sufficiently illuminating to warrant quotation in detail. As a whole, however, they show the same order of magnitude as those we have analyzed.

A summary of our data shows a population of 4,700,000 in an area roughly embracing the present states of Tlaxcala, eastern Mexico, northern Morelos, central Puebla, southern Hidalgo, and much of Michoacán. If we omit Michoacán, the value for the central region is 3,700,000. Reverting briefly to the baptism figures cited in the preceding section, if we deduct the number ascribed by Motolinía to the South Sea coast, we find that the remaining area coincides with that to which the military estimates apply. The population of this region, according to records of baptisms, approximates 4,200,-000, against our military estimate of 3,700,000. The correspondence is therefore close.

For purposes of speculation we may use an intermediate figure of 4,000,000. There should be added 1,000,000 for Michoacán and 800,000 for Guerrero, although these estimates may not do justice to such large areas. As for the rest of central Mexico, our estimates based on later documents show a probable population of 3,150,000 for Hidalgo, Vera Cruz, and Oaxaca. The total, then, for our entire territory, based principally on military figures, would be 8,950,000, exclusive of Nueva Galicia.

ESTIMATES DERIVED FROM LATER DATA

A third method for estimating the population in 1519 is to utilize the data presented for 1565. If we can establish for a reasonable sample of towns or provinces the ratio of population in 1519 to that in 1565, the factor may be applied to the region as a whole with some likelihood of approximation. It will be necessary to consider certain localities separately and in some detail.

a) Tenochtitlán-Tlatelolco. The size of the capital and most important city of New Spain has been a subject of speculation and discussion from the conquest to the present day. There have been certain definite affirmations, however, three of which merit consideration. One is by the "Anonymous Conqueror,"[19] to the effect that "the majority of those who have visited it [Tenochtitlán] estimate the population at seventy thousand inhabitants, rather more than less." Some controversy has arisen concerning the meaning of "inhabitants" in this passage. In a note to the Anonymous Con-

---

[19] The Anonymous Conqueror, *Narrative of Some Things of New Spain*, trans. M. H. Saville (New York, Cortés Society, 1917), p. 61.

queror's narrative (p. 90, n. 44) Joaquín García Icazbalceta suggests that a mistake was made by the person who translated the lost MS into Italian and that the author actually said *casas*. It seems more likely that the original employed the word *vecinos* or *vasallos*, as was the universal custom in Spain, which would make the Anonymous Conqueror's estimate correspond with that of other observers. Ixtlilxochitl (Vol. 2, p. 378) says that the city had "en medio más de quinientos mil vasallos," a fantastic exaggeration, as Alfredo Chavero pointed out in a note to the same passage. Whether Ixtlilxochitl meant 500,000 *vasallos* or 500,000 *inhabitants*, there is no way of determining. With some misgiving, we may take the latter interpretation; reckoning by inhabitants is fairly characteristic of the author. Oviedo (Vol. 3, p. 528), on the other hand, relying upon a statement of Fray Diego de Loaysa, says that the population of the capital "sería de cincuenta mil vecinos." It is customary and probably most nearly correct to calculate the population by multiplying the number of *vecinos* by five, on the assumption that the mean family number prior to the conquest was five. The three estimates just discussed, then, would give us values of 350,000, 500,000, and 250,000, respectively.

Firmly embedded in the historical literature is the statement that the city contained 60,000 houses, which would imply a population of 300,000. This estimate first appears in Gómara (Vol. 1, p. 231), who adds that each house contained from two to ten persons. No explicit statement of the sort, however, is contained in the letters of Cortés, the *True History* of Bernal Díaz, the narrative of the Anonymous Conqueror, or in Andrés de Tapia. Thomas Gage,[20] who saw the city in 1625, says (p. 96) that it "was [at the time of the conquest] as some say of sixty, but more probably it is reported to have been of fourscore thousand houses." Torquemada (Vol. 1, p. 291) raises the number of houses to 120,000—to all appearances too high a value.

---

[20] Thomas Gage, *A New Survey of the West Indies* (London, 1677).

Emphasis has been placed upon the size of the market at Tlatelolco. Cortés (Vol. 1, p. 257) states that at the market "there are daily more than sixty thousand souls." The Anonymous Conqueror (p. 65) is more conservative, placing the average attendance at between 20,000 and 25,000, and on market days at between 40,000 and 50,000. Gómara (Vol. 1, p. 236) says that the market would hold 60,000 or even 100,000. The size of the market, however, save by comparison with those of other cities, is not a valid criterion of the population, since a very large proportion of the people present must have been merchants and produce sellers from the surrounding country.

We have some information respecting the size of the city which may be of use. Bancroft,[21] basing his assertion upon a statement of the Anonymous Conqueror, gives the circumference of the city as twelve miles, which would make its area 11.9 square miles. But elsewhere[22] he states that there was constructed around the southern half of the city a levee which was three leagues, or nine miles, in length, which would imply a circumference of eighteen miles and an area of 17.5 square miles. In the same volume (p. 280) Bancroft reproduces a map of Tenochtitlán originally published in the Nuremberg edition of the letters of Cortés. If his statement is correct that the Tlacapan causeway was half a league long, and if the map is drawn to an accurate scale, it can be shown that the diameter of the city was 1½ leagues, or 4½ miles, which would give an area of 19.6 square miles. León y Gama[23] claims that both the north–south and east–west axes were two leagues long, which would give an area of 26.3 square miles. However, as he points out, the eastern side of the city included a large lagoon or basin within the levee, for the docking of boats. On the whole, the various sources are in

---

[21] H. H. Bancroft, *Native Races of the Pacific States* (3 vols., San Francisco, 1875), Vol. 2, p. 561, n. 24.
[22] H. H. Bancroft, *History of Mexico* (6 vols., San Francisco, 1883–1888), Vol. 1, p. 277.
[23] Antonio de León y Gama, *Descripción de la Ciudad de México*, published from the original MS in *Revista Mexicana de Estudios Históricos* (Mexico, 1927), Vol. 1, App. pp. 5–58.

moderately good agreement on a figure approximating 20 square miles for the area of the city. We have only one concrete clue to the density of the city's population. In 1909, A. P. Maudslay published[24] a fragment of a map entitled "Plano hecho en papel de maguey," which purports to represent a section of the western part of Tenochtitlán, at or near Tlatelolco. It clearly shows the houses and lots (*solares*) of the section. The author gives 30 by 40 meters as the dimensions of a standard *solar*. From this figure it can be calculated that there were 2,132 *solares* (and therefore houses) per square mile, and that the density of population of this part of the city would be 10,660 persons per square mile. If we assume a total area of twenty square miles we get an over-all population of 213,200. The criticism may be made that we have not made allowance for palaces, temples, and other public areas. It may be answered that the palaces and temples house large permanent staffs of officials, priests, servants and their families. Moreover, it may be doubted, to judge by the accounts of eyewitnesses, whether, in much of the city, each house was provided with as large a plot of land as is shown on the map. The distortion produced by using this fragmentary sample is therefore not as great as might be supposed.

In 1803, Alexander von Humboldt[25] gave some attention to the size of ancient Tenochtitlán: "What is now the Barrio of Santiago comprises but a part of the ancient Tlatelolco. We proceed for more than an hour on the road to Tlalnepantla and Ahuehuetes among the ruins of the old city. We perceive there as well as on the road to Tacuba and Ixtapalapan how much the Mexico rebuilt by Cortés is smaller than Tenochtitlán under the last of the Montezumas." If by "We proceed for more than an hour" Humboldt refers to walking, then the ruins he observed must have extended in 1803 at least three or, possibly, four miles beyond the built-up sec-

[24] *Anales del Museo Nacional de México*, Ser. 3, Vol. 1, pp. 51–54.
[25] Alexander von Humboldt, *Political Essay on the Kingdom of New Spain*. English translation by John Black (4 vols., London, 1814), Vol. 2, p. 21.

tions. The edge of the latter must have extended at least a mile and a half beyond the Zócalo, which would imply an original diameter of some six miles or more, making an area larger than that indicated by earlier writers. Humboldt (Vol. 2, p. 60) also set a high estimate on the population of Tenochtitlán, to judge by the following: "Were we to judge from the fragments of ruined houses and the recital of the first conquerors, and especially from the number of combatants whom the kings ... opposed to ... the Spaniards, we should pronounce the population of Tenochtitlán three times greater than that of the Mexico of our days." The latter he calculated to be 140,000, which would give 420,000 as the aboriginal population.

We now have four sets of values: (1) direct estimates of 350,000, 500,000, and 250,000; (2) house counts yielding 300,000; (3) area-density calculations giving 213,000; and (4) Humboldt's estimate of 420,000. Of these (3) appears too low and (4) too high. The arithmetical mean of all six values is 340,000, a figure which is somewhat larger than the frequently quoted 300,000, but which is perhaps warranted on the basis of available evidence.

For Mexico City in 1565 we have three estimates of some credibility, the average of which gives an Indian population of 74,895. The ratio of the population in 1565 to that in 1519 is 0.22, or approximately one-fifth. In view of the total destruction of the city in 1521, this large reduction is reasonable.

b) Texcoco. Cortés (Vol. 1, p. 248), after his first visit to Texcoco, wrote that the city "may have thirty thousand households." Mendieta (Vol. 2, p. 59) repeated that Texcoco must have had "al pie de treinta mil vecinos," and Torquemada (Vol. 3, p. 28) said that in 1524 Texcoco had "más de treinta mil vezinos que le avían quedado [de ?] el estrago de la guerra." 30,000 *vecinos* indicates a population of 150,000. Nevertheless, Herrera (Dec. II, Lib. VIII, p. 245) says that Texcoco was as large as Tenochtitlán, a statement which is repeated by nearly all ancient and modern writers. Torquemada (Vol. 1, p. 304) affirms that, "según cuenta segura y verdadera," the city had 140,000 houses and covered a *distance* of three to four leagues, "desde el corazón de ella (que era la morada y palacios del rey) que se iba dilatando por tres o cuatro leguas." Clavigero explains this wide discrepancy in the following passage: "De la capital de Texcoco sabemos por las cartas de Carlos V que tenía cerca de 30,000 casas; mas esto debe entenderse de aquella parte de la población que propiamente se llamaba *Texcoco*; pues comprendidas las otras tres ciudades de Coatlinchán, Huexotla y Atenco ... su circuito era mayor que el de México. Torquemada, apoyado en el testimonio de Sahagún y en el de los indios, asegura que en aquellas cuatro ciudades se contaban 140,000 casas."[26]

If we allow this correction and take Torquemada's estimate for the four towns literally, they would have had, together, five times 140,000, or 700,000 inhabitants. This number appears excessive on grounds of general probability and because it makes each of the subsidiary towns larger than Texcoco itself. Even by arbitrarily reducing the number of houses to 90,000 (fifty per cent greater than the number for Mexico City) we still get a population for the four towns of 450,000.

Torquemada says that the houses "iban dilatando" three or four leagues from the center of Texcoco, evidently in the form of an almost continuous city. The four towns are strung out from north to south along the old lake shore for twenty kilometers, or nearly four leagues. The buildings probably extended eastward well into the lower foothills, a distance of fully ten kilometers. In Texcoco, however, the congestion must have been much less than in the capital—more open space between houses, more gardens and truck farming. Therefore it would not be justifiable to ascribe to Texcoco more than half the density of Tenochtitlán, or, say, 2,000 persons per square kilometer, which would yield a population

---
[26] Francisco Javier Clavigero, *Historia Antigua de México* (2 vols., Mexico, 1844). Disertación VII, Vol. 2, p. 272.

of 400,000. If we adopt this latter value and neglect Torquemada's inflated figure, we still have Texcoco larger than Tenochtitlán. This value would, moreover, allow Texcoco itself the 30,000 houses which Cortés ascribed to it and allow the three satellite towns 50,000. In 1565, according to our data, Texcoco had 83,966 inhabitants, and the 1565–1519 ratio is 0.21, which is almost the same as that for Tenochtitlán.

c) Tlaxcala. The ancient province of Tlaxcala coincided almost exactly with the present state. Cortés (Vol. I, p. 211) wrote, ". . . according to the visitation which I ordered made, this province [Tlaxcala] has five hundred thousand householders"—an incredible number. Gómara, on the other hand, who usually is fairly reliable in his figures and who, indeed, drew most of his data from the papers of Cortés, says (Vol. I, p. 184) that the province of Tlaxcala had 150,000 *vecinos*. Multiplied by our customary factor of five, this figure gives us a population of 750,000. Herrera, in one place (Dec. II, Lib. VI, p. 199), says that the province had eighteen pueblos with "más de ciento y cincuenta mil vecinos," and elsewhere (Dec. II, Lib. X, p. 360) he puts the number at more than 120,000. Other writers, ancient and modern, have held rather consistently to these two latter estimates, or a population of between 600,000 and 750,000. In view of our later estimate, the value of 750,000 seems substantially correct. The population of Tlaxcala in 1565, according to good contemporary testimony, was 400,000. The rate of diminution was therefore only 0.53, as contrasted with the five-to-one reduction in Tenochtitlán and Texcoco. The difference is explained by the favored treatment which the Tlaxcalans enjoyed and by the relatively easier economic circumstances in which they passed the first half century of Spanish domination.

d) The populations of several towns are given specifically in Cortés' letters. He gives either *vecinos* or houses in round numbers, and states that on occasion he caused actual counts to be made. Since for most of these places we have adequate data from 1565, a direct comparison is possible. We have reduced Cortés' figures to population by multiplying by five.

LOCALITY	CORTES' ESTIMATE	1565	RATIO
Otumba	17,500	23,635	1.35
Coyoacán	30,000	18,120	.60
Churubusco	22,500	7,900	.35
Mexicalcingo	15,000	1,108	.07
Huaquechula	27,500	14,660	.53
Izúcar	17,500	7,568	.43
Ixtacamaxtitlán	27,500	9,600	.35
Chalco	100,000	41,623	.42
Huejotzingo	250,000	45,272	.18
Cholula	200,000	50,714	.25
Acolman	17,500	5,616	.32
Ixtapalapa	40,000	2,680	.07

The mean ratio is 0.41, with both the standard deviation and the standard error large.

e) In C. O. Sauer's recent *Colima of New Spain in the Sixteenth Century* (Univ. Calif. Publ., Ibero-Americana: 29 [Berkeley and Los Angeles, 1948]), which followed exhaustive examination of the local records of the sixteenth century, he places the aboriginal population of the ancient province (somewhat larger than the present state) at 140,000. Our adjusted value for 1565 for the area of the present state is 43,471. The 1565–1519 ratio is therefore somewhat greater than 0.31.

f) An isolated sample is available from Oaxaca. Burgoa[27] states that at the time of the entrance of the Dominican missionaries (*ca.* 1540) the town of Yanhuitlán and its subject towns "... hacían más de doce mil familias en lo espacioso y ameno de aquel valle." Also (p. 286), "... tenía este pueblo doce mil vecinos de familia." This number indicates a population of at least 48,000 in 1540, which was several years after the first Spanish penetration into that area, and which, therefore, was probably smaller than that of 1519. Nevertheless, if we assume that there had been no significant decline prior to

---

[27] Francisco de Burgoa, *Geográfica Descripción* (2 vols., Mexico, 1934), Vol. I, p. 284.

1540, we may use 48,000 as a possible figure for 1519. By 1565 the population had sunk to 24,368. The ratio is 0.51. The six examples discussed above yield ratios respectively of 0.22, 0.21, 0.53, 0.41, 0.31, 0.51. The mean is 0.365. If we consider the twelve towns mentioned by Cortés as separate items and include them with the other five, the mean is 0.394. There is variation from place to place, owing both to inadequacy of the data and inherent differences in local conditions. It seems reasonably clear, however, that by 1565 the population had been generally reduced to at least one-half, and in some places to one-fifth, of its preconquest value. The averages just cited center around two-fifths, or 40 per cent, a figure which we may accept as being not too distant from the truth.

The population at or near 1565 has been shown to have been very close to 4,409,180. If this value is 40 per cent of the 1519 level, then the latter becomes 11,022,450. The rounded number of 11,000,000 is a sufficiently close approximation. If Nueva Galicia be excluded, the corresponding figure is 10,500,000.

Reviewing the three methods employed to calculate the aboriginal population of central Mexico, we find the results to be in essential agreement: by baptismal figures, 9,030,000; by army sizes, 8,950,000; by ratios of 1565 to 1519, 10,500,000 —all exclusive of Nueva Galicia. The first two methods are based on incomplete evidence and are therefore less to be trusted than the third, but they are confirmatory in that they reach the same order of magnitude. On the whole, the ratio method may be accepted as the best of the three, and the 1519 population of all central Mexico may be set at 11,000,000.[28]

---

[28] Gonzalo Aguirre Beltrán, in his study cited in the Introduction, follows modern scholars in rejecting all early estimates of the preconquest population, and accepts Rosenblat's figure of 4,500,000 as the most reasonable; but Rosenblat includes the bishoprics of Yucatán, Tabasco, and Chiapas, and the unknown northern territory—all of which lie outside the area of this study. If we deduct the 400,000 which he assigns to those areas, his figure must be reduced to 4,100,000, against our 11,000,-000. For 1570, Aguirre Beltrán accepts Pérez Bustamante's reasonable estimate of

The Population Trend, 1540–1570

Between the conquest and the year 1560 no clear single record of population exists save the *Suma de Visitas*, which does not give a true picture for any given year. A document which affords us a more tangible clue is the *Relación de las tasaciones* (document C), although the approach must be indirect. It cites, for numerous towns, the tribute assessed in specific years between 1550 and 1571. The trend of assessments may be followed throughout this period, although the returns are incomplete. For some towns only one year is mentioned; for others, two years are given; for still others, several. We tabulated the populations of sixty-six towns according to their assessments, breaking them down into five periods of three or four years each: 1553–1557; 1558–1561; 1562–1564; 1565–1567; 1568–1571. The population (converted from tribute) was then entered for each period and town. The result was an incomplete table, with most spaces unfilled. Then, in order to derive the *relative* (rather than the absolute) values, we made the tabulation which appears below. In it the population of each town has been set at the arbitrary value of 100 for period five. For 26 towns there are data for both period five and period four. The ratio of period four to

---

2,942,248 for our area, which would allow a decline of only 26 per cent from 1519 to 1570, against our estimate of a greater than 60 per cent decline. This violent discrepancy arises from the conviction among most scholars that the ancient observers were not to be trusted—a conviction which we do not share,—and from their resultant habit of dividing early estimates by some arbitrary factor, ranging from two to five. It seems to us that if the testimony of respectable witnesses can be discarded so easily, then all history would have to be rewritten in the light of later assumptions.

The single exception to the general trend is the study made by Miguel O. de Mendizábal (cited above, p. 1). Mendizábal arrives at a preconquest value for *all* Mexico of 9,170,400 and a value for 1574 of 3,056,800—which, by his method of calculation, would give for the area to which we have limited ourselves values of 6,843,000 and 2,281,000, respectively. Mendizábal erred: (1) by depending upon too few sources, using the *Suma de Visitas* and Lopez de Velasco's *Geografía* only for his statistical analysis; (2) by establishing a tributary-population ratio of 3.2 (against our ratio of 4.0); and (3) by adopting an arbitrary factor of 2/3 for the decline between 1519 and 1574, based upon no apparent evidence. Even so, he made an intelligent attempt to use contemporary sources and derived a curve of population decline fairly close to ours.

Population of Central Mexico

Ratios of Population Decline, 1553–1571

Period 1 1553–1557	Period 2 1558–1561	Period 3 1562–1564	Period 4 1565–1567	Period 5 1568–1571
(207)	(151)	123	104	100
(207)	(151)	150	(137)	100
163	(151)	(151)	(137)	100
(207)	(151)	(151)	102	100
102	(151)	(151)	(137)	100
(207)	169	(151)	140	100
(207)	159	(151)	135	100
(207)	(151)	73	(137)	100
(207)	148	(151)	160	100
230	(151)	171	(137)	100
(207)	(151)	124	(137)	100
(207)	(151)	142	(137)	100
176	117	(151)	(137)	100
152	(151)	(151)	129	100
(207)	56	(151)	(137)	100
(207)	(151)	(151)	149	100
162	(151)	168	139	100
56	(151)	(151)	(137)	100
(207)	(151)	(151)	213	100
(207)	134	(151)	(137)	100
199	(151)	233	(137)	100
(207)	(151)	(151)	161	100
251	(151)	(151)	248	100
(207)	(151)	196	(137)	100
(207)	(151)	177	(137)	100
(207)	148	(151)	(137)	100
227	(151)	(151)	(137)	100
(207)	(151)	138	(137)	100
(207)	(151)	(151)	73	100
175	164	(151)	(137)	100
(207)	(151)	180	(137)	100
(207)	(151)	(151)	103	100
(207)	(151)	(151)	223	100
(207)	157	(151)	(137)	100
(207)	(151)	(151)	90	100
(207)	(151)	123	109	100
102	171	(151)	(137)	100
(207)	(151)	110	(137)	100
796	(151)	(151)	(137)	100
(207)	(151)	200	(137)	100
130	568	(151)	(137)	100

Population Trend: 1519-1600

RATIOS OF POPULATION DECLINE, 1553-1571—*Continued*

Period 1 1553-1557	Period 2 1558-1561	Period 3 1562-1564	Period 4 1565-1567	Period 5 1568-1571
(207)	(151)	(151)	(137)	100
(207)	139	(151)	(137)	100
418	(151)	(151)	(137)	100
(207)	77	(151)	(137)	100
(207)	(151)	136	(137)	100
(207)	86	(151)	(137)	100
256	(151)	(151)	(137)	100
(207)	(151)	(151)	(137)	100
(207)	(151)	222	(137)	100
(207)	(151)	(151)	107	100
(207)	(151)	171	131	100
(207)	52	(151)	112	100
(207)	(151)	(151)	244	100
129	(151)	182	(137)	100
(207)	(151)	(151)	135	100
98	(151)	(151)	120	100
(207)	(151)	104	(137)	100
131	(151)	(151)	89	100
(207)	(151)	(151)	118	100
253	(151)	(151)	(137)	100
(207)	(151)	118	(137)	100
(207)	145	(151)	(137)	100
137	(151)	(151)	117	100
(207)	85	(151)	(137)	100
(207)	(151)	85	120	100

period five was then determined for each of the 26 examples, and their mean of 137 was entered in column four for all the remaining towns.

The same procedure was followed with respect to column three (corresponding to 1562-1564), which was equated to period four or to period five, depending upon which figures were available. Their mean, with reference to the 100 of period five, is 151. Period two (1558-1561), treated in a similar fashion, yielded a mean of 151, and period one, 207. The entries in parentheses are ratios derived from the means; those without parentheses represent direct ratios derived from the tribute rates of the *Relación de las tasaciones*.

We should not be justified in concluding from this scant evidence that the population diminished by half between 1555 and 1570. A clue to the solution of the difficulty lies in the changes in assessment methods made during this period. Prior to 1553 the tribute was paid in kind or commodities, and the lists were compiled in terms of grain, textiles, manu-

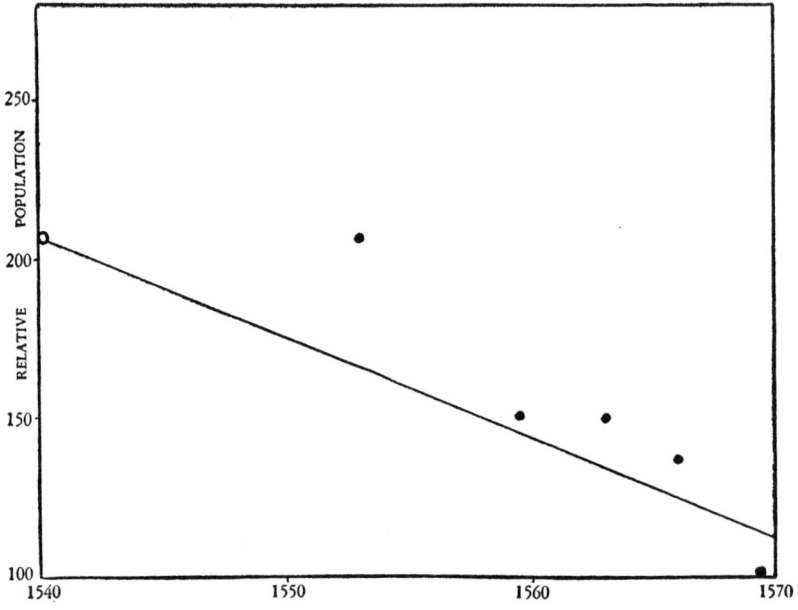

Fig. 1. Population decline, 1540–1570.

factured goods, farm produce, and the like. The rationalization of the tribute into *fanegas* of maize and *pesos de oro común* brought about a long period of readjustment in the Crown's attempt to bring the tribute into line with the actual number of tributaries. By the middle of the decade 1560–1570 this readjustment was substantially complete; but at the beginning of the period of rationalization (1553) the assessed tribute and the tribute collected were seriously out of adjustment. At that time the tribute was based upon the capacity to pay considered appropriate some years earlier, and, indeed,

Population Trend: 1519–1600   43

it often coincided with the rate given in the *Suma de Visitas*, which has been shown to have extended no later than 1544. The rate in 1553 was apparently based upon a rough approximation of the population as it existed about 1540. Between 1540 and 1553 the population diminished but the tribute rate did not. Hence we may assume that the rate for our period one (1553–1557) did not represent the population of that period, but that of some ten or more years earlier, or, say, that of 1540. If we retain 100 as the value for the population of 1568–1571, the population of 1565 becomes equivalent to 142, and the decline from 1540 (not 1555) to 1565 is relatively from 207 to 142. We have already established a probable total population of 4,409,180 for 1565. Then, by proportion, the population for 1540 becomes $\frac{4,409,180 \times 207}{142}$, or 6,427,466.

These relationships are shown graphically in figure 1. On the abscissas are plotted the dates and on the ordinates the relative populations, that of 1570 being set equivalent to 100. The calculated points are indicated by solid dots; that of 1553 is set back to 1540, indicated by a circle. The line is drawn to emphasize the trend of population between 1540 and 1570.

The Population in 1597–1610

During the last thirty years of the sixteenth century the population suffered further serious reduction. The exact loss is impossible to determine, but there is sufficient evidence to indicate that it was great. In 1597 a petition (document P) was sent to the Crown by the encomenderos, requesting permanent tenure. Their argument was based upon their extreme poverty, which, in turn, they ascribed to the diminution of the tribute-paying population. The testimony accompanying the petition is in the usual form of an *interrogatorio*, the third question of which states that the total number of tributaries in New Spain had dropped to the low level of 400,000.[29]

---
[29] Since the petition of 1597 (document P) did not include Nueva Galicia, we must add approximately 20,000 tributaries for that area, which would yield an adjusted total of 420,000 for our territory.

All the witnesses called give a blanket endorsement to this statement, attributing the loss to the big epidemics of 1576–1578 and to those of the early years of the decade 1590–1600. At least two of these witnesses ascribe a mortality of 500,000 tributaries to these epidemics.

The 420,000 tributaries of document P would yield a population of 1,680,000, which seems definitely too low. In 1565, according to our estimate, there were about 1,100,000 tributaries. If we allow for exaggeration on the part of the interested witnesses and assume that 500,000 was the loss from *all* causes, rather than from epidemics alone, 600,000 would remain for 1597 and a population of 2,400,000.

In the 1597 list there are 65 towns for which we also have adequate data for the period 1560–1570 (C–N in the tables). The 1597–1565 ratio has been calculated for them. The mean is 0.668, or, say, 0.67. By applying this factor to the 1565 population of 4,409,180, we get a value of 2,954,150 for 1597.

In the petition of 1597 the statement occurs that of the total number of tributaries then in existence "los más están en la corona." In other words, more than half were Crown towns, the rest being held by the encomenderos. Since the petition allows that the encomienda towns had 213,553 tributaries (plus 20,000 for Nueva Galicia), the total, according to it, must have been in excess of 447,106, rather than the 400,000 stated in the third question of the *interrogatorio*.

A closer approximation to the relative numbers under encomienda and Crown may be reached by considering the situation in the period 1560–1570. Of the towns listed in our tables we know that some were held in encomienda, a group which we may designate by *A*. Others were under the Crown, group *C*. A third group, *B*, were encomienda towns at the time of the *Suma de Visitas*, but we have no sure evidence of their status in 1565. A fourth group, *D*, is unknown, but since they do not appear in the *Suma*, or in the encomienda list of 1565–1570 (document L), or in the list of 1597, we may assume that they were held by the Crown.

The total population in 1565 for the four groups, rounded to the nearest thousand, was: A, 1,799,000; B, 91,000; C, 2,094,000; D, 158,000. The ratio C/A is 1.16, and that of $C + D/A + B$ is 1.19. If we now apply the second ratio to the sum of encomienda tributaries in 1597 (i.e., 213,553), on the assumption that there was no change in the ratio during those thirty years, the Crown tributaries in 1597 would have been 252,000, the total 465,553, and the total population 1,862,222. It is known, however, that some encomiendas were absorbed by the Crown within that period. Certainly a large number of the small encomiendas of 1540–1550 (group B) had been taken over. Therefore the ratio 1.19 is undoubtedly too low. If we assume, conservatively, that one-half of group B and one-tenth of group A had come under royal jurisdiction, then the ratio $C + D/A + B$ would be 1.49, or, for simple reckoning, 1.50. Applying this factor to the admitted 213,553 encomienda tributaries in 1597, we get for the Crown a total of 317,000; for both, 530,553; for the corresponding population, 2,122,000.

We may disregard, then, the 400,000 tributaries claimed in the petition, and we still have three estimates, one based on the stated population loss, the second on the 1597–1565 ratio, and the third on the relationship between encomienda and royal towns. The three estimates are, respectively, 2,400,000, 2,959,000, and 2,122,000. Their average is 2,493,-000, or approximately 2,500,000.

This value appears surprisingly low. We have, however, one piece of confirmatory, independent evidence. In the *Fuentes para la Historia del Trabajo en Nueva España*,[30] Volume 6, are reports of litigation which include data on the number of laborers supplied to the mines by certain towns. The dates center around 1607. By that time the number of tributaries which a town might be obliged to give to this service was fixed at 4 per cent, and hence at 1 per cent of the population. For eleven scattered towns mentioned in the

---

[30] Edited by Silvio Zavala and María Castelo (8 vols., Mexico, 1939–1945).

Fuentes we have, therefore, the population in 1607. The mean ratio of these values to those for the same towns in 1565 is 0.456. The calculated population for the country in 1607 is 2,014,000, considerably smaller than the value we got for 1597.

Although we may concede the possibility that all these calculations are based upon underestimates, there is no clear

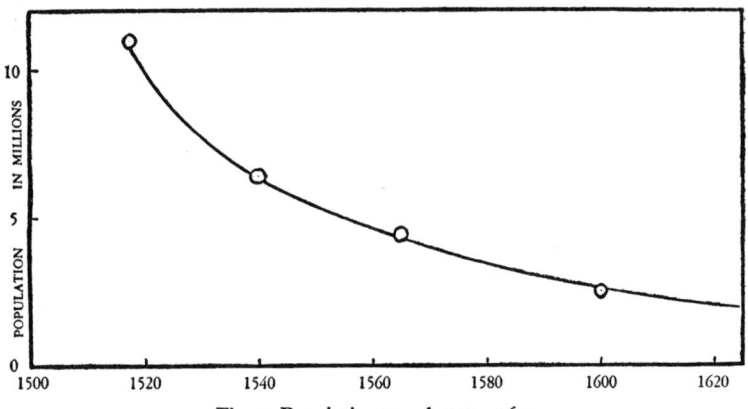

Fig. 2. Population trend, 1519–1600.

source of information pointing to a higher figure. In the absence of such evidence we may tentatively assign the approximate value of 2,500,000 to the population at the end of the century.

Conclusion

In the accompanying graph (fig. 2) the computed populations for the four critical dates of 1519, 1540, 1565, and 1600 have been plotted. The smoothed curve passing through them ignores minor fluctuations and irregularities, since we have no data complete enough to warrant such detail. We believe, nevertheless, that the trend here depicted is entirely reasonable and a fairly close representation of the decline of population in the sixteenth century.

III. SUBSEQUENT POPULATION CHANGES

IT IS APPARENT that the closing years of the sixteenth century had not yet seen the end of the decline in population. Both the numerical data and the slope of the curve lead to the inference that the decline continued at a perceptible rate well into the seventeenth century. A casual extrapolation of the curve would suggest that the population curve leveled off, around 1650, at a value approaching 1,500,000. The next period for which good population data are available does not occur until 1793, when Viceroy Revillagigedo took the first modern census of Mexico. It may be of interest to compare some of his figures with those for the mid-sixteenth century.

In the *Ramo de Censos* of the National Archive of Mexico there is a long series of detailed returns for 1793 from numerous towns of central Mexico for which we also have sixteenth-century data, and a direct comparison indicates a very great diminution in population between the two periods. The territorial subdivisions, however, do not clearly coincide. In the Revillagigedo census each pueblo, rancho, and hacienda is listed separately, whereas in the early lists the minor units are consistently included with the *cabecera*. This difference in treatment makes direct comparison by towns or *jurisdicciones* impossible. There is, however, in the same archive, in the *Ramo de Historia* (Vols. 72, 73, 522, and 523), a group of tabulations for the 1793 census which cover large territorial divisions, particularly provinces. Three of the provinces coincide reasonably well with modern states and allow us to make a direct comparison.

PROVINCE OR STATE	POPULATION IN 1565	POPULATION IN 1793
Tlaxcala	400,000	59,177
Oaxaca	693,680	411,336
Mexico and the Federal District	826,672	1,043,223
Totals	1,920,352	1,513,736

The 1793–1565 ratio is 0.788.

For purposes of comparison another approach is possible. The total population of Mexico in 1793 was found to be 5,200,000, but it includes a great deal of territory outside of that covered in our study, for example: Guanajuato, Sonora, Yucatán, Durango, Nuevo México, Baja California, Querétaro, Aguas Calientes, and Nuevo León, the population of which is given as 1,152,609. We must also eliminate Chiapas, Tabasco, Chihuahua, Tamaulipas, and most of San Luis Potosí and Zacatecas. For the latter areas 300,000 would probably be an adequate value. In all, then, we must deduct 1,452,609 from the total of 5,200,000, which leaves, in round numbers, 3,750,000 as the population of central Mexico and Nueva Galicia in 1793. The ratio of this value to that of 1565 (4,409,180) is 0.849, a result reasonably close to the 0.788 found by comparing the three provinces. Without attempting to press beyond the accuracy of the data, we may conclude that the population of our area in 1793 was somewhere near four-fifths that in 1565. A total of 3,700,000 may be taken as a working approximation.

There is some evidence that the population was definitely on the increase during the eighteenth century. It was pointed out by one of us in a recent paper[1] that the inhabitants of Michoacán nearly doubled in numbers between 1730 and 1793, and that if the same rate of increase held throughout the country the value for all of Mexico in 1730 would have been 2,450,000. For the central provinces alone it would have been 1,770,000. To be sure, an estimate based upon a single province cannot be conclusive. It does, however, support the strong likelihood that in 1700 there were not more than 2,000,000 people in the area of our study. If so we again encounter the probability that the minimum was reached somewhere in the seventeenth century and that the value at the bottom of the curve was as low as 1,500,000.

[1] S. F. Cook, "The Population of Mexico in 1793," *Human Biology*, Vol. 14 (1942), pp. 499–515.

APPENDIX I

Tables of Population in 1565

Half brackets are used to denote two or more towns for which the data are consolidated. Full brackets indicate numerical items not used in calculating totals. Parentheses are used for items obtained by calculation (see text). For Jalisco, Nayarit, Colima, and Zacatecas the population is based upon column A (see text, § I).

The sources for the entries under *special items* are as follows:

No. 11, Cuernavaca: the value was derived from calculations based upon the entire holdings of the Marqués del Valle as listed in Documents H and N.

No. 59, Tecamachalco: directly from the *Suma de Visitas*.

No. 216, Teotlalco and Centayuca: from the *Visita* of 1556, in the *Archivo General de Indias, Aud. Mex.*, leg. 168 (59-4-3).

No. 475, Texcoco; no. 599, Huejotzingo; no. 600, Tlaxcala; no. 601, Mexico City: All from the expert testimony found in the document entitled: *Ynformación para su magestad de las provincias en que es defraudado y de la gente que en ellas hay. 1562.* A.G.I., *Patronato*, leg. 182 (2-2-3).

MEXICO

No.	Name	A	B	C	D	E	F	G
87	Acaxuchitlan...................	1300t	830p	......	......	......	......	......
		5200	3320	......	......	......	......	......
38	Acolman [pueblo]..............	1324t	1000p	......	......	......	......	......
		5296	4000	......	......	......	......	......
	Acolman [province]..............	......	......	......	......	......	......	......
		......	......	......	......	......	......	......
407	Amatepec.....................	698t	950p	1234p	......	667p	......	......
		2792	3800	4936	......	2668	......	......
4	Apaxco.......................	532t	600p	......	......	......	......	......
		2128	2400	......	......	......	......	......
164	Atlacomulco...................	343t	1238p	......	......	......	......	......
		1372	4952	......	......	......	......	......
220	Xocotitlan....................	620t	1700p	......	......	......	......	......
		2480	6800	......	......	......	......	......
2	Atlapulco.....................	......	1000p	......	......	......	......	......
		(2307)	4000	......	......	......	......	......
607	Atlatlauca + Xochiac...........	......	300p	350p	......	174p	......	......
		(952)	1200	1400	......	696	......	......
158	Atzcapozalco..................	......	1500p	......	......	......	......	......
		(5538)	6000	......	......	......	......	......
167	Axapusco + Zaguala............	......	940p	1929p	......	695p	......	......
		(4032)	3760	7716	......	2780	......	......
233	Ayucan.......................	1000p	1000p	......	......	......	......	......
		4000	4000	......	......	......	......	......
233	Capulhuac....................	......	......	......	......	......	......	......
		......	......	......	......	......	......	......
233	Tepexoxuca...................	......	......	......	......	......	......	......
		......	......	......	......	......	......	......
233	Caquete......................	......	......	......	......	......	......	......
		......	......	......	......	......	......	......
206	Calcoyuca + Tecoloapan.........	......	1750p	......	......	......	......	......
		(8745)	7000	......	......	......	......	......
770	Coatepec.....................	......	......	......	......	......	......	......
		(1538)	......	......	......	......	......	......
95	Coyoacan + Tacubaya..........	......	2130p	......	......	......	......	......
		(8991)	8520	......	......	......	......	......
777	Coyotepec....................	......	......	......	......	......	......	......
		(741)	......	......	......	......	......	......
166	Cuautitlan....................	......	3400p	7430p	......	6752p	......	......
		(21818)	13600	29720	......	27008	......	......
10	Cuevas (Cuitlavaca)............	......	800p	......	......	......	......	......
		(4111)	3200	......	......	......	......	......
8	Culhuacan....................	......	560p	......	......	......	......	......
		(3136)	2240	......	......	......	......	......
423	Tlamanalco...................	......	......	4993p	......	4267p	......	......
		(13600)	......	19972	......	17068	......	......
423	Amecameca...................	......	......	1523p	......	1522p	......	......
		(4668)	......	6092	......	6088	......	......
423	Tenango......................	......	......	2048p	......	1921p	......	......
		(6635)	......	8192	......	7684	......	......
423	Chimalhuacan.................	......	......	1869p	......	1619p	......	......
		(5421)	......	7476	......	6476	......	......

Appendix I: Population in 1565

MEXICO

H	I	J	K	L	M	N	O	P	Special items	Population
.....	.....	.....	700t	.....	.....	.....	830t	.....	.....	.....
.....	.....	.....	2800	.....	.....	.....	3320	.....	.....	2800
404t	.....	.....	.....	.....	.....	.....	.....	.....	.....	.....
5616	.....	.....	.....	.....	.....	.....	.....	.....	.....	.....
64t	3000t	.....	2560t	.....	.....	4100t	.....	.....	.....	.....
10256	12000	.....	10240	.....	.....	16400	.....	.....	.....	12224
.....	.....	.....	.....	.....	.....	.....	.....	.....	.....	.....
.....	.....	.....	.....	.....	.....	.....	.....	.....	.....	3802
.....	.....	.....	1155t	1155t	.....	.....	.....	331t	.....	.....
.....	.....	.....	4620	4620	.....	.....	.....	1324	.....	4620
.....	.....	.....	4422t	.....	.....	3500t	.....	.....	.....	.....
.....	.....	.....	17688	.....	.....	14000	.....	.....	.....	15844
.....	.....	.....	.....	.....	.....	.....	.....	.....	.....	.....
.....	.....	.....	800t	700t	.....	2200t	.....	440t	.....	.....
.....	.....	.....	3200	2800	.....	8800	.....	1760	.....	3000
.....	.....	.....	.....	404t	.....	.....	.....	.....	.....	.....
.....	.....	.....	.....	1616	.....	.....	.....	.....	.....	1237
.....	.....	.....	.....	.....	.....	1800t	.....	.....	.....	.....
.....	.....	.....	.....	.....	.....	7200	.....	.....	.....	7200
.....	.....	.....	.....	.....	.....	.....	.....	334t	.....	.....
.....	.....	.....	.....	.....	.....	.....	.....	1336	.....	5248
.....	.....	.....	360t	.....	.....	.....	.....	852t	.....	.....
.....	.....	.....	1440	.....	.....	.....	.....	3408	.....	1440
.....	600t	.....	573t	.....	.....	.....	.....	548t	.....	.....
.....	2400	.....	2292	.....	.....	.....	.....	2192	.....	2346
.....	.....	.....	358t	.....	.....	.....	.....	.....	.....	.....
.....	.....	.....	1432	.....	.....	.....	.....	.....	.....	1432
.....	.....	.....	.....	.....	.....	.....	.....	.....	.....	.....
.....	.....	.....	2922t	.....	.....	.....	.....	.....	.....	.....
.....	.....	.....	11688	.....	.....	.....	.....	.....	.....	11688
.....	.....	.....	500t	500t	.....	.....	.....	.....	.....	.....
.....	.....	.....	2000	2000	.....	.....	.....	.....	.....	2000
.....	.....	.....	.....	.....	.....	4530t	.....	.....	.....	.....
.....	.....	.....	.....	.....	.....	18120	.....	.....	.....	18120
.....	.....	.....	.....	241t	.....	.....	.....	.....	.....	.....
.....	.....	.....	.....	964	.....	.....	.....	.....	.....	964
.....	.....	.....	.....	.....	.....	.....	.....	.....	.....	28364
.....	.....	.....	1254t	1254t	.....	1500t	.....	.....	.....	.....
.....	.....	.....	5016	5016	.....	6000	.....	.....	.....	5344
.....	1000t	.....	1030t	.....	.....	1030t	.....	.....	.....	.....
.....	4000	.....	4120	.....	.....	4120	.....	.....	.....	4080
.....	.....	.....	.....	.....	.....	4000t	.....	.....	.....	.....
.....	.....	.....	.....	.....	.....	16000	.....	.....	.....	17680
.....	.....	.....	.....	.....	.....	1500t	.....	.....	.....	.....
.....	.....	.....	.....	.....	.....	6000	.....	.....	.....	6068
.....	.....	.....	.....	.....	.....	2500t	.....	.....	.....	.....
.....	.....	.....	.....	.....	.....	10000	.....	.....	.....	8625
.....	.....	.....	.....	.....	.....	1800t	.....	.....	.....	.....
.....	.....	.....	.....	.....	.....	7200	.....	.....	.....	7050

Population of Central Mexico

MEXICO—(Continued)

No.	Name	A	B	C	D	E	F	G
423	Atengo.................	...... (1692)	2800p 11200	......	......	......	......	......
702	Chapa de Mota.........	...... (8861)	......	......	......	......	......	......
425	Chiconautla............	...... (1625)	330p 1320	528p 2112	......	528p 2112	......	......
9	Chimalhuacan..........	...... (2769)	800p 3200	......	......	......	......	......
119	Churubusco + Cuamoxtitlan.....	...... (6077)	2170p 8680	......	......	......	......	......
546	Ecatepec...............	...... (8000)	1390p 5560	......	......	......	......	......
546	Coatitlan..............	...... (10461)	......	......	......	......	......	......
776	Huehuetoca............	...... (4935)	......	......	......	......	......	......
697	Huexotla..............	...... (7692)	......	......	......	......	......	......
179	Hueypoxtla............	1927t 7708	1800p 7200	......	......	......	......	......
179	Tianguistengo..........	...... (8877)	......	......	......	......	......	......
179	Tlacotlapilco..........	......	......	......	......	......	......	......
476	Huitzilapan............	601t 2404	450p 1800	......	......	......	......	......
611	Huixquilucan...........	...... (1846)	580p 2400	......	......	......	......	......
699	Ixtapalapa.............	...... (2062)	......	......	......	......	......	......
110	Ixtapaluca.............	...... (1138)	370p 1480	......	......	......	......	......
433	Ixtlahuaca.............	1004t 4016	1400p 5600	1591p 6364	......	1013p 4052	......	......
117	Malinalco..............	1895t 7580	1870p 7480	2000p 8000	......	2000p 8000	......	......
34	Metepec...............	...... (14206)	1100p 4400	......	......	......	......	......
34	Tepemachalco..........	......	......	......	......	......	......	......
13	Calimaya..............	......	1440p 5760	......	......	......	......	......
613	Mexicalcingo...........	...... (853)	300p 1200	277p 1108	......	277p 1108	......	......
601	Mexico City............	...... (57611)	......	16164p 64656	......	20752p 83008	......	......
116	Michimaloya...........	1390t 5560	800p 3200	......	......	......	......	......
708	Milpa Alta.............	...... (8615)	......	......	......	......	......	......
36	Mizquic...............	...... (2064)	550p 2200	......	......	......	......	......

Appendix I: Population in 1565

MEXICO—(Continued)

H	I	J	K	L	M	N	O	P	Special items	Population
.....	.....	.....	.....	.....	.....	550t	.....	.....	.....	
.....	.....	.....	.....	.....	.....	2200	.....	.....	.....	2200
.....	.....	.....	3360t	.....	.....	2400t	.....	.....	.....	
.....	.....	.....	13440	.....	.....	9600	.....	.....	.....	11520
.....	.....	.....	.....	.....	.....	.....	.....	.....	.....	2112
.....	.....	.....	.....	1000t	.....	800t	.....	.....	.....	
.....	.....	.....	.....	4000	.....	3200	.....	.....	.....	3600
.....	.....	.....	.....	1975t	.....	.....	.....	.....	.....	
.....	.....	.....	.....	7900	.....	.....	.....	.....	.....	7900
.....	.....	.....	.....	.....	.....	2600t	.....	450t	.....	
.....	.....	.....	.....	.....	.....	10400	.....	1800	.....	10400
.....	.....	.....	.....	.....	.....	3400t	.....	.....	.....	
.....	.....	.....	.....	.....	.....	13600	.....	.....	.....	13600
.....	.....	.....	1605t	.....	.....	.....	.....	.....	.....	
.....	.....	.....	6420	.....	.....	.....	.....	.....	.....	6420
.....	.....	.....	.....	.....	.....	2500t	.....	.....	.....	
.....	.....	.....	.....	.....	.....	10000	.....	.....	.....	10000
.....	.....	.....	⎡3070t	1701t	.....	⎡2700t	.....	.....	.....	
.....	.....	.....	⎣12280	6804	.....	⎢10800	.....	.....	.....	11540
.....	.....	.....	.....	216t	.....	⎢	.....	.....	.....	
.....	.....	.....	.....	864	.....	⎢	.....	.....	.....	......
.....	.....	.....	.....	.....	.....	⎢	.....	.....	.....	
.....	.....	.....	.....	.....	.....	⎣	.....	.....	.....	⎣......
.....	.....	.....	.....	.....	.....	[2700t]	.....	.....	.....	
.....	.....	.....	.....	.....	.....	.....	.....	.....	.....	2404
.....	.....	.....	.....	.....	.....	.....	.....	.....	.....	2400
.....	.....	.....	.....	640t	.....	700t	.....	.....	.....	
.....	.....	.....	.....	2560	.....	2800	.....	.....	.....	2680
.....	.....	.....	.....	.....	.....	.....	.....	.....	.....	1480
.....	.....	.....	.....	.....	.....	1300t	.....	.....	.....	
.....	.....	.....	.....	.....	.....	5200	.....	.....	.....	5205
.....	3000p	2000t	.....	2000p	.....	2500t	.....	.....	.....	
.....	12000	8000	.....	8000	.....	10000	.....	.....	.....	9200
.....	.....	.....	.....	⎡3834t	.....	1900t	.....	.....	.....	⎡
.....	.....	.....	.....	⎢15336	.....	7600	.....	.....	.....	⎢18468
.....	.....	.....	.....	⎢	.....	.....	.....	367t	.....	⎢
.....	.....	.....	.....	⎢	.....	.....	.....	1468	.....	⎢......
.....	.....	.....	.....	⎢	.....	3500t	.....	.....	.....	⎢
.....	.....	.....	.....	⎣	.....	14000	.....	.....	.....	⎣......
.....	.....	.....	.....	.....	.....	.....	.....	.....	.....	
.....	.....	.....	.....	.....	.....	.....	.....	.....	.....	1108
.....	.....	.....	.....	.....	.....	.....	.....	.....	77022tp	74895
.....	.....	.....	.....	1547t	.....	.....	.....	.....	.....	
.....	.....	.....	.....	6188	.....	.....	.....	.....	.....	6188
.....	.....	.....	.....	.....	.....	2800t	.....	.....	.....	
.....	.....	.....	.....	.....	.....	11200	.....	.....	.....	11200
t	700t	.....	.....	645t	.....	[1200t]	.....	.....	.....	
2668	2800	.....	.....	2580	.....	.....	.....	.....	.....	2683

Population of Central Mexico

MEXICO—(Continued)

No.	Name	A	B	C	D	E	F	G
37	Nextlalpan......................	400t	350p	......	......	......	......	......
		1600	1400	......	......	......	......	......
190	Ocuilan.........................	1646t	1500p	......	......	......	......	......
		6584	6000	......	......	......	......	......
615	Otumba.........................	..,....	1600p	6184p	......	5042p	......	......
		(18180)	6400	24736	......	20168	......	......
299	Otzolotepec.....................	190t	......	......	......	......	......	......
		760	......	......	......	......	......	......
299	Xilotzingo......................	186t	......	......	......	......	......	......
		744	......	......	......	......	......	......
299	Mimiapam......................	80t	......	......	......	......	......	......
		320	......	......	......	......	......	......
241	Soyanaquilpan...................	487t	850p	......	......	645p	......	......
		1948	3400	......	......	2580	......	......
43	Tacuba.........................	......	2700p	......	......	......	......	......
		(14461)	10800	......	......	......	......	......
335	Teacalco........................	239t	......	......	......	......	......	......
		956	......	......	......	......	......	......
303	Tecama.........................	550t	600p	632p	......	632p	......	......
		2200	2400	2528	......	2528	......	......
53	Tenango........................	......	1400p	1000p	......	777p	......	......
		(3058)	5600	4000	......	3108	......	......
528	Tenayuca.......................	720p	570p	......	......	1025p	......	......
		2880	2280	......	......	4100	......	......
778	Teoloyucan......................	......	......	......	......	......	......	......
		(2517)	......	......	......	......	......	......
42	Teotihuacan.....................	690t	1400p	......	......	1703p	......	......
		2760	5600	......	......	6812	......	......
127	Tepetlaoxtoc....................	......	1100p	......	......	......	......	......
		(9068)	4400	......	......	......	......	......
50	Tepexpa........................	965t	850p	......	......	......	......	......
		3860	3400	......	......	......	......	......
768	Temaxcalapa....................	......	......	......	......	......	......	......
		(4858)	......	......	......	......	......	......
617	Tepotzotlan.....................	......	870p	2971p	......	......	......	......
		(7895)	3480	11884	......	......	......	......
51	Tequisistlan....................	⎡235t	⎡420p	⎡500p	......	⎡462p	......	......
		940	1680	2000	......	1848	......	......
51	Totolcingo......................	......	......	......	......	......	......	......
		⎣......	⎣......	⎣......	......	⎣......	......	......
44	Tequixquiac.....................	1090t	1600p	......	......	......	......	......
		4360	6400	......	......	......	......	......
208	Texaquique.....................	......	500p	......	......	......	......	......
		(1537)	2000	......	......	......	......	......
129	Texcaltitlan.....................	⎡554t	⎡2000p	......	......	......	......	......
		2216	8000	......	......	......	......	......
129	Temascaltepec...................	......	......	......	......	......	......	......
		(5062)	......	......	......	......	......	......
129	Texupilco......................	⎣......	⎣......	......	......	......	......	......
		......	......	......	......	......	......	......

Appendix I: Population in 1565

MEXICO—(Continued)

H	I	J	K	L	M	N	O	P	Special items	Population
.....	.....	.....	.....	820t	.....	.....	.....	.....	.....	
.....	.....	.....	.....	3280	.....	.....	.....	.....	.....	3280
800t	1800t	.....	.....	1804t	.....	1900t	.....	.....	.....	
7200	7200	.....	.....	7216	.....	7600	.....	.....	.....	7304
.....	.....	.....	.....	.....	.....	6500t	.....	.....	.....	
.....	.....	.....	.....	.....	.....	26000	.....	.....	.....	23635
.....	.....	.....	.....	.....	.....	.....	.....	.....	.....	760
.....	.....	.....	.....	.....	.....	.....	.....	.....	.....	744
.....	.....	.....	.....	.....	.....	.....	.....	136t	.....	
.....	.....	.....	.....	.....	.....	.....	.....	544	.....	320
.....	.....	.....	.....	700t	.....	.....	.....	.....	.....	
.....	.....	.....	.....	2800	.....	.....	.....	.....	.....	2690
.....	.....	.....	.....	.....	.....	4700t	.....	.....	.....	
.....	.....	.....	.....	.....	.....	18800	.....	.....	.....	18800
00t	.....	.....	.....	.....	.....	.....	.....	.....	.....	
800	.....	.....	.....	.....	.....	.....	.....	.....	.....	800
.....	.....	.....	.....	.....	.....	.....	.....	.....	.....	2528
.....	.....	.....	1205t	.....	.....	(2600t)	.....	.....	.....	
.....	.....	.....	4820	.....	.....	.....	.....	.....	.....	3976
.....	.....	.....	.....	.....	.....	.....	.....	.....	.....	4100
.....	.....	.....	818t	.....	.....	.....	.....	.....	.....	
.....	.....	.....	3272	.....	.....	.....	.....	.....	.....	3272
.....	.....	.....	.....	1655t	.....	.....	.....	.....	.....	
.....	.....	.....	.....	6620	.....	.....	.....	.....	.....	6716
.....	.....	.....	.....	2947t	.....	.....	.....	1604t	.....	
.....	.....	.....	.....	11788	.....	.....	.....	6416	.....	11788
43t	.....	.....	.....	⎡1579t	.....	.....	.....	.....	.....	⎧
2172	.....	.....	.....	6316	.....	.....	.....	.....	.....	6316
.....	.....	.....	197t	788	.....	.....	.....	.....	.....	⎩.....
.....	.....	.....	2733t	.....	.....	2400t	.....	.....	.....	
.....	.....	.....	10932	.....	.....	9600	.....	.....	.....	10264
22t	.....	.....	.....	.....	.....	.....	.....	.....	.....	⎧
1688	.....	.....	.....	.....	.....	.....	.....	.....	.....	1845
.....	.....	.....	.....	.....	.....	.....	.....	.....	.....	⎩.....
.....	.....	.....	1676t	1650t	.....	[3700t]	.....	.....	.....	
.....	.....	.....	6704	6600	.....	.....	.....	.....	.....	6652
.....	.....	.....	.....	.....	.....	.....	.....	.....	.....	2000
.....	.....	.....	⎡1526t	1509t	.....	⎡1900t	.....	.....	.....	
.....	.....	.....	6104	6036	.....	7600	.....	.....	.....	6580
.....	.....	.....	.....	.....	.....	.....	.....	.....	.....	.....
.....	.....	.....	.....	.....	.....	.....	.....	.....	.....	.....
.....	.....	.....	⎣.....	.....	.....	⎣.....	.....	.....	.....	.....

MEXICO—(Continued)

No.	Name	A	B	C	D	E	F	G
475	Texcoco	...... (64589)	2700p 10800	15975p 63900	......	......	......	......
54	Tlacotepec	...... (2200)	550p 2200	......	......	......	......	......
173	Tlacotepec	....	⌠3300p 13200	......	......	......	......	......
173	Xochicuatla	551t 2204	....	......	......	......	......	......
173	Quetzala	...... (4185)	....	......	......	......	......	......
46	Tlachichilpa	⌠905t 3620	⌠1050p 4200	......	......	......	......	......
46	Malacatepec	...... ⌊	...... ⌊	......	......	......	......	......
666	Tlalnepantla	...... (10461)	....	......	......	......	......	......
49	Tlanalapa	...... (3200)	⌠800p 3200	......	......	......	......	......
49	Talistaca	....	...... ⌊	......	......	......	......	......
305	Tlapanaloyan	118t 472	150p 600	......	......	......	......	......
45	Toluca	2869t 11476	3700p 14800	......	......	......	......	......
621	Totolapan	...... (12409)	3500p 14000	4379p 17516	......	4643p 18572	......	......
56	Tultitlan	...... (6917)	1500p 6000	2832p 11328	......	1664p 6656	......	......
296	Xalatlaco	...... (4923)	1200p 4800	......	......	......	......	......
198	Xaltocan	...... (894)	600p 2400	352p 1408	......	......	......	......
73	Xilotepec [province]	...... (68208)	17000p 68000	......	......	......	......	......
72	Xilotzingo	660t 2640	1100p 4400	......	......	......	......	......
74	Xiquipilco	2800t 11200	3300p 13200	......	......	......	......	......
445	Xochimilco	2250p 9000	2250p 9000	10584p 42336	......	8941p 35764	......	......
773	Xoquicingo	...... (668)	....	......	......	......	......	......
97	Zacualpan	1000t 4000	⌠2500p 10000	......	......	......	......	......
97	Tenancingo	786t 3144	...... ⌊	......	......	......	......	......
14	Zinacantepec	815t 3260	2750p 11000	......	......	......	......	......
608	Zitlaltepec	...... (2198)	500p 2000	806p 3224	......	......	......	......

Appendix I: Population in 1565

MEXICO—(Continued)

H	I	J	K	L	M	N	O	P	Special items	Population
						22000t			25000t	
						88000			100000	83966
										2200
				1360t				489t		
				5440				1956		5440
			1410t	1555t		1400t				
			5640	6220		5600				5820
						3400t		1162t		
						13600		4648		13600
										3200
			209t	150t						
			836	600						718
						5800t				
						23200				23200
10p	4000t					3000t				
16440	16000					12000				16132
										8992
			1500t	[592t]		1700t		972t		
			6000			6800		3888		6400
			229t							
			916							1162
				18335t		26000t		13131t		
				73340		104000		52524		88670
			584t							
			2336							2336
			3208t	3500t		2300t				
			12832	14000		9200				12011
						5800t				
						23200				33766
			217t							
			868							868
	2000t		700t	2150t		1050t				
	8000		2800	8600		4200				8533
						1200t				
						4800				
				1500t		1300t				
				6000		5200				5600
			623t							
			2492							2858

MEXICO—(Concluded)

No.	Name	A	B	C	D	E	F	G
219	Zumpahuacan	868t 3472	1500p 6000					
219	Soacango							
237	Zumpango	(6554)	1020p 4080	2364p 9456		1978p 7912		
605	Coatepec	(4000)	1330p 5320			1000p 4000		
165	Ixtapa	(1844)	1000p 4000					
774	Ziotepec	(960)						
	Cuapanoya	(462)						
240	Tlanacopan	(1846)	270p 1080					
288	Oxtotipac	(1800)	600p 2400					
843	Huitzizilapan			437p 1748				

HIDALGO

No.	Name	A	B	C	D	E	F	G
273	Acatlan	571t 2284						
149	Acaxuchitlan	(2769)			900t 3600			
152	Acayuca	(2443)	700p 2800					
156	Actopan [province]	(34138)						
204	Achiotepec	(4308)	1500p 6000					
541	Ahuatipan	700t 2800						
272	Atengo	430t 1720	250p 1000	713p 2852		463p 1852		
402	Atitlaquia	1248t 4992	400p 1600	1907p 7629		1409p 5636		
157	Atotonilco (el grande)	5803t 23212	5500p 22000					
1	Atotonilco	820t 3280	1050p 4200					
1	Zacamal							
3	Axacuba	2985t 11940	1840p 7360					
171	Chapantongo	2876t 11504	1430p 5720	1578p 6312		1578p 6312		

Appendix I: Population in 1565   59

MEXICO—(Concluded)

H	I	J	K	L	M	N	O	P	Special items	Population
....	.....	.....	.....	.....	.....	1500t	.....	658t	.....	⎧ 6000
....	.....	.....	.....	.....	.....	6000	.....	2632	.....	⎨
....	.....	.....	.....	.....	.....	.....	.....	.....	.....	⎩ .....
....	.....	.....	2048t	.....	.....	[2900t]	.....	.....	.....	
....	.....	.....	8192	.....	.....	.....	.....	.....	.....	8520
....	.....	.....	.....	.....	.....	1600t	.....	.....	.....	
....	.....	.....	.....	.....	.....	6400	.....	.....	.....	5200
....	.....	.....	.....	600t	.....	.....	.....	.....	.....	
....	.....	.....	.....	2400	.....	.....	.....	.....	.....	2400
....	.....	.....	312t	.....	.....	.....	.....	.....	.....	
....	.....	.....	1248	.....	.....	.....	.....	.....	.....	1248
....	.....	.....	150t	.....	.....	.....	.....	.....	.....	
....	.....	.....	600	.....	.....	.....	.....	.....	.....	600
....	.....	.....	.....	600t	.....	.....	.....	.....	.....	
....	.....	.....	.....	2400	.....	.....	.....	.....	.....	2400
....	.....	.....	.....	.....	.....	.....	.....	.....	.....	
....	.....	.....	.....	.....	.....	.....	.....	.....	.....	2400
....	.....	.....	.....	.....	.....	.....	.....	.....	.....	1748

HIDALGO

H	I	J	K	L	M	N	O	P	Special items	Population
t	.....	.....	.....	.....	.....	.....	800t	.....	.....	
3200	.....	.....	.....	.....	.....	.....	3200	.....	.....	3200
....	.....	.....	.....	.....	.....	.....	.....	529t	.....	
....	.....	.....	.....	.....	.....	.....	.....	2116	.....	3600
....	.....	.....	848t	740t	.....	[2400t]	848t	.....	.....	
....	.....	.....	3392	2960	.....	.....	3392	.....	.....	3176
0t	12500t	.....	.....	7190t	.....	15000t	.....	3818t	.....	
28800	50000	.....	.....	28760	.....	60000	.....	15272	.....	44380
....	.....	.....	.....	1400t	.....	.....	.....	.....	.....	
....	.....	.....	.....	5600	.....	.....	.....	.....	.....	5600
....	.....	.....	.....	.....	.....	.....	.....	.....	.....	2800
....	.....	.....	456p	.....	.....	.....	.....	.....	.....	
....	.....	.....	1824	.....	.....	.....	.....	.....	.....	2176
....	.....	.....	1409t	.....	.....	[5500t]	2819t	.....	.....	
....	.....	.....	5636	.....	.....	.....	11276	.....	.....	6300
0t	6000t	.....	.....	5200t	.....	4900t	5000t	.....	.....	
20400	24000	.....	.....	20800	.....	19600	20000	.....	.....	21200
....	.....	.....	⎡ 1610t	⎡ 1550t	.....	.....	⎡ 1810t	⎡ 343t	.....	⎧
....	.....	.....	6440	6200	.....	.....	7240	1372	.....	6320
....	.....	.....	⎣	⎣	.....	.....	⎣	⎣	.....	⎩ .....
4t	.....	.....	4365t	.....	.....	5600t	4284t	.....	.....	
17136	.....	.....	17460	.....	.....	22400	17136	.....	.....	22400
8t	1400t	.....	.....	.....	.....	[3200t]	1568t	.....	.....	
6312	5600	.....	.....	.....	.....	.....	6272	.....	.....	6134

Population of Central Mexico

HIDALGO—(Continued)

No.	Name	A	B	C	D	E	F	G
238	Chichatlan....................	......	800p	......	......	......	......	......
		(3200)	3200	......	......	......	......	......
701	Chichicaxtla.................	......	......	......	......	......	......	......
		(3685)	......	......	......	......	......	......
94	Chilcuautla..................	961t	800p	......	......	......	......	......
		3844	3200	......	......	......	......	......
457	Tlacotlapilco................	772t	......	......	......	......	......	......
		3088	......	......	......	......	......	......
553	Chilpopocatlan...............	500t	......	......	......	......	......	......
		2000	......	......	......	......	......	......
289	Huautla......................	169t	......	......	......	......	......	......
		676	......	......	......	......	......	......
27	Huazalingo...................	531t	1500p	......	......	......	......	......
		2124	6000	......	......	......	......	......
696	Huichapan....................	......	......	......	......	......	......	......
		(13538)	......	......	......	......	......	......
612	Ixcuinquitlapilco [pueblo]...	......	430p	4558p	......	3877p	......	......
		(12753)	1720	18232	......	15508	......	......
612	Ixcuinquitlapilco [sugetos]..	......	......	......	......	......	......	......
		(10615)	......	......	......	......	......	......
183	Ixmiquilpam..................	2800t	2121p	1595p	......	4972p	......	......
		11200	8484	6380	......	19888	......	......
183	Tlacintla....................	......	......	......	......	......	......	......
71	Jasso (Xipacoya).............	1793t	800p	......	......	......	......	......
		7172	3200	......	......	......	......	......
236	Macuilsuchitl................	1264t	1560p	......	......	......	......	......
		5056	6240	......	......	......	......	......
492	Malila.......................	1663t	2200p	......	......	......	......	......
		6652	8800	......	......	......	......	......
437	Molango......................	4126t	......	......	......	......	......	......
		16504	......	......	......	......	......	......
35	Metztitlan...................	7318t	13500p	......	......	......	......	......
		29272	54000	......	......	......	......	......
394	Nexpa + Tauzan...............	560t	480p	219p	......	219p	......	......
		2240	1920	876	......	876	......	......
121	Pachuca [pueblo].............	432t	550p	......	......	......	......	......
		1728	2200	......	......	......	......	......
121	Pachuca [mines]..............	......	......	......	......	......	......	......
		(1796)	......	......	......	......	......	......
240	Talnacopan...................	......	270p	......	......	......	......	......
		(1080)	1080	......	......	......	......	......
502	Sayula.......................	400t	150p	......	......	352p	......	......
		1600	600	......	......	1408	......	......
514	Tepatepec....................	429t	......	......	......	......	......	......
		1716	......	......	......	......	......	......
514	Tepeitic.....................	......	......	......	......	......	......	......
230	Mizquiahuala.................	486t	340p	......	......	806p	......	......
		1944	1360	......	......	3224	......	......

Appendix I: Population in 1565

HIDALGO—(Continued)

H	I	J	K	L	M	N	O	P	Special items	Population
.....	.....	.....	.....	.....	.....	.....	.....	.....	.....	
.....	.....	.....	.....	.....	.....	.....	.....	.....	.....	3200
.....	.....	1295t	.....	.....	.....	1100t	940t	.....	.....	
.....	.....	5180	.....	.....	.....	4400	3760	.....	.....	4790
18t	2500t	.....	.....	1200t	.....	.....	.....	.....	.....	
4871	10000	.....	.....	4800	.....	.....	.....	.....	.....	9036
0t	.....	.....	.....	.....	.....	.....	800t	.....	.....	
3200	.....	.....	.....	.....	.....	.....	3200	.....	.....	
.....	.....	.....	.....	.....	.....	.....	.....	.....	.....	.....
.....	.....	.....	.....	.....	.....	.....	.....	.....	.....	2000
.....	.....	.....	.....	.....	.....	.....	100t	.....	.....	
.....	.....	.....	.....	.....	.....	.....	400	.....	.....	400
.....	.....	.....	.....	800t	.....	.....	600t	.....	.....	
.....	.....	.....	.....	3200	.....	.....	2400	.....	.....	3200
.....	.....	.....	.....	.....	.....	4400t	.....	.....	.....	
.....	.....	.....	.....	.....	.....	17600	.....	.....	.....	17600
00t	.....	.....	.....	.....	.....	.....	4000t	.....	.....	
16000	.....	.....	.....	.....	.....	.....	16000	.....	.....	16580
50t	.....	.....	.....	.....	.....	.....	3450t	.....	.....	
13800	.....	.....	.....	.....	.....	.....	13800	.....	.....	13800
26t	4000t	.....	.....	.....	.....	3100t	.....	.....	.....	
16104	16000	.....	.....	.....	.....	12400	.....	.....	.....	16098
.....	.....	.....	.....	.....	.....	.....	.....	.....	.....	
.....	.....	.....	.....	.....	.....	.....	.....	.....	.....	.....
.....	.....	.....	.....	2182t	.....	.....	.....	.....	.....	
.....	.....	.....	.....	8728	.....	.....	.....	.....	.....	8728
.....	.....	.....	.....	.....	.....	.....	.....	.....	.....	
.....	.....	.....	.....	.....	.....	.....	.....	.....	.....	6240
.....	3000t	.....	.....	.....	.....	4400t	1186t	.....	.....	
.....	12000	.....	.....	.....	.....	17600	4744	.....	.....	14880
.....	.....	.....	.....	.....	.....	.....	1174t	.....	.....	
.....	.....	.....	.....	.....	.....	.....	4696	.....	.....	.....
.....	11000t	.....	.....	9650t	.....	13000t	16114c	.....	.....	
.....	44000	.....	.....	38600	.....	52000	21432	.....	.....	44866
.....	.....	.....	.....	.....	.....	.....	.....	.....	.....	
.....	.....	.....	.....	.....	.....	.....	.....	.....	.....	876
.....	.....	.....	651t	710t	.....	(2700t)	652t	.....	.....	
.....	.....	.....	2604	2840	.....	.....	2608	.....	.....	2722
.....	.....	.....	584t	.....	.....	.....	532t	.....	.....	
.....	.....	.....	2336	.....	.....	.....	2128	.....	.....	2336
.....	.....	.....	.....	.....	.....	.....	.....	.....	.....	
.....	.....	.....	.....	.....	.....	.....	.....	.....	.....	1080
.....	.....	.....	.....	.....	.....	.....	300t	.....	.....	
.....	.....	.....	.....	.....	.....	.....	1200	.....	.....	1408
t	.....	.....	588t	.....	.....	.....	588t	.....	.....	
800	.....	.....	2352	.....	.....	.....	2352	.....	.....	2352
.....	.....	.....	.....	.....	.....	.....	.....	.....	.....	
.....	.....	.....	.....	.....	.....	.....	.....	.....	.....	.....
.....	.....	.....	806t	800t	.....	(2500t)	806t	.....	.....	
.....	.....	.....	3224	3200	.....	.....	3224	.....	.....	3216

Population of Central Mexico

HIDALGO—(Continued)

No.	Name	A	B	C	D	E	F	G
652	Tepeapulco................	...... (15750)	1350p 5400	4493p 17972	....	4463p 17852	....	....
232	Tepetitlan.................	352t 1408	550p 2200	....	....	....	....	....
123	Tepexi.....................	2850t 11400	2200p 8800	....	....	....	....	....
456	Tetepango.................	931t 3724	540p 2160	....	....	858t 3432	....	....
55	Texcatepec................	2313t 9252	1400p 5600	....	....	....	....	....
130	Tezontepec................	80t 320	250p 1000	....	....	....	....	....
336	Tezontepec................	601t 2404	530p 2120	....	....	....	....	....
52	Tianguistengo.............	543t 2172	400p 1600	....	....	....	....	....
775	Tilcuautla.................	...... (1908)	....	....	....	....	....	....
125	Tizayuca..................	1021t 4084	1360p 5440	....	....	2382p 9528	....	....
125	Tolcayuca.................	1006t 4024	....	....	....	1055p 4220	....	....
460	Tlahuelilpa................	609t 2436	600p 2400	....	....	[222p]	....	....
122	Tlamaco...................	400t 1600	550p 2200	....	....	....	....	....
47	Tlanchinol................	1033t 4132	⎧8100p⎨ 32400	....	....	....	....	....
47	Acuimantla................	1040t 4160	⎩......⎭	....	....	....	....	....
293	Tlaquilpa.................	271t 1084	900p 3600	866p 3464	....	866p 3464	....	....
211	Tornacustla...............	...... (2541)	550p 2200	....	....	....	....	....
474	Tula......................	7800t 31200	1300p 5200	....	....	3080p 12320	....	....
48	Tulancingo................	...... (16923)	1700p 6800	....	....	....	....	....
245	Tututepec.................	...... 14260tp	4500p 18000	....	....	....	....	....
513	Xochicoatlan..............	1710t 6840	1500p 6000	....	....	....	....	....
629	Yahualica.................	...... (3385)	600p 2400	....	....	....	....	....
413	Zapotlan..................	456t 1824	220p 880	....	....	392p 1568	....	....
92	Zempoala.................	...... (10233)	880p 3520	3352p 13408	....	3352p 13408	....	....
807	Zinguilucan...............	...... (2573)	....	887p 3549	757t 3028	757t 3028	....	....
811	Zimapan..................	...... (1231)	....	....	....	....	....	....

Appendix I: Population in 1565

HIDALGO—(Continued)

H	I	J	K	L	M	N	O	P	Special Items	Population
.....	.....	.....	.....	.....	.....	6400t	6356t	.....	.....	.....
.....	.....	.....	.....	.....	.....	25600	25424	.....	.....	20475
.....	.....	.....	.....	[766t]	.....	3500t	3510t	.....	.....	.....
.....	.....	.....	.....	.....	.....	14000	14040	.....	.....	14000
.....	.....	.....	.....	3980t	.....	3500t	.....	.....	.....	.....
.....	.....	.....	.....	15920	.....	14000	.....	.....	.....	14960
68t	.....	.....	.....	.....	.....	.....	.....	.....	.....	.....
3472	.....	.....	.....	.....	.....	.....	.....	.....	.....	3452
.....	.....	.....	.....	3071t	.....	1600t	1453t	.....	.....	.....
.....	.....	.....	.....	12284	.....	6400	5812	.....	.....	9342
.....	.....	.....	.....	.....	.....	.....	.....	195t	.....	.....
.....	.....	.....	.....	.....	.....	.....	.....	780	.....	1000
00t	800t	.....	487t	807t	.....	800t	487t	.....	.....	.....
3200	3200	.....	1948	3228	.....	3200	1948	.....	.....	2955
.....	.....	.....	.....	600t	.....	.....	.....	.....	.....	.....
.....	.....	.....	.....	2400	.....	.....	.....	.....	.....	2400
.....	.....	.....	620t	.....	.....	.....	620t	.....	.....	.....
.....	.....	.....	2480	.....	.....	.....	2480	.....	.....	2480
.....	.....	.....	1277t	.....	.....	⎰4400t	.....	.....	.....	⎰
.....	.....	.....	5108	.....	.....	17600	.....	.....	.....	13552
.....	.....	.....	1050t	1054t	.....	⎱	.....	.....	.....	⎱
.....	.....	.....	4200	4216	.....	.....	.....	.....	.....	.....
.....	.....	.....	.....	.....	.....	.....	.....	.....	.....	.....
.....	.....	.....	.....	.....	.....	.....	.....	.....	.....	2418
.....	.....	.....	800t	793t	.....	.....	800t	.....	.....	.....
.....	.....	.....	3200	3172	.....	.....	3200	.....	.....	3186
.....	⎰5000t	⎰4500t	.....	⎰4389t	.....	⎰4500t	⎰4500t	.....	.....	.....
.....	20000	18000	.....	17556	.....	18000	18000	.....	.....	18389
.....	.....	.....	.....	.....	.....	.....	.....	.....	.....	.....
.....	.....	.....	.....	⎱	.....	.....	⎱	.....	.....	⎱.....
.....	.....	.....	351t	866t	.....	.....	600t	241t	.....	.....
.....	.....	.....	1404	3464	.....	.....	2400	964	.....	2949
.....	.....	.....	.....	826t	.....	.....	400t	147t	.....	.....
.....	.....	.....	.....	3304	.....	.....	1600	588	.....	3304
.....	.....	.....	.....	.....	.....	9000t	7980t	.....	.....	.....
.....	.....	.....	.....	.....	.....	36000	31920	.....	.....	24160
.....	.....	.....	.....	.....	.....	5500t	5481t	.....	.....	.....
.....	.....	.....	.....	.....	.....	22000	21924	.....	.....	22000
500t	3000t	.....	.....	4000t	.....	3600t	3600t	.....	.....	.....
14400	12000	.....	.....	16000	.....	14400	14400	.....	.....	14200
.....	1500t	.....	.....	.....	.....	.....	1563t	.....	.....	.....
.....	6000	.....	.....	.....	.....	.....	6252	.....	.....	6000
.....	.....	.....	.....	.....	.....	1100t	.....	.....	.....	.....
.....	.....	.....	.....	.....	.....	4400	.....	.....	.....	4400
.....	.....	.....	392t	.....	.....	.....	392t	.....	.....	.....
.....	.....	.....	1568	.....	.....	.....	1568	.....	.....	1568
.....	.....	.....	.....	[533t]	.....	3300t	2670t	272t	.....	.....
.....	.....	.....	.....	.....	.....	13200	10680	1088	.....	13304
.....	900t	947t	.....	.....	.....	770t	947t	.....	.....	.....
.....	3600	3788	.....	.....	.....	3080	3788	.....	.....	3345
.....	.....	.....	.....	.....	.....	.....	400t	.....	.....	.....
.....	.....	.....	.....	.....	.....	.....	1600	.....	.....	1600

Population of Central Mexico

HIDALGO—(Concluded)

No.	Name	A	B	C	D	E	F	G
24	Epazoyuca	......	900p	......	......	......	......	......
		(6319)	3600	......	......	......	......	......
428	Huejutla	609t	1180p	......	......	......	......	......
		2436	4720	......	......	......	......	......
	Oztatlahuauca	......	......	......	......	......	......	......
		(2052)	......	......	......	......	......	......
	Ixquilpa	......	......	......	......	......	......	......
		(4000)	......	......	......	......	......	......
	Hueoquilpa	......	200p	......	......	......	......	......
		(800)	800	......	......	......	......	......
	Talhuacpa	429t	......	......	......	......	......	......
		1716	......	......	......	......	......	......
	Tezapotitlan	......	1100p	......	......	......	......	......
		(4400)	4400	......	......	......	......	......
	Teotlalpa	......	......	......	......	400t	......	......
		(1231)	......	......	......	1600	......	......
	Tlacachique	118t	......	......	......	......	......	......
		472	......	......	......	......	......	......
	Icitecomal	......	600p	......	......	......	......	......
		(2400)	2400	......	......	......	......	......

PUEBLA

No.	Name	A	B	C	D	E	F	G
401	Acatlan	......	370p	1024p	......	......	......	......
		(2806)	1480	4096	......	......	......	......
554	Acatzingo	......	......	......	......	......	......	......
		(9784)	......	......	......	......	......	......
405	Ahuatlan	100t	200p	72p	40t	72p	......	......
		400	800	288	160	288	......	......
710	Aljojuca	......	......	......	......	......	......	......
		(431)	......	......	......	......	......	......
552	Alpatlahuac	......	......	......	......	......	......	......
		(3295)	......	......	......	......	......	......
754	Ameluca	......	......	......	20t	......	......	......
		(62)	......	......	80	......	......	......
404	Atempan	......	400p	......	400t	......	......	......
		(1231)	1600	......	1600	......	......	......
815	Atzalą	......	......	......	......	......	......	......
		(2770)	......	......	......	......	......	......
271	Axochitlan	......	......	......	......	1109p	......	......
		(3245)	......	......	......	4436	......	......
722	Calmeca	......	......	......	......	......	......	......
		(462)	......	......	......	......	......	......
203	Castilblanco	......	1000p	......	......	......	......	......
		(4615)	4000	......	......	......	......	......
723	Coatepec	......	......	......	......	......	......	......
		(184)	......	......	......	......	......	......

Appendix I: Population in 1565

HIDALGO—(Concluded)

H	I	J	K	L	M	N	O	P	Special items	Population
.....	2000t	1865t	.....	1350t	.....	3000t	[979t]	689t	.....	.....
.....	8000	7460	.....	5400	.....	12000	.....	2756	.....	8215
.....	1000t	814t	.....	.....	.....	[2300t]	814t	.....	.....	.....
.....	4000	3256	.....	.....	.....	.....	3256	.....	.....	3763
.....	.....	.....	.....	.....	.....	.....	667t	.....	.....	.....
.....	.....	.....	.....	.....	.....	.....	2668	.....	.....	2668
.....	.....	.....	.....	.....	.....	1300t	.....	.....	.....	.....
.....	.....	.....	.....	.....	.....	5200	.....	.....	.....	5200
.....	.....	.....	.....	.....	.....	.....	.....	.....	.....	.....
.....	.....	.....	.....	.....	.....	.....	.....	.....	.....	800
.....	.....	.....	.....	.....	.....	.....	.....	.....	.....	1716
.....	.....	.....	.....	.....	.....	.....	.....	.....	.....	4400
.....	.....	.....	.....	.....	.....	.....	.....	.....	.....	1600
.....	.....	.....	.....	.....	.....	.....	.....	.....	.....	472
.....	.....	.....	.....	.....	.....	.....	.....	.....	.....	2400

PUEBLA

H	I	J	K	L	M	N	O	P	Special items	Population
.....	.....	.....	.....	.....	.....	800t	.....	.....	.....	.....
.....	.....	.....	.....	.....	.....	3200	.....	.....	.....	3648
.....	.....	.....	.....	.....	.....	3180t	.....	.....	.....	.....
.....	.....	.....	.....	.....	.....	12720	.....	.....	.....	12720
.....	.....	.....	.....	.....	.....	70p	105t	.....	.....	.....
.....	.....	.....	.....	.....	.....	280	420	.....	.....	254
.....	.....	.....	.....	.....	.....	140t	.....	.....	.....	.....
.....	.....	.....	.....	.....	.....	560	.....	.....	.....	560
.....	.....	.....	.....	.....	.....	1071t	.....	.....	.....	.....
.....	.....	.....	.....	.....	.....	4284	.....	.....	.....	4284
.....	.....	.....	.....	.....	.....	.....	.....	.....	.....	80
.....	.....	.....	.....	.....	.....	400t	.....	.....	.....	.....
.....	.....	.....	.....	.....	.....	1600	.....	.....	.....	1600
.....	.....	.....	.....	.....	.....	.....	900t	.....	.....	.....
.....	.....	.....	.....	.....	.....	.....	3600	.....	.....	3600
.....	.....	.....	.....	.....	.....	1000t	.....	.....	.....	.....
.....	.....	.....	.....	.....	.....	4000	.....	.....	.....	4218
.....	.....	.....	.....	.....	.....	150t	.....	.....	.....	.....
.....	.....	.....	.....	.....	.....	600	.....	.....	.....	600
.....	.....	.....	.....	1500t	.....	.....	.....	945t	.....	.....
.....	.....	.....	.....	6000	.....	.....	.....	3780	.....	6000
.....	.....	.....	.....	.....	.....	60t	200t	.....	.....	.....
.....	.....	.....	.....	.....	.....	240	800	.....	.....	240

PUEBLA—(Continued)

No.	Name	A	B	C	D	E	F	G
281	Coatzingo	80t	36p					
		320	144					
410	Colucan	314t				234p		
		1256				936		
414	Coxcatlan	769t	400p	480p	455t			
		3076	1600	1920	1820			
28	Cuatinchan	1560t	1500p	1668p				
		6240	6000	6672				
700	Chalchicomula							
		(1661)						
721	Chalma							
		(734)						
222	Chapulco	228t	400p		300t			
		912	1600		1200			
12	Chiapa	1455t	1923p					
		5820	7692					
107	Chichiquila				⎡1508t	141p		
		(3042)			6032	564		
107	Quimixtitlan					328p		
					⎣	1312		
411	Chietla	1086t	870p			904p		
		4344	3480			3616		
99	Chila		600p					
		(1850)	1200					
174	Chila	331t	⎡2260p					
		1324	9040					
174	Mecatlan							
			⎣					
609	Chinantla		700p					
		(2923)	2800					
412	Cholula	9340t	2700p	13640p		12610p		
		37360	10800	54560		50440		
25	Eloxuchitlan	246t	600p		250t			
		984	2400		1000			
178	Epatlan	667t	560p	614p	734t	735t		
		2668	2240	2456	2936	2940		
29	Huaquechula	3499t	2000p					
		13996	8000					
106	Huachinango	1143t	⎡3900p					
		4572	15600					
106	Otzolotepec	390t						
		1560	⎣					
426	Huatlavaca	600t	500p	610p		691p		
		2400	2000	2440		2764		
111	Huehuetlan	449t	500p					
		1796	2000					
599	Huejotzingo		8000p	11308p		7360p		
		(34824)	32000	45238		29440		
610	Hueytlalpan		1000p		1710t			
		(5292)	4000		6840			
755	Huitzila				120t			
		(369)			480			

Appendix I: Population in 1565

PUEBLA—(Continued)

H	I	J	K	L	M	N	O	P	Special items	Population
						60t	60t			
						240	240			240
										936
						[4500t]	483t			
							1932			1870
				1284t		1071t				
				5136		4284				5364
						540t				
						2160				2160
						240t				
						960				960
				200t						
				800						1200
										7692
							160t			
							640			3954
							800t			
							3200			⎩......
906t	900t					920t	906t			
3624	3600					3680	3624			3640
				600t		600t				
				2400		2400				2400
						⎧1600t				
						6400				6400
						......				
						⎩				⎩......
					900t	1000t				
					3600	4000				3800
						11786t				
						47144				50714
				400t			230t			
				1600			920			1300
				730t		600t	[110t]			
				2920		2400				2730
						3665t				
						14660				14660
3683t	3700t			⎧2900t		⎧3000t	⎧3683t			
14732	14800			11600		12000	14732			13284
				⎩		⎩	⎩			⎩......
300t										
3200										2801
				700t	900t		900t			
				2800	3600		3600			3200
						[3769t]			11318t	
									45272	45272
						1730t	1730t			
						6920	6920			6880
										480

PUEBLA—(Continued)

No.	Name	A	B	C	D	E	F	G
512	Ixtacamaxtitlan [pueblo]......	...... (2230)	....	....	1000t 4000	....	....	....
512	Ixtacamaxtitlan [sugeto]......	...... (3077)	....	....	1000t 4000	....	....	....
598	Ixtayucan...................	...... (4308)	....	....	....	....	....	....
686	Ixtayuca....................	...... (1692)	320p 1280	....	....	....	....	....
432	Izucar.......................	906t 3624	1800p 7200	1892p 7568	....	1892p 7568	....	....
432	Tonala.......................	...... (9050)	220p 880	3716p 14864	....	2167p 8668	....	....
753	Jalpan.......................	...... (923)	....	....	300p 1200	....	....	....
531	Jicotepec....................	476t 1904	1100p 4400	....	1000t 4000	....	....	....
70	Jojupango....................	605t 2420	2600p 10400	....	800t 3200	....	....	....
70	Matlaque.....................	...... (308)	600p 2400	....	100t 400	....	....	....
70	Tonatico.....................	....	....	....	....	....	....	....
243	Jolalpan.....................	...... (400)	100p 400	....	....	....	....	....
485	Jonotla......................	...... (2461)	450p 1800	....	800t 3200	[190p]	....	....
151	Metlaltoyuca.................	...... (480)	120p 480	....	....	....	....	....
326	Mexcalcingo..................	1300t 5200	3900p 15600	....	1608t 6432	....	....	....
689	Mitepec......................	...... (2615)	800p 3200	....	700t 2800	....	....	....
486	Necoxtla.....................	181t 724	117p 468	....	....	....	....	....
690	Nopalucan....................	...... (928)	120p 480	333p 1332	300t 1200	333p 1332	....	....
337	Pantepec.....................	...... (285)	....	....	30t 120	....	....	....
41	Papalocticpa.................	...... (1534)	300p 1200	....	300t 1200	....	....	....
41	Tlacolultepec................	....	390p 1560	....	....	....	....	....
766	Petlalcingo..................	104t 416	....	....	150t 600	....	....	....
137	Piaxtla......................	217t 868	1000p 4000	....	535t 2140	710p 2840	....	....
693	Puebla.......................	...... (2310)	1004p 4016	....	....	903p 3612	....	....
100	Quecholac + Villanueva.......	4392t 17568	3360p 13440	....	....	....	....	....
112	La Rinconada................	...... (308)	300p 1200	....	100t 400	....	....	....

Appendix I: Population in 1565

PUEBLA—(Continued)

H	I	J	K	L	M	N	O	P	Special items	Population
……	……	……	……	……	……	450t 1800	750t 3000	……	……	2900
……	……	……	……	……	……	……	……	……	……	4000
……	……	……	……	……	……	1400t 5600	……	……	……	5600
……	……	……	……	550t 2200	……	……	……	……	……	2200
……	……	……	……	……	……	……	……	……	……	7568
……	……	……	……	……	……	[830p]	……	……	……	11766
……	……	……	……	……	……	……	……	……	……	1200
……	……	……	……	……	……	1500t 6000	1500t 6000	……	……	5000
……	……	……	……	800t 3200	……	……	400t 1600	……	……	3200
……	……	……	……	……	……	……	……	……	……	⎧ 400
……	……	……	……	……	……	……	……	……	……	⎨ ……
……	……	……	……	……	……	……	……	……	……	⎩ 400
……	……	……	……	……	……	……	758t 3032	……	……	3200
……	……	……	……	……	……	……	……	……	……	480
……	……	……	……	1300t 5200	……	……	1700t 6800	……	……	5200
……	……	……	……	……	……	1000t 4000	1000t 4000	……	……	3400
……	……	……	……	……	……	110t 440	110t 440	……	……	440
……	……	……	……	……	……	242t 962	219t 876	……	……	1206
……	……	……	……	……	……	155t 620	……	……	……	370
……	……	……	……	300t 1200	……	……	⎧ 500t 2000	……	……	⎧ 2000
……	……	……	……	……	……	……	⎩ ……	113t 452	……	⎩ …… 600
……	……	……	……	710t 2840	……	700t 2800	720t 2880	……	……	2655
……	……	550t 2200	……	……	……	800t 3200	……	……	……	3004
……	……	……	……	7000t 28000	……	3360t 13440	……	……	……	20720
……	……	……	……	……	……	……	……	……	……	400

Population of Central Mexico

PUEBLA—(Continued)

No.	Name	A	B	C	D	E	F	G
698	Seco...................	(5077)	......	......	1200t 4800	......	......	......
698	Telitlatzingo...........	(1231)	......	......	......	......	......	......
655	Tatetla.................	222t 888	......	......	......	328p 1312	......	......
205	Tecali..................	3314t 13256	2050p 8200	......	......	......	......	......
59	Tecamachalco...........	13982t 55928	3330p 13320	......	......	......	......	......
209	Tehuacan...............	2015t 8060	2540p 10160	4400p 17600	......	2497p 9988	......	......
450	Tejaluca................	70t 280	......	......	50t 200	50p 200	......	......
131	Tenampulco.............	160t 640	150p 600	......	200t 800	......	......	......
244	Teopantlan.............	470t 1880	575p 2300	......	545t 2180	545p 2180	......	......
216	Teotlalco...............	......	5190p 20760	......	1600t 6400	3533p 14132	......	......
216	Centayuca..............	(15569)	......	......	......	688p 2752	......	......
547	Tepanco................	(8000)	......	......	......	......	......	......
63	Tepapayeca [pueblo]....	1745t 6980	2000p 8000	......	......	......	......	......
63	Tepapayeca [sugetos]...	1292t 5168	......	......	......	......	......	......
452	Tepeaca................	9878t 39512	4800p 19200	10473p 41892	......	9400p 37600	......	......
62	Tepeoxuma.............	685t 2740	800p 3200	......	800t 3200	......	......	......
675	Tepexco................	(4800)	1200p 4800	......	......	......	......	......
566	Tepexi.................	(8093)	......	......	......	2584p 10336	......	......
235	Tetela..................	2000t 8000	1820p 7280	1800p 7200	......	1678p 6712	......	......
461	Tetela..................	305t 1220	300p 1200	......	500t 2000	519p 2076	......	......
814	Texmelucan............	(2461)	......	......	......	......	......	......
654	Teziutlan...............	745t 2980	......	......	1368t 5472	995p 3980	......	......
453	Tilapa..................	958t 3832	......	......	......	434p 1736	......	......
761	Tlacotepec..............	(8355)	......	......	2820t 11280	2611p 10444	......	......
128	Tlacuilotepec...........	(2960)	390p 1560	......	......	......	......	......
606	Tlapaxala...............	(1769)	......	......	......	......	......	......

Appendix I: Population in 1565

PUEBLA—(Continued)

H	I	J	K	L	M	N	O	P	Special items	Population
						2100t				
						8400				6600
						400t				
						1600				1600
										1312
				5473t		5000t	5000t	4042t		
				21892		20000	20000	16168		20946
						3930t			48423tp	
						15720			48423	48423
				3000t		2730t				
				12000		10920				12627
							70t			
							280			200
				150t						
				600						700
				524t		509t				
				2096		2036				2123
						1421t	1430t		⎡5060t	
						5684	5720		⎣20240	20240
						2600t				
						10400				10400
						1346t				
						5384				5384
										5168
						6120t	8000t			
						24480	32000			34657
				800t		1000t	1000t			
				3200		4000	4000			3466
										4800
						2677t				
						10708				10522
										6856
						470t	470t			
						1880	1880			1989
							800t			
							3200			3200
										4726
										1736
										10862
t							950t			
3848							3800			3848
						575t				
						2300				2300

PUEBLA—(Concluded)

No.	Name	A	B	C	D	E	F	G
603	Tlapotongo	44t 176	30p 120					
451	Tlatlauquitepec	825t 3300	1700p 6800		1190t 4760			
692	Tlaxco	(1588)	500p 2000	516p 2064		516p 2064		
218	Totimehuacan	835t 3340	650p 2600					
304	Tuzapan	1023t 4092						
817	Verde	(1231)						
139	Xiutetelco	(5538)						
757	Zacapoaxtla	(5643)			1834t 7336			
15	Zacatlan	(9246)	1840p 7360					
16	Zapotitlan	1347t 5388	2000p 8000		2200t 8800			
16	Tequistepec	(6461)						
16	Caltican							
101	Zoquitlan	300t 1200	440p 1760		422t 1688			
484	Zoyatitlanapa	290t 1160						
	Cuahualulco	(1723)						
	Jonacatlan	(3538)			1000t 4000			
	Tuchitlan	(462)						
	Ixtepec	(616)			200t 800			
846	Teotlalcingo	(1231)						
845	Tlaxcoapan	(5538)						
	Xocoyolo	(677)						
222	Cuapan	1381t 5524						
93	Tochimilco (Ocopetlayuca)	(5659)	1700p 6800	2309p 9236		2309p 9236		

Appendix I: Population in 1565

PUEBLA—(Concluded)

H	I	J	K	L	M	N	O	P	Special items	Population
				10t						
				40						40
						700t	2200c			
						2800	2926			3780
										2064
				1000t				516t		
				4000				2064		4000
								880t		
								3520		4092
							400t			
							1600			1600
						1800t				
						7200				7200
										7336
				3150t		2860t				
				12600		11440				12020
						2000t	2052t			
						8000	8248			8400
						320t	310t			
						1280	1240			1484
						200t	200t			
						800	800			800
						560t				
						2240				2240
						1300t		470t		
						5200		1880		4600
						150t				
						600				600
										800
							400t			
							1600			1600
							1800t			
							7200			7200
							220t			
							880			880
69t						4876t	4069t	2131t		
16276						19504	16276	8524		16570
						900t				
						3600				7357

GUERRERO

No.	Name	A	B	C	D	E	F	G
259	Acaguapisca...............	22t 88	45p 180	......	......	......	......	......
583	Acalpica................	11t 44	....	......	......	......	......	......
161	Acamixtlavaca...........	...... (1178)	400p 1600	......	......	......	......	......
126	Acapulco [province]......	...... (9554)	1726p 6904	......	......	......	......	......
282	Acapuzalco..............	...... (616)	200p 800	......	......	......	......	......
491	Ajuchitlan...............	...... (3682)	1500p 6000	1190p 4760	......	......	......	......
271	Alahuixtlan..............	600t 2400	⎡1350p 5400	......	......	......	......	......
271	Ostuma..................	800t 3200	....	......	......	......	......	......
260	Atenchancaleca..........	57t 228	⎨200p 800	......	......	......	......	......
260	Zapotitlan...............	33t 132	...... ⎣......	......	......	......	......	......
295	Atempa.................	457t 1828	....	......	......	......	......	......
409	Atenango...............	535t 2140	640p 2560	809p 3236	....	809p 3236	......	......

88	Ayutla..................	⎡227t
		  908
			⎡500p
			  2000
				......
				......
					260t
					1040
						......
						......
							160t
							640
								......

88	Tultepec................	⎣......
		  ......
			⎣......
			  ......
				......	200t
					800
						......	......	......

580	Ayutla..................	87t 348	80p 320	......	......	......	......	......
242	Cacahuatepec...........	116t 464	700p 2800	......	......	[39p]	......	......
584	Camutla................	86t 344	....	......	......	......	......	......
597	Cayaco.................	140t 560	150p 600	......	......	......	......	......
284	Cicapuzalco.............	...... (616)	....	......	......	......	......	......
593	Cihuatlan...............	128t 512	....	......	......	......	......	......
772	Coatlan.................	...... (1565)	....	......	......	......	......	......
772	Acuitlapan..............	....	....	......	......	......	......	......
522	Copala..................	...... (4231)	....	......	......	......	......	......
522	Juchitlan...............	...... (923)	....	......	......	......	......	......
522	Cuezala................	...... (677)	....	......	......	......	......	......
522	Ciquila.................	...... (308)	....	......	......	......	......	......

Appendix I: Population in 1565

GUERRERO

H	I	J	K	L	M	N	O	P	Special items	Population
										180
										44
			383t				272t	272t		
			1532				1088	1088		1532
					3105t		810t			
					12420		3240			12420
										800
				1200t	1200t					
				4800	4800					4787
			250t	528t						
			1000	2112						2156
			300t			320t				
			1200			1280				
										800
										1828
										3236
				400t		160t				
				1600		640				1393
						100t				
						400				
										348
				600t						
				2400						2400
										344
										600
			200t	200t				230t		
			800	800				940		800
										512
			200t	600t			300t			
			800	2400			1200			2034
			217t							
			868							
						1375t				
						5500				5500
						300t				
						1200				1200
						220t				
						880				880
						100t				
						400				400

Population of Central Mexico

GUERRERO—(Continued)

No.	Name	A	B	C	D	E	F	G
522	Cacatipa	(372)						
146	Coyuca	(1609)	300p 1200					
168	Coyoquilla	(677)	325p 1300					
292	Cuautepec	103t 412	500p 2000					
707	Cuetzala	(5692)						
172	Cutzamala	3606t 14424	4000p 16000					
17	Chilapa	1130t 4520						
261	Chipila	124t 496	100p 400					
301	Huamuxtitlan	2247t 8988		637p 2548	1500t 6000			
262	Huitlalotla	313t 1252	150p 600					
769	Huitziltepec	(415)						
555	Huixtac	(1357)						
263	Huiztlan	87t 348	130p 520					
109	Huizuco [province]	1384t 5536	900p 3600					
436	Iguala	5400t 21600	1170p 4680	1092p 4368		831p 3324		
574	Ixtapa	44t 176	150p 600					
480	Jalapa [province]	(3557)		911p 3644				
269	Japutica	96t 384	100p 400					
234	Juchitlan	80t 320						
266	Mila	32t 128	36p 144					
767	Mochtitlan	(1732)			489t 1956	637p 2548		
193	Noxtepe	(4305)	900p 3600					
592	Nuxco	60t 240	54p 216					
39	Oapan	(2499)	1900p 7600	866p 3464		866p 3464		

Appendix I: Population in 1565

GUERRERO—(Continued)

H	I	J	K	L	M	N	O	P	Special items	Population
......	......	......	......	......	......	121t	......	......	......	
......	......	......	......	......	......	484	......	......	......	484
......	......	......	......	446t	600t	600t	350t	......	......	
......	......	......	......	1784	2400	2400	1400	......	......	2092
......	......	......	......	200t	......	......	......	......	......	
......	......	......	......	800	......	......	......	......	......	800
......	......	......	......	......	......	......	......	......	......	
......	......	......	......	......	......	......	......	......	......	2000
......	......	......	......	......	......	1850t	......	......	......	
......	......	......	......	......	......	7400	......	......	......	7400
......	......	......	......	850t	......	900t	830t	......	......	
......	......	......	......	3400	......	3600	3320	......	......	3500
......	3000t	......	......	......	......	4009t	3000t	2794t	......	
......	12000	......	......	......	......	16036	12000	11176	......	13500
......	......	......	......	......	......	......	......	......	......	496
......	......	......	......	......	......	1600t	......	440t	......	
......	......	......	......	......	......	6400	......	1760	......	4983
......	......	......	......	......	......	......	......	......	......	1252
......	......	......	135t	......	......	......	......	......	......	
......	......	......	540	......	......	......	......	......	......	540
......	......	......	441t	......	......	......	......	......	......	
......	......	......	1764	......	......	......	......	......	......	1764
......	......	......	......	60t	......	......	......	......	......	
......	......	......	......	240	......	......	......	......	......	240
......	......	......	......	1500t	......	1500t	......	......	......	
......	......	......	......	6000	......	6000	......	......	......	6000
......	......	......	840t	......	......	1200t	......	......	......	
......	......	......	3360	......	......	4800	......	......	......	3963
......	......	......	......	......	......	......	......	......	......	600
......	......	......	......	......	......	1401t	......	......	......	
......	......	......	......	......	......	5604	......	......	......	4624
......	......	......	......	......	......	......	......	......	......	400
......	......	......	......	......	......	......	......	......	......	320
......	......	......	......	......	......	......	......	......	......	144
......	......	......	......	......	......	......	......	......	......	2252
......	......	......	......	1398t	......	1400t	......	......	......	
......	......	......	......	5592	......	5600	......	......	......	5596
......	......	......	......	......	......	......	......	......	......	240
......	......	......	705t	......	......	......	......	......	......	
......	......	......	2820	......	......	......	......	......	......	3249

GUERRERO—(Continued)

No.	Name	A	B	C	D	E	F	G
191	Olinala	1679t	2000p	1351p	1100t	1351p	......	......
		6716	8000	5404	4400	5404	......	......
191	Papalutla	......	......	319p	380t	285p	......	......
		......	......	1276	1520	1140	......	......
138	Ometepec	340t	1500p	......	......	......	......	......
		1360	6000	......	......	......	......	......
138	Igualapa	450t	......	......	......	......	......	......
		2200	......	......	......	......	......	......
138	Xochistavaca	307t	......	......	......	......	......	......
		1228	......	......	......	......	......	......
594	Pamutla	64t	30p	......	......	......	......	......
		256	120	......	......	......	......	......
573	Pantla	120t	100p	......	......	......	......	......
		480	400	......	......	......	......	......
586	Paxalo	112t	......	......	......	......	......	......
		448	......	......	......	......	......	......
589	Petatlan	160t	......	......	......	......	......	......
		640	......	......	......	......	......	......
579	Pechique	15t	......	......	......	......	......	......
		60	......	......	......	......	......	......
532	Pochotitlan	362t	420p	......	550t	......	275t	......
		1448	1680	......	2200	......	1100	......
267	Puchutlan	78t	83p	......	......	......	......	......
		312	332	......	......	......	......	......
197	Pungarabato	2109t	1250p	......	......	......	......	......
		8436	5000	......	......	......	......	......
581	Pustlan	60t	120p	......	......	......	......	......
		240	480	......	......	......	......	......
468	Taxco	523t	1200p	2384t	......	1384p	......	......
		2092	4800	9536	......	5536	......	......
468	Tamacasapa	267t	......	......	......	......	......	......
		1068	......	......	......	......	......	......
468	Atzala	82t	......	......	......	......	......	......
		328	......	......	......	......	......	......
575	Tecomatlan	87t	......	......	......	......	......	......
		348	......	......	......	......	......	......
595	Tecpan	320t	......	......	......	228p	......	......
		1280	......	......	......	912	......	......
544	Teloloapan + Ixcatempa	......	......	......	......	......	......	......
		(2861)	......	......	......	......	......	......
585	Temalhuacan	54t	......	......	......	......	......	......
		216	......	......	......	......	......	......
515	Tenango	......	365p	836p	......	836p	......	......
		(2328)	1460	3344	......	3344	......	......
213	Tepecuacuilco	2299t	2500p	......	......	......	......	......
		9196	10000	......	......	......	......	......
215	Tetela	1488t	2000p	......	......	......	......	......
		5952	8000	......	......	......	......	......
226	Tetipac	......	750p	......	......	......	......	......
		(1441)	3000	......	......	......	......	......
64	Tixtla	......	3500p	1190p	901t	1122p	......	......
		(3280)	14000	4760	3604	4488	......	......

Appendix I: Population in 1565

GUERRERO—(Continued)

H	I	J	K	L	M	N	O	P	Special items	Population
.....	.....	.....	.....	.....	.....	1300t	.....	.....	1555t	
.....	.....	.....	.....	.....	.....	5200	.....	.....	6220	6561
.....	.....	.....	.....	.....	.....	.....	.....	.....	220t	
.....	.....	.....	.....	.....	.....	.....	.....	.....	880	......
.....	.....	.....	.....	⎧1820t	600t	⎧1500t	.....	.....	.....	
.....	.....	.....	.....	⎨ 7280	2400	⎨ 6000	.....	.....	.....	6220
.....	.....	.....	.....	⎪	600t	⎪	.....	.....	.....	
.....	.....	.....	.....	⎪	2400	⎪	.....	.....	.....	......
.....	.....	.....	.....	⎪	200t	⎪	.....	.....	.....	
.....	.....	.....	.....	⎩	800	⎩	.....	.....	.....	......
.....	.....	.....	.....	.....	.....	.....	.....	.....	.....	
.....	.....	.....	.....	.....	.....	.....	.....	.....	.....	256
.....	.....	.....	.....	.....	.....	.....	.....	.....	.....	
.....	.....	.....	.....	.....	.....	.....	.....	.....	.....	480
.....	.....	.....	.....	.....	.....	.....	.....	.....	.....	
.....	.....	.....	.....	.....	.....	.....	.....	.....	.....	448
.....	.....	.....	.....	.....	.....	.....	.....	.....	.....	
.....	.....	.....	.....	.....	.....	.....	.....	.....	.....	640
.....	.....	.....	.....	.....	.....	.....	.....	.....	.....	
.....	.....	.....	.....	.....	.....	.....	.....	.....	.....	60
.....	.....	.....	.....	.....	.....	193t	.....	.....	.....	
.....	.....	.....	.....	.....	.....	772	.....	.....	.....	1357
.....	.....	.....	.....	.....	.....	.....	.....	.....	.....	
.....	.....	.....	.....	.....	.....	.....	.....	.....	.....	332
.....	.....	.....	.....	600t	1500t	1500t	549t	.....	.....	
.....	.....	.....	.....	2400	6000	6000	2196	.....	.....	4800
.....	.....	.....	.....	.....	.....	.....	.....	.....	.....	
.....	.....	.....	.....	.....	.....	.....	.....	.....	.....	480
.....	.....	.....	600t	.....	.....	.....	.....	.....	.....	⎧
.....	.....	.....	2400	.....	.....	.....	.....	.....	.....	6725
.....	.....	.....	337t	.....	.....	.....	362t	.....	.....	⎨
.....	.....	.....	1348	.....	.....	.....	1448	.....	.....	......
.....	.....	.....	339t	.....	.....	.....	289t	.....	.....	⎪
.....	.....	.....	1356	.....	.....	.....	1156	.....	.....	⎩......
.....	.....	.....	.....	.....	.....	.....	.....	.....	.....	
.....	.....	.....	.....	.....	.....	.....	.....	.....	.....	348
.....	.....	.....	.....	.....	.....	.....	.....	.....	.....	
.....	.....	.....	.....	.....	.....	.....	.....	.....	.....	912
.....	.....	.....	930t	.....	.....	.....	.....	.....	.....	
.....	.....	.....	3720	.....	.....	.....	.....	.....	.....	3720
.....	.....	.....	.....	.....	.....	.....	.....	.....	.....	
.....	.....	.....	.....	.....	.....	.....	.....	.....	.....	216
.....	.....	.....	598t	.....	.....	.....	.....	.....	.....	
.....	.....	.....	2392	.....	.....	.....	.....	.....	.....	3026
.....	.....	.....	2040t	[600t]	.....	2200t	.....	.....	.....	
.....	.....	.....	8160	.....	.....	8800	.....	.....	.....	8480
.....	.....	.....	.....	645t	.....	[80t]	660t	.....	.....	
.....	.....	.....	.....	2580	.....	.....	2640	.....	.....	2580
.....	.....	.....	468t	469t	.....	.....	345t	.....	.....	
.....	.....	.....	1872	1876	.....	.....	1380	.....	.....	1874
.....	.....	.....	.....	.....	.....	.....	.....	.....	.....	
.....	.....	.....	.....	.....	.....	.....	.....	.....	.....	4264

80   Population of Central Mexico

GUERRERO—(Continued)

No.	Name	A	B	C	D	E	F	G
446	Tlacotepec.................	(4923)	......	......	......	......	......	......
61	Tlacozautitlan.............	(8855)	2400p 9600	3360p 13440	......	......	......	......
60	Tlapa [province]..........	(15851)	4000p 16000	4000p 16000	......	4000p 16000	......	......
225	Tlaxmalac + Mayanala....	(2895)	1400p 5600	......	......	......	......	......
268	Toliman...................	115t 460	170p 680	......	......	......	......	......
455	Totoltepec................	300t 1200	230p 920	......	......	......	100t 400	......
88	Tultepec..................	72t 288	......	286p 1144	......	285p 1140	......	......
588	Xihuacan..................	340t 1360	......	......	......	......	......	......
590	Ximalcota.................	212t 484	......	......	......	......	......	......
596	Zacalutla.................	132t 528	60p 240	......	......	......	......	......
582	Zacatula..................	176t 704	220p 880	......	......	......	......	......
260	Zapotitlan................	132t 528	140p 560	......	......	......	......	......
587	Zihuatanejo...............	60t 240	......	......	......	......	......	......
302	Zirandaro.................	(907)	......	350p 1400	......	294p 1176	......	......
221	Zumpango.................	200t 800	900p 3600	700p 2800	......	481p 1924	......	......
	Anacuilco.................	26t 104	......	22p 88	......	......	......	......
	Autepec...................	...... (280)	70p 280	......	......	......	......	......
	Cacalotepec...............	80p 320	......	......	......	......	......	......
	Colutla....................	80t 320	......	......	......	......	......	......
	Coyuca....................	...... (680)	170p 680	......	......	......	......	......
	Coyuca....................	...... (140)	35p 140	......	......	......	......	......
	Quezala...................	...... (25)	......	......	......	......	......	......
	Cuitlatenamic.............	...... (2766)	......	......	899t 3596	......	......	......
	Cuyuca....................	...... (140)	35p 140	......	......	......	......	......
	Hinhitlan..................	...... (140)	35p 140	......	......	......	......	......
	Ixhuatlan..................	...... (409)	......	133p 532	......	133p 532	......	......

Appendix I: Population in 1565

GUERRERO—(Continued)

H	I	J	K	L	M	N	O	P	Special items	Population
......	......	......	......	......	......	1600t	650t	.....	.....	
......	......	......	......	......	......	6400	2600	.....	.....	6400
......	......	......	......	......	......	2396t	......	.....	.....	
......	......	......	......	......	......	9584	......	.....	.....	11512
......	5500t	5331t	......	5520p	......	6550t	......	.....	.....	
......	22000	21364	......	22080	......	26200	......	.....	.....	20607
......	......	......	927t	845t	......	1800t	......	505t	.....	
......	......	......	3708	3380	......	7200	......	2020	.....	3763
......	......	......	......	80t	......	......	......	.....	.....	
......	......	......	......	320	......	......	......	.....	.....	320
......	......	......	......	......	......	100t	......	.....	.....	
......	......	......	......	......	......	400	......	.....	.....	400
......	......	......	......	......	......	......	......	140t	.....	
......	......	......	......	......	......	......	......	560	.....	1142
......	......	......	......	......	......	......	......	.....	.....	1360
......	......	......	......	......	......	......	......	.....	.....	848
......	......	......	......	......	......	......	......	.....	.....	528
......	......	......	......	......	......	......	......	..···	.....	880
......	......	......	......	......	......	......	......	.....	.....	560
......	......	......	......	......	......	......	......	.....	.....	240
......	......	......	......	......	......	......	300t	.....	.....	
......	......	......	......	......	......	......	1200	.....	.....	1288
......	......	......	......	......	......	500t	400t	.....	.....	
......	......	......	......	......	......	2000	1600	.....	.....	2241
......	......	......	......	......	......	......	......	.....	.....	88
......	......	......	......	......	......	......	......	.....	.....	280
......	......	......	......	......	......	......	......	.....	.....	320
......	......	......	......	......	......	......	......	.....	.....	320
......	......	......	......	......	......	......	......	.....	.....	680
......	......	......	......	......	......	......	......	.....	.....	140
......	......	......	......	......	......	8t	......	.....	.....	
......	......	......	......	......	......	32	......	.....	.....	32
......	......	......	......	......	......	......	......	.....	.....	3596
......	......	......	......	......	......	......	......	.....	.....	140
......	......	......	......	......	......	......	......	.....	.....	140
......	......	......	......	......	......	......	......	20t	.....	
......	......	......	......	......	......	......	......	80	.....	532

GUERRERO—(Concluded)

No.	Name	A	B	C	D	E	F	G
	Ixtapa...................	...... (880)	300p 1200	286p 1144	....	....	....	....
	Laguancoyula.............	...... (768)	537p 2148	....	....	....	....	....
	Miquitla.................	...... (480)	120p 480	....	....	....	....	....
	Nexuca...................	...... (800)	200p 800	....	....	....	....	....
	Potuctla.................	28t 112	....	....	....	12p 48	....	....
	Tonatla..................	...... (2154)	....	....	....	....	....	....
	Cocoalco.................	....	....	....	....	....	....	....
826	Totolapa.................	...... (1692)	600p 2400	550p 2200	....	....	....	....
	Xaputigua................	...... (1680)	420p 1680	....	....	....	....	....
	Yacapul..................	68t 272	....	....	....	....	....	....
	Zahuatlan................	...... (240)	60p 240	....	....	....	....	....
	Zimatlan.................	135t 540	....	....	....	....	....	....
	Zitlaltomagua............	...... (320)	80p 320	....	....	....	....	....
	Zolcoacoa................	...... (336)	84p 336	....	....	....	....	....
199	Cocula...................	326t 1304	1550p 6200	....	....	....	....	....
619	Tliztaca.................	...... (6923)	(540p)	....	....	....	....	....
591	Juluchuga................	68t 272	....	....	....	....	....	....

MORELOS

No.	Name	A	B	C	D	E	F	G
673	Amayuca.................	...... (615)	....	....	....	....	....	....
682	Atlacahualoya...........	...... (168)	....	....	....	....	....	....
11	Cuernavaca [province]...	...... (68236)	11840p 47360	....	....	....	....	....

Appendix I: Population in 1565

GUERRERO—(Concluded)

H	I	J	K	L	M	N	O	P	Special items	Population
....	.....	.....	.....	.....	.....	.....	.....	.....	.....	
....	.....	.....	.....	.....	.....	.....	.....	.....	.....	1144
....	.....	.....	.....	250t	.....	.....	.....	.....	.....	
....	.....	.....	.....	1000	.....	.....	.....	.....	.....	1000
....	.....	.....	.....	.....	.....	.....	.....	.....	.....	
....	.....	.....	.....	.....	.....	.....	.....	.....	.....	480
....	.....	.....	.....	.....	.....	.....	.....	.....	.....	
....	.....	.....	.....	.....	.....	.....	.....	.....	.....	800
....	.....	.....	.....	.....	10t	.....	.....	.....	.....	
....	.....	.....	.....	.....	40	.....	.....	.....	.....	44
....	.....	.....	.....	.....	.....	⎰700t	.....	.....	.....	⎧
....	.....	.....	.....	.....	.....	⎱2800	.....	.....	.....	2800
....	.....	.....	.....	.....	.....	.....	.....	.....	.....	⎩......
....	.....	.....	.....	.....	.....	.....	.....	.....	.....	
....	.....	.....	.....	.....	.....	.....	.....	.....	.....	2200
....	.....	.....	.....	.....	.....	.....	.....	.....	.....	1680
....	.....	.....	.....	.....	.....	.....	.....	.....	.....	272
....	.....	.....	.....	.....	.....	.....	.....	.....	.....	240
....	.....	.....	.....	.....	.....	.....	.....	.....	.....	540
....	.....	.....	.....	.....	.....	.....	.....	.....	.....	320
....	.....	.....	.....	.....	.....	.....	.....	.....	.....	336
....	.....	.....	348t	856t	.....	.....	.....	.....	.....	
....	.....	.....	1392	3424	.....	.....	.....	.....	.....	2408
....	.....	.....	.....	.....	.....	2250t	.....	.....	.....	
....	.....	.....	.....	.....	.....	9000	.....	.....	.....	9000
...	.....	.....	.....	.....	.....	.....	.....	.....	.....	272

MORELOS

H	I	J	K	L	M	N	O	P	Special items	Population
800	.....	.....	.....	.....	.....	.....	.....	116t	.....	
800	.....	.....	.....	.....	.....	.....	.....	464	.....	800
...	.....	164c	.....	.....	.....	.....	.....	51t	.....	
...	.....	218	.....	.....	.....	.....	.....	204	.....	218
...	.....	.....	.....	.....	.....	.....	.....	.....	22177t	
...	.....	.....	.....	.....	.....	.....	.....	.....	88708	88708

Population of Central Mexico

MORELOS—(Continued)

No.	Name	A	B	C	D	E	F	G
667	Jonacatepec [province]	...... (7637)	......	......	......	......	......	......
231	Jumiltepec	1122t 4488	1100p 4400	......	......	......	......	......
671	Jantetelco	...... (1231)	......	......	......	......	......	......
228	Oaxtepec	...... (27692)	3412p 13648	......	......	......	......	......
506	Ocuituco	1681t 6724	1200p 4800	......	......	1576p 6304	......	......
674	Telistac	...... (283)	......	......	......	......	......	......
124	Tlacotepec	190t 760	⎰2300p ⎱9200	......	......	......	......	......
124	Temoac	700t 2800	......	......	......	......	......	......
124	Zacualpa	180t 720	......	......	......	......	......	......
124	Huaculco	223t 892	......	......	......	......	......	......
709	Tlacuiltenango	...... (15230)	......	......	......	......	......	......
806	Tlayacapan	...... (4624)	......	......	......	......	......	......
679	Tlayecac	...... (516)	......	......	......	......	......	......
678	Xalostoc	...... (584)	......	......	......	......	......	......
142	Yautepec	...... (21846)	⎰4200p ⎱16800	......	......	......	......	......
142	Tepoztlan	......	......	......	......	......	......	......
5	Yecapixtla [province]	...... (9615)	2670p 10680	......	......	......	......	......
770	Zacango	...... (241)	......	94p 376	......	78p 312	......	......
	Matlayac	...... (677)	......	......	......	......	......	......

OAXACA

No.	Name	A	B	C	D	E	F	G
786	Acaltepec	...... (923)	......	......	......	......	......	......
154	Achiutla [province]	2866t 11464	2000p 8000	......	......	......	......	......
742	Alotepec	...... (369)	......	......	......	......	......	......

Appendix I: Population in 1565

MORELOS—(Continued)

H	I	J	K	L	M	N	O	P	Special items	Population
.....	2000t	2964t	.....	.....	.....	.....	.....	.....	.....	
.....	8000	11856	.....	.....	.....	.....	.....	.....	.....	9928
)40t	1200t	.....	.....	1000t	.....	1100t	.....	.....	.....	
4160	4800	.....	.....	4000	.....	4400	.....	.....	.....	4340
•0t	.....	.....	.....	.....	.....	400t	.....	295t	.....	
1600	.....	.....	.....	.....	.....	1600	.....	1180	.....	1600
.....	.....	.....	.....	.....	.....	9000t	.....	.....	.....	
.....	.....	.....	.....	.....	.....	36000	.....	.....	.....	36000
66t	1600t	.....	.....	.....	.....	1600t	.....	.....	.....	
6264	6400	.....	.....	.....	.....	6400	.....	.....	.....	6355
.....	.....	277c	.....	.....	.....	.....	.....	90t	.....	
.....	.....	368	.....	.....	.....	.....	.....	360	.....	368
•0t	.....	.....	.....	1630t	.....	.....	.....	.....	.....	
2000	.....	.....	.....	6520	.....	.....	.....	.....	.....	6660
•0t	.....	.....	.....	.....	.....	.....	.....	.....	.....	
3200	.....	.....	.....	.....	.....	.....	.....	.....	.....	.....
0t	.....	.....	.....	.....	.....	.....	.....	.....	.....	
1000	.....	.....	.....	.....	.....	.....	.....	.....	.....	.....
)t	.....	.....	.....	.....	.....	.....	.....	.....	.....	
600	.....	.....	.....	.....	.....	.....	.....	.....	.....	
.....	.....	.....	.....	.....	.....	4950t	.....	.....	.....	
.....	.....	.....	.....	.....	.....	19800	.....	.....	.....	19800
.....	1500t	1508t	.....	.....	.....	1500t	.....	.....	.....	
.....	6000	6032	.....	.....	.....	6000	.....	.....	.....	6011
.....	.....	.....	.....	.....	.....	.....	.....	129t	.....	
.....	.....	.....	.....	.....	.....	.....	.....	516	.....	516
)t	.....	.....	.....	.....	.....	.....	.....	125t	.....	
760	.....	.....	.....	.....	.....	.....	.....	500	.....	760
.....	.....	.....	.....	.....	.....	4500t	.....	.....	.....	
.....	.....	.....	.....	.....	.....	18000	.....	.....	.....	28400
.....	.....	.....	.....	.....	.....	2600t	.....	.....	.....	
.....	.....	.....	.....	.....	.....	10400	.....	.....	.....	.....
.....	.....	3125t	.....	.....	.....	.....	.....	.....	.....	
.....	.....	12500	.....	.....	.....	.....	.....	.....	.....	12500
.....	.....	.....	63t	.....	.....	.....	.....	.....	.....	
.....	.....	.....	252	.....	.....	.....	.....	.....	.....	313
)t	.....	.....	.....	.....	.....	.....	.....	.....	.....	
880	.....	.....	.....	.....	.....	.....	.....	.....	.....	880

OAXACA

H	I	J	K	L	M	N	O	P	Special items	Population
.....	.....	.....	.....	.....	300t	.....	.....	.....	.....	
.....	.....	.....	.....	.....	1200	.....	.....	.....	.....	1200
.....	.....	.....	.....	.....	[1200t]	[1460t]	.....	1231t	.....	
.....	.....	.....	.....	.....	.....	.....	.....	4924	.....	11464
.....	.....	.....	.....	.....	.....	120t	.....	.....	.....	
.....	.....	.....	.....	.....	.....	480	.....	.....	.....	480

OAXACA—(Continued)

No.	Name	A	B	C	D	E	F	G
163	Amaltepec........	...... (184)	240p 960	......	......	......	......	......
6	Amusgos.........	240t 960	400p 1600	......	......	......	......	......
90	Apoala..........	709t 2836	352p 1408	......	......	......	......	......
90	Apasco..........	......	......	......	......	......	......	......
90	Jocotipac........	......	......	......	......	......	......	......
278	Atlahuaca........	658t 2632	......	952p 3808	......	698p 2792	......	......
150	Ayacastepec.....	327t 1308	800p 3200	......	......	......	......	......
630	Ayautla.........	223t 892	150p 600	......	......	......	......	......
751	Ayoquezco.......	...... (597)	......	208p 832	......	208p 832	......	......
739	Ayutla..........	80t 320	......	......	......	......	......	......
274	Ayutla..........	35t 140	......	......	......	......	......	......
499	Cacalotepec......	150t 600	......	......	......	......	......	......
141	Cacalotepec......	150t 600	600p 2400	......	......	......	......	......
816	Cahuitlan........	...... (1301)	170p 680	......	......	423p 1692	......	......
714	Calihuala........	...... (523)	......	......	......	......	......	......
202	Calpulalpan......	386t 1544	500p 2000	......	......	......	......	......
217	Coatepec........	...... (852)	500p 2000	277p 1108	......	......	......	......
22	Coatlan.........	10655t 42620	2000p 8000	......	......	......	......	......
22	Miahuatlan......	......	......	......	......	......	......	......
22	Ejutla...........	......	......	......	......	......	......	......
22	Almolonga.......	......	......	......	......	......	......	......
22	Cuixtlan.........	......	......	......	......	......	......	......
22	Suchixtepec......	......	......	......	......	......	......	......
22	Rio Hondo.......	......	......	......	......	......	......	......
22	Amatlan.........	......	......	......	......	......	......	......
104	Coixtlahuaca.....	...... (7636)	1000p 4000	1899p 7596	......	1899p 7596	......	......

Appendix I: Population in 1565

OAXACA—(Continued)

H	I	J	K	L	M	N	O	P	Special items	Population
......	......	......	......	60t	......	......	......	......	......	
......	......	......	......	240	......	......	......	......	......	240
......	......	......	......	......	300t	300t	......	307t	......	
......	......	......	......	......	1200	1200	......	1228	......	1200
......	......	......	......	......	⌠500t	⌠550t	......	⌠223t	......	⌠
......	......	......	......	......	2000	2200	......	892	......	2100
......	......	......	......	......	......	......	......	......	......	
......	......	......	......	......	⌊......	⌊......	......	⌊......	......	⌊......
......	......	......	......	......	120t	150t	......	115t	......	
......	......	......	......	......	480	600	......	460	......	600
......	......	......	......	......	800t	800t	......	......	......	
......	......	......	......	......	3200	3200	......	......	......	3250
......	......	......	......	......	......	360t	236t	150t	......	
......	......	......	......	......	......	1440	944	600	......	1440
......	......	......	......	......	......	......	......	......	......	
......	......	......	......	......	......	......	......	......	......	892
......	......	......	......	......	200t	160t	......	......	......	
......	......	......	......	......	800	640	......	......	......	776
......	......	......	......	......	......	60t	......	......	......	
......	......	......	......	......	......	240	......	......	......	240
......	......	......	......	......	......	......	......	......	......	
......	......	......	......	......	......	......	......	......	......	140
......	......	......	......	......	......	......	......	......	......	
......	......	......	......	......	......	......	......	......	......	600
......	......	......	......	[10t]	......	100t	......	33t	......	
......	......	......	......	......	......	400	......	132	......	400
......	......	......	......	......	......	......	150t	......	......	
......	......	......	......	......	......	......	600	......	......	1692
......	......	......	......	......	......	170t	160t	......	......	
......	......	......	......	......	......	680	640	......	......	680
......	......	......	......	200t	200t	200t	......	......	......	
......	......	......	......	800	800	800	......	......	......	800
......	......	......	......	......	......	......	......	......	......	1108
......	......	......	......	⌠4000t	1400t	1400t	1700t	......	......	⌠
......	......	......	......	16000	5600	5600	6800	......	......	17066
......	......	......	......	......	1300t	1400t	1400t	......	......	
......	......	......	......	......	5200	5600	5600	......	......	......
......	......	......	......	......	250t	500t	......	......	......	
......	......	......	......	......	1000	2000	......	......	......	......
......	......	......	......	⌊......	......	......	......	......	......	
......	......	......	......	......	......	......	......	......	......	......
......	......	......	......	......	300t	......	255p	......	......	
......	......	......	......	......	1200	......	1020	......	......	......
......	......	......	......	......	......	......	......	......	......	
......	......	......	......	......	......	150t	......	......	......	
......	......	......	......	......	......	600	......	......	......	⌊......
......	......	......	......	2600t	3200t	2800t	......	......	......	
......	......	......	......	10400	12800	11200	......	......	......	9928

OAXACA—(Continued)

No.	Name	A	B	C	D	E	F	G
500	Comaltepec............	340t						
		1360						
821	Cotahuistla...........	......						
		(769)						
155	Astata................	160t			200p	200p		
		640			800	800		
103	Coyotepec............	......	258p					
		(1061)	1032					
624	Cozoaltepec..........	......	⎡235p	45p				
		(110)	940	180				
624	Amatlan..............	......	......	107p				
		(329)	⎣......	428				
20	Cuilapa..............	......	1400p					
		(18461)	5600					
784	Cuquila..............	......						
		(369)						
727	Cuyotepexi...........	......						
		(615)						
246	Chachoapam..........	......	380p					
		(1538)	1520					
730	Chalcatongo..........	......						
		(2153)						
280	Chayuco..............	200t						
		800						
533	Chazumba............	150t			⎡400t			
		600			1600			
529	Huapanapa...........	95t	300p		⎣			
		380	1200					
21	Chicomezuchil........	682t						
		2728						
543	Chichicapa...........	1455t	......	1064p		1064p		
		5820		4256		4256		
322	Chichicastepec........	70t	84p					
		280	336					
744	Chisme...............	......						
		(154)						
498	Choapan..............	7643tp	250p					
		7643	1000					
26	Etla..................	......	1000p					
		(4615)	4000					
136	Etlatongo + Huautla...	......	500p					
		(924)	2000					
431	Huajolotitlan..........	......						
		(308)						
725	Huajuapam............	......				572p		
		(1784)				2288		
430	Huamelula............	63t	400p			650p		
		252	1600			2600		
430	Tlacolula.............	345t						
		1380						

Appendix I: Population in 1565

OAXACA—(Continued)

H	I	J	K	L	M	N	O	P	Special Items	Population
				150t	150t					
				600	600					600
						250t				
						1000				1000
					200t	200t				
					800	800				800
					500t	190t				
					2000	760				1380
						30t				
						120				150
							200t			
							800			428
						6000t				
						24000				24000
					120t					
					480					480
						200t				
						800				800
				600t	400t					
				2400	1600					2000
					600t	800t		401t		
					2400	3200		1604		2800
										800
										1600
										......
				550t	800t	500t				
				2200	3200	2000				2466
					1200t					
					4800					4428
						90t				
						360				360
						50t				
						200				200
						240t				
						960				960
					2200t	800t				
					8800	3200				6000
					300t					
					1200					1200
					100t					
					400					400
				668p		500t				
				2672		2000				2320
					700t	700t				
					2800	2800				2733
					100t	100t				
					400	400				400

OAXACA—(Continued)

No.	Name	A	B	C	D	E	F	G
316	Huatulco...................	190t	......	......	......	......	......	......
		760	......	......	......	......	......	......
144	Ocotepec...................	350t	800p	......	......	......	......	......
		1440	3200	......	......	......	......	......
316	Suchitepec.................	135t	300p	340p	......	......	......	......
		540	1200	1360	......	......	......	......
762	Huatusco...................	......	......	......	350t	......	......	......
		(1306)	......	......	1400	......	......	......
778	Huauclilla..................	......	......	......	......	......	......	......
		(246)	......	......	......	......	......	......
177	Huautla....................	190t	960p	......	......	......	......	......
		760	3840	......	......	......	......	......
177	Nanatiquipac................	30t	......	......	......	......	......	......
		120	......	......	......	......	......	......
728	Ixcatlan...................	......	......	......	......	......	......	......
		(462)	......	......	......	......	......	......
783	Huiltepec..................	......	......	......	......	......	......	......
		(462)	......	......	......	......	......	......
782	Huajolotitlan...............	1793t	825p	1800p	......	1084p	......	......
		7172	3300	7200	......	4336	......	......
32	Igualtepec + Suchiquizala...	......	2000p	......	......	......	......	......
		(6153)	8000	......	......	......	......	......
724	Igualtepec..................	......	......	......	......	......	......	......
		(1231)	......	......	......	......	......	......
181	Ixcatlan + Nopala...........	......	400p	......	......	......	......	......
		(2153)	1600	......	......	......	......	......
685	Ixcuintepec + Elotepec......	......	200p	246p	......	......	......	......
		(919)	800	984	......	......	......	......
392	Ixcuintepec.................	471t	......	......	......	......	......	......
		1884	......	......	......	......	......	......
435	Ixtepec....................	1217t	......	1204p	......	1204p	......	......
		4868	......	4816	......	4816	......	......
325	Ixtepexi...................	451t	250p	306p	......	306p	......	......
		1804	1000	1224	......	1224	......	......
114	Ixtlan.....................	420t	400p	......	......	......	......	......
		1680	1600	......	......	......	......	......
182	Ixcatoya...................	170t	300p	......	......	......	......	......
		680	1200	......	......	......	......	......
749	Jalahui....................	......	......	......	......	......	......	......
		(123)	......	......	......	......	......	......
363	Jalapa.....................	220t	......	......	......	......	......	......
		880	......	......	......	......	......	......
76	Jalapa.....................	......	750p	......	......	......	......	......
		(2923)	3000	......	......	......	......	......
483	Jaltepec...................	303t	210p	......	......	......	......	......
		1212	840	......	......	......	......	......
184	Jaltepetongo...............	......	360p	......	......	......	......	......
		(1384)	1440	......	......	......	......	......
184	Tiltepec...................	......	......	......	......	......	......	......
		......	......	......	......	......	......	......
314	Jamiltepec.................	200t	......	......	......	......	......	......
		800	......	......	......	......	......	......

Appendix I: Population in 1565

OAXACA—(Continued)

H	I	J	K	L	M	N	O	P	Special items	Population
……	……	……	……	⎧ 550t	250t	300t	……	……	……	
……	……	……	……	| 2200	1000	1200	……	……	……	1466
……	……	……	……	⎩ ……	……	……	……	……	……	
……	……	……	……	……	……	……	……	……	……	……
……	……	……	……	……	……	……	……	……	……	
……	……	……	……	……	……	……	……	……	……	1360
……	……	……	……	……	……	500t	1000t	……	……	
……	……	……	……	……	……	2000	4000	……	……	1700
……	……	……	……	80t	……	……	……	……	……	
……	……	……	……	320	……	……	……	……	……	320
……	……	……	……	⎧ 600t	400t	……	236t	……	……	
……	……	……	……	| 2400	1600	……	944	……	……	2140
……	……	……	……	| ……	……	70t	77t	……	……	
……	……	……	……	⎩ ……	……	280	308	……	……	……
……	……	……	……	……	200t	100t	……	……	……	
……	……	……	……	……	800	400	……	……	……	600
……	……	……	……	……	……	150t	……	……	……	
……	……	……	……	……	……	600	……	……	……	600
……	……	……	……	……	1200t	……	……	……	……	
……	……	……	……	……	4800	……	……	……	……	5445
……	……	……	……	……	……	……	……	……	……	
……	……	……	……	……	……	……	……	……	……	8000
……	……	……	……	……	……	400t	……	……	……	
……	……	……	……	……	……	1600	……	……	……	1600
……	……	……	……	800t	600t	……	……	……	……	
……	……	……	……	3200	2400	……	……	……	……	2800
……	……	……	……	……	400t	250t	……	……	……	
……	……	……	……	……	1600	1000	……	……	……	1195
……	……	……	……	600t	……	……	……	……	……	
……	……	……	……	2400	……	……	……	……	……	2400
……	……	……	……	……	700t	699t	……	……	……	
……	……	……	……	……	2800	2796	……	……	……	3807
……	……	……	……	……	250t	300t	……	……	……	
……	……	……	……	……	1000	1200	……	……	……	1162
……	……	……	……	400t	400t	400t	……	……	……	
……	……	……	……	1600	1600	1600	……	……	……	1600
……	……	……	……	……	……	……	……	……	……	
……	……	……	……	……	……	……	……	……	……	1200
……	……	……	……	……	……	40t	……	……	……	
……	……	……	……	……	……	160	……	……	……	160
……	……	……	……	……	150t	……	……	158t	……	
……	……	……	……	……	600	……	……	632	……	600
……	……	……	……	……	1000t	900t	……	……	……	
……	……	……	……	……	4000	3600	……	……	……	3800
……	……	……	……	……	……	……	……	……	……	
……	……	……	……	……	……	……	……	……	……	1212
……	……	……	……	⎧ 400t	200t	200t	……	114t	……	
……	……	……	……	| 1600	800	800	……	456	……	1800
……	……	……	……	| ……	300t	……	……	146t	……	
……	……	……	……	⎩ ……	1200	……	……	584	……	……
……	……	……	……	……	……	……	……	……	……	
……	……	……	……	……	……	……	……	……	……	800

OAXACA—(Continued)

No.	Name	A	B	C	D	E	F	G
140	Jicayan	400t 1600	400p 1600					
154	Justlavaca	460t 1840	520p 2080	463p 1852		463p 1852		
734	Lapaguia	90t 360						
224	Macuiltianguez	(3076)	1000p 4000					
224	Cusmiquila							
504	Macuilzochitl	405t 1620		338p 1352		338p 1352		
504	Teotitlan (del Valle)	518t 2072		501p 2004		501p 2004		
189	Malinaltepec	621tp 621	200p 800					
687	Maninaltepec	300t 1200	650p 2600					
247	Mazatlan	70t 280	100p 400					
743	Metlaltepec	(185)						
439	Miahuatlan	100t 400						
668	Mitla	718t 2872		870p 3480		287p 1148		
188	Mitlantongo	523t 2092	562p 2248					
312	Mixtepec	50t 200						
185	Mixtepec	(1076)	600p 2400					
472	Mixtepec	(3558)			1070t 4280			
740	Moctun	(123)						
153	Zoquitlan	242t 968						
153	Azuntepec	260t 1040						
153	Epustepec	280t 1120						
153	Necotepec	120t 480						
153	Olintepec	80t 320						
153	Tepexistepec	85t 340						
441	Nejapa	840p 3360	600p 2400	786p 3144		590p 2360		
440	Nochistlan	1159tp 1159	500p 2000	1077p 4308		1077p 4308		

Appendix I: Population in 1565

OAXACA—(Continued)

H	I	J	K	L	M	N	O	P	Special items	Population
					200t					
					800					800
										1852
					250t	250t				
					1000	1000				1000
				500t	250t			39t		
				2000	1000			156		4000
					300t	214t				
					1200	856				1190
					400t	300t				
					1600	1200				1702
				300t	300t	200t				
				1200	1200	800				1066
				[30t]		100t				
						400				400
					20t	40t				
					80	160				120
						60t				
						240				240
										400
					600t	600t				
					2400	2400				2332
						300t		175t		
						1200		700		1200
										200
				350t						
				1400						1400
				1070t		1480t				
				4280		5920				4626
						40t				
						160				160
				[800t	200t			221t		
				3200	800			881		3120
					200t			356t		
					800			1424		
					200t			453t		
					800			1812		
					100t		75t	75t		
					400		300	300		
					60t			74t		
					240			296		
								133t		
								532		
					600t	[4770t]				
					2400					2635
					1000t		720t			
					4000		2880			4205

Population of Central Mexico

OAXACA—(Continued)

No.	Name	A	B	C	D	E	F	G
30	Oaxaca	(2615)	1500p 6000					
223	Oaxaca	(1231)	440p 1760					
736	Ocotepec	(569)						
144	Ocotepec	303t 1212	425p 1700					
40	Ocotlan	(3144)	400p 1600					
442	Ocotlan	1566t 6264						
558	Ojitlan	60t 240	150p 600	150p 600		133p 532		
120	Ozolotepec	[393t] (2769)	700p 2800					
443	Papalotepec	507t 2028	100p 400			427p 1708		
	Cuizala							
530	Tepeucila	143t 572	160p 640					
443	Tutepetongo	106t 424	750p 3000	250p 1000				
632	Peñoles	(1846)	365p 1460					
560	Pinotepa	515t 2060						
511	Pochutla	(112)	100p 400			40p 160		
196	Puctla	600t 2400	240p 960					
444	Quiotepec	300t 1200				289p 1156		
735	San Miguel Grande	(1231)						
713	Silacayoapam [province]	(3692)			1200t 4800			
23	Sola	(2717)	850p 3400					
556	Ixtayutla	284t 1136						
105	Sosola	402t 1608	550p 2200					
631	Soyaltepec	57t 228	270p 1080					
631	Zoyatlan	(188)				72p 288		
490	Soyaltepec	1150tp 1150		438p 1752		438p 1752		
490	Tonaltepec	(850)	200p 800	328p 1312		328p 1312		

Appendix I: Population in 1565

OAXACA—(Continued)

H	I	J	K	L	M	N	O	P	Special items	Population
......	......	......	......	......	......	850t	......	.....	.....	
......	......	......	......	......	......	3400	......	.....	.....	3400
......	......	......	......	......	......	400t	......	.....	.....	
......	......	......	......	......	......	1600	......	.....	.....	1600
......	......	......	......	......	150t	220t	......	.....	.....	
......	......	......	......	......	600	800	......	.....	.....	740
......	......	......	......	450t	......	......	......	.....	.....	
......	......	......	......	1800	......	......	......	.....	.....	1800
......	......	......	......	1022t	......	......	......	.....	.....	
......	......	......	......	4088	......	......	......	.....	.....	4088
......	......	......	......	......	1200t	1020t	......	.....	.....	
......	......	......	......	......	4800	4080	......	.....	.....	4440
......	......	......	......	......	......	......	......	.....	.....	566
......	......	......	......	600t	1200t	......	2000t	.....	.....	
......	......	......	......	2400	4800	......	8000	.....	.....	3600
......	......	......	......	......	600t	1400t	......	.....	.....	
......	......	......	......	......	2400	5600	......	.....	.....	5600
......	......	......	......	......	......	......	......	.....	.....	......
......	......	......	......	......	150t	......	......	.....	.....	
......	......	......	......	......	600	......	......	.....	.....	......
......	......	......	......	......	......	......	......	.....	.....	......
......	......	......	......	......	......	600t	......	.....	.....	
......	......	......	......	......	......	2400	......	.....	.....	2400
......	......	......	......	......	......	......	......	.....	.....	2060
......	......	......	......	......	30t	40t	......	.....	.....	
......	......	......	......	......	120	160	......	.....	.....	146
......	......	......	......	300t	200t	......	......	.....	.....	
......	......	......	......	1200	800	......	......	.....	.....	1000
......	......	......	......	......	250t	......	......	.....	.....	
......	......	......	......	......	1000	......	......	.....	.....	1078
......	......	......	......	......	......	400t	......	.....	.....	
......	......	......	......	......	......	1600	......	.....	.....	1600
......	......	......	......	......	......	......	......	.....	.....	4800
......	......	......	......	800t	800t	800t	......	.....	.....	
......	......	......	......	3200	3200	3200	......	.....	.....	3533
......	......	......	......	......	......	250t	......	.....	.....	
......	......	......	......	......	......	1000	......	.....	.....	......
......	......	......	......	600t	400t	600t	......	.....	.....	
......	......	......	......	2400	1600	2400	......	.....	.....	2133
......	......	......	......	......	30t	......	......	.....	.....	
......	......	......	......	......	120	......	......	.....	.....	120
......	......	......	......	......	50t	......	......	.....	.....	
......	......	......	......	......	200	......	......	.....	.....	244
......	......	......	......	......	300t	200t	......	.....	.....	
......	......	......	......	......	1200	800	......	.....	.....	1376
......	......	......	......	......	250t	200t	......	.....	.....	
......	......	......	......	......	1000	800	......	.....	.....	1106

96 Population of Central Mexico

OAXACA—(Continued)

No.	Name	A	B	C	D	E	F	G
180	Suchixtepec	(123)	150p 600					
527	Talea	125t 500						
544	Talistaca	1021t 4084	460p 1840	545p 2180		545p 2180		
69	Tamazulapa	3735tp 3735	900p 3600					
200	Tamazola	605t 2420	670p 2680					
780	Tataltepec	(308)						
210	Tehuantepec [province]	18805tp 18805	2200p 8800	4650t 18600				
465	Tejupam	(1144tp) 1144				1567p 6268		
747	Temascalapa	40t 160	170p 680					
313	Temascaltepec	301t 1204						
374	Tenango	60t 240						
785	Tenexpa	(772)						
463	Teococuilco	910t 3640	330p 1320			129p 516		
463	Zoquiapan							
463	Jaltianguis					107p 428		
463	Atepec		330p 1320			308p 1232		
310	Teotalcingo	1039t 4156	740p 2960					
448	Teotitlan (del Camino)	1260t 5040	700p 2800	1111p 4444		996p 3984		
471	Teotlaxco	76t 304						
318	Teozacualco	1789t 7156	740p 2960	1160p 4640		1394p 5576		
523	Teozapotlan	2126t 8504	540p 2160	1434p 5736		1434p 5736		
249	Teozatlan	1384tp 1384	600p 2400					
371	Tepanzacualco	59t 236						
68	Tepetlolutla	(1538)	900p 3600					
464	Teposcolula	10560tp 10560	1000p 4000	6833p 27332		5026p 20104		

Appendix I: Population in 1565

OAXACA—(Continued)

H	I	J	K	L	M	N	O	P	Special items	Population
.....	.....	.....	.....	150t	.....	150t	.....	.....	.....	
.....	.....	.....	.....	600	.....	600	.....	.....	.....	600
.....	.....	.....	.....	.....	.....	40t	.....	.....	.....	
.....	.....	.....	.....	.....	.....	160	.....	.....	.....	160
.....	.....	.....	.....	.....	400t	600t	430t	.....	.....	
.....	.....	.....	.....	.....	1600	2400	1720	.....	.....	2090
.....	.....	.....	.....	1672t	1500t	[400t]	.....	.....	.....	
.....	.....	.....	.....	6688	6000	.....	.....	.....	.....	6344
.....	.....	.....	.....	.....	300t	800t	.....	102t	.....	
.....	.....	.....	.....	.....	1200	3200	.....	408	.....	2200
.....	.....	.....	.....	.....	100t	.....	.....	.....	.....	
.....	.....	.....	.....	.....	400	.....	.....	.....	.....	400
.....	.....	.....	.....	.....	3000t	3320t	.....	.....	.....	
.....	.....	.....	.....	.....	12000	13280	.....	.....	.....	12640
.....	.....	.....	.....	.....	900t	1000t	750p	.....	.....	
.....	.....	.....	.....	.....	3600	4000	3000	.....	.....	4623
.....	.....	.....	.....	.....	.....	60t	.....	.....	.....	
.....	.....	.....	.....	.....	.....	240	.....	.....	.....	240
.....	.....	.....	.....	.....	.....	.....	.....	.....	.....	
.....	.....	.....	.....	.....	.....	.....	.....	.....	.....	1204
.....	.....	.....	.....	.....	.....	.....	.....	.....	.....	
.....	.....	.....	.....	.....	.....	.....	.....	.....	.....	240
.....	.....	.....	.....	302t	200t	.....	.....	71t	.....	
.....	.....	.....	.....	1208	800	.....	.....	284	.....	1004
.....	.....	.....	.....	.....	⎡890t	⎡1000t	.....	.....	.....	⎡
.....	.....	.....	.....	.....	3560	4000	.....	.....	.....	3780
.....	.....	.....	.....	.....	.....	.....	.....	.....	.....	
.....	.....	.....	.....	.....	.....	.....	.....	.....	.....	
.....	.....	.....	.....	.....	.....	.....	.....	.....	.....	
.....	.....	.....	.....	.....	⎣	⎣	.....	.....	.....	⎣
.....	.....	.....	.....	.....	.....	.....	.....	.....	.....	4156
.....	.....	.....	.....	.....	900t	.....	916t	.....	.....	
.....	.....	.....	.....	.....	3600	.....	3664	.....	.....	4009
.....	.....	.....	.....	.....	.....	.....	.....	.....	.....	304
.....	.....	.....	.....	.....	[600t]	[600t]	.....	.....	.....	
.....	.....	.....	.....	.....	.....	.....	.....	.....	.....	5108
.....	.....	.....	.....	.....	1300t	1808t	.....	.....	.....	
.....	.....	.....	.....	.....	5200	7232	.....	.....	.....	5976
.....	.....	.....	.....	.....	.....	500t	.....	.....	.....	
.....	.....	.....	.....	.....	.....	2000	.....	.....	.....	2000
.....	.....	.....	.....	800t	.....	.....	.....	.....	.....	
.....	.....	.....	.....	3200	.....	.....	.....	.....	.....	3200
.....	.....	.....	.....	.....	500t	500t	.....	.....	.....	
.....	.....	.....	.....	.....	2000	2000	.....	.....	.....	2000
.....	.....	.....	.....	.....	4500t	4000t	.....	.....	.....	
.....	.....	.....	.....	.....	18000	16000	.....	.....	.....	20357

OAXACA—(Continued)

No.	Name	A	B	C	D	E	F	G
311	Tequixistlan	286t	......	......	......	......	......	......
		1144	......	......	......	......	......	......
373	Tequixtepec	1000t	......	......	......	1740p	......	......
		4000	......	......	......	6960	......	......
618	Tequixtepec	......	120p	......	......	......	......	......
		(769)	480	......	......	......	......	......
317	Tetepec	88t	......	......	......	41p	......	......
		352	......	......	......	164	......	......
473	Teutila	1516t	1100p	1291p	......	1291p	......	......
		6064	4400	5164	......	5164	......	......
827	Lachichivia	148t	220p	......	......	......	......	......
		592	880	......	......	......	......	......
828	Xuquila	......	......	......	......	......	......	......
		(369)	......	......	......	......	......	......
829	Teiticpac	......	......	851p	......	......	......	......
		(2386)	......	3404	......	......	......	......
830	Teiticpac	......	520p	1183p	......	1183p	......	......
		(3321)	2080	4732	......	4732	......	......
831	Tepuxtepec	......	......	......	......	......	......	......
		(185)	......	......	......	......	......	......
832	Huitepec	56t	45t	......	......	......	......	......
		224	180	......	......	......	......	......
833	Yoveo	......	......	......	......	......	......	......
		(185)	......	......	......	......	......	......
834	Camotlan	......	......	......	......	......	......	......
		(77)	......	......	......	......	......	......
835	Camotlan	153t	......	......	......	......	......	......
		612	......	......	......	......	......	......
836	Zochila	......	......	......	......	......	......	......
		(369)	......	......	......	......	......	......
837	Lalopa	140t	250p	......	......	......	......	......
		560	1000	......	......	......	......	......
838	Tagni	116t	130p	......	......	......	......	......
		464	520	......	......	......	......	......
838	Lazagaya	77t	......	......	......	......	......	......
		308	......	......	......	......	......	......
839	Yacoche	42t	60p	......	......	......	......	......
		168	240	......	......	......	......	......
370	Tiltepec	148t	200p	......	......	......	......	......
		592	800	......	......	......	......	......
542	Titicapa	2080t	......	......	......	......	......	......
		8320	......	......	......	......	......	......
207	Tlacamama	91t	200p	......	......	......	......	......
		364	800	......	......	......	......	......
340	Tlacochahuaya	855t	......	......	......	......	......	......
		3420	......	......	......	......	......	......
462	Tlacolula	498t	280p	427p	......	300p	......	......
		1992	1120	1708	......	1200	......	......
319	Tlacotepec	190t	......	......	......	......	......	......
		760	......	......	......	......	......	......

Appendix I: Population in 1565

OAXACA—(Continued)

H	I	J	K	L	M	N	O	P	Special items	Population
......	......	......	......	......	800t	700t	......	......	......	
......	......	......	......	......	3200	2800	......	......	......	3000
......	......	......	......	500t	......	1000t	......	......	......	
......	......	......	......	2000	......	4000	......	......	......	4320
......	......	......	......	......	250t	......	......	......	......	
......	......	......	......	......	1000	......	......	......	......	1000
......	......	......	......	......	120t	......	......	......	......	
......	......	......	......	......	480	......	......	......	......	322
......	......	......	......	......	[120t]	1500t	......	......	......	
......	......	......	......	......	......	6000	......	......	......	5443
......	......	......	......	50t	......	120t	......	52t	......	
......	......	......	......	200	......	480	......	204	......	340
......	......	......	......	......	......	120t	......	......	......	
......	......	......	......	......	......	480	......	......	......	480
......	......	......	......	......	700t	......	......	......	......	
......	......	......	......	......	2800	......	......	......	......	3102
......	......	......	......	......	1000t	952t	1000t	......	......	
......	......	......	......	......	4000	3808	4000	......	......	4318
......	......	......	......	......	......	60t	......	......	......	
......	......	......	......	......	......	240	......	......	......	240
......	......	......	......	......	......	......	......	......	......	
......	......	......	......	......	......	......	......	......	......	224
......	......	......	......	......	......	60t	......	......	......	
......	......	......	......	......	......	240	......	......	......	240
......	......	......	......	......	......	25t	......	......	......	
......	......	......	......	......	......	100	......	......	......	100
......	......	......	......	......	......	......	......	......	......	
......	......	......	......	......	......	......	......	......	......	612
......	......	......	......	......	......	120t	......	......	......	
......	......	......	......	......	......	480	......	......	......	480
......	......	......	......	......	......	150t	......	......	......	
......	......	......	......	......	......	600	......	......	......	600
......	......	......	......	......	......	50t	......	......	......	
......	......	......	......	......	......	200	......	......	......	200
......	......	......	......	......	......	......	......	......	......	308
......	......	......	......	......	......	60t	......	......	......	
......	......	......	......	......	......	240	......	......	......	240
......	......	......	......	200t	......	240t	......	......	......	
......	......	......	......	800	......	960	......	......	......	980
......	......	......	......	......	......	......	......	......	......	8320
......	......	......	......	......	100t	100t	......	......	......	
......	......	......	......	......	400	400	......	......	......	400
......	......	......	......	......	500t	600t	......	......	......	
......	......	......	......	......	2000	2400	......	......	......	2200
......	......	......	......	......	400t	300t	......	......	......	
......	......	......	......	......	1600	1200	......	......	......	1427
......	......	......	......	......	......	......	......	......	312t	
......	......	......	......	......	......	......	......	......	1248	760

Population of Central Mexico

OAXACA—(Continued)

No.	Name	A	B	C	D	E	F	G
788	Tlacoatzintepec	152t						
		608						
788	Quezalapa							
		(185)						
788	Tecomaltepec	127t						
		508						
741	Tlahuilotepec	228t						
		912						
133	Tlaxiaco [province]	6541t						
		26164						
469	Tonaguia	181t						
		724						
469	Tupetongo	34t				134p		
		136				536		
669	Tonala	765p						
		3060						
787	Topiltepec							
		(123)						
135	Totolapan	262t	400p					
		1048	1600					
372	Totolapilla	125t						
		500						
251	Tulantongo	2662tp	750p	1240p		1240p		
		2662	3000	4960		4960		
443	Tutepetongo	106t	750p	250p				
		424	3000	1000				
737	Tutla							
		(923)						
57	Tutotepec	900t	3000p					
		3600	12000					
57	Nopala	695t						
		2780						
470	Tuxtepec	162t						
		648						
478	Usila	1075tp	320p					
		1075	1280					
686	Villa Alta							
		(92)						
252	Xaltepec	2098t	4000p					
		8392	16000					
748	Yagoni							
		(154)						
750	Yalalag							
		(185)						
33	Yanhuitlan	13733tp	1500p					
		13733	6000					
434	Yautepec			90p				
		(200)		360				
746	Yaviche							
		(92)						
781	Yococui							
		(277)						

Appendix I: Population in 1565

OAXACA—(Continued)

H	I	J	K	L	M	N	O	P	Special items	Population
.....	.....	.....	.....	.....	200t	500t	.....	.....	.....	
.....	.....	.....	.....	.....	800	2000	.....	.....	.....	1820
.....	.....	.....	.....	.....	60t	.....	.....	.....	.....	
.....	.....	.....	.....	.....	240	.....	.....	.....	.....	.....
.....	.....	.....	.....	.....	150t	.....	.....	.....	.....	
.....	.....	.....	.....	.....	600	.....	.....	.....	.....	.....
.....	.....	.....	.....	.....	80t	200t	.....	.....	.....	
.....	.....	.....	.....	.....	320	800	.....	.....	.....	560
.....	.....	.....	.....	4281t	4900t	4355t	.....	.....	.....	
.....	.....	.....	.....	17124	19600	17420	.....	.....	.....	16036
.....	.....	.....	.....	.....	.....	100t	.....	.....	.....	
.....	.....	.....	.....	.....	.....	400	.....	.....	.....	400
.....	.....	.....	.....	.....	.....	.....	.....	.....	.....	
.....	.....	.....	.....	.....	.....	.....	.....	.....	.....	536
.....	.....	.....	.....	.....	.....	.....	.....	.....	.....	
.....	.....	.....	.....	.....	.....	.....	.....	.....	.....	3060
.....	.....	.....	.....	.....	150t	.....	.....	.....	.....	
.....	.....	.....	.....	.....	600	.....	.....	.....	.....	600
.....	.....	.....	.....	550t	300t	.....	.....	.....	.....	
.....	.....	.....	.....	2200	1200	.....	.....	.....	.....	1700
.....	.....	.....	.....	.....	.....	60t	.....	91t	.....	
.....	.....	.....	.....	.....	.....	240	.....	364	.....	240
.....	.....	.....	.....	.....	1000t	1000t	.....	.....	.....	
.....	.....	.....	.....	.....	4000	4000	.....	.....	.....	4480
.....	.....	.....	.....	.....	.....	.....	.....	.....	.....	1000
.....	.....	.....	.....	.....	300t	300t	.....	.....	.....	
.....	.....	.....	.....	.....	1200	1200	.....	.....	.....	1200
.....	.....	.....	.....	3463t	3000t	3400t	.....	.....	.....	
.....	.....	.....	.....	13852	12000	13600	.....	.....	.....	13151
.....	.....	.....	.....	.....	.....	.....	.....	.....	.....	.....
.....	.....	.....	.....	.....	.....	.....	.....	.....	.....	648
.....	.....	.....	.....	.....	400t	500t	.....	.....	.....	
.....	.....	.....	.....	.....	1600	2000	.....	.....	.....	1800
.....	.....	.....	.....	.....	.....	30t	.....	.....	.....	
.....	.....	.....	.....	.....	.....	120	.....	.....	.....	120
.....	.....	.....	.....	1584t	1500t	1600t	.....	.....	.....	
.....	.....	.....	.....	6336	6000	6400	.....	.....	.....	6245
.....	.....	.....	.....	.....	.....	50t	.....	.....	.....	
.....	.....	.....	.....	.....	.....	200	.....	.....	.....	200
.....	.....	.....	.....	.....	.....	60t	.....	.....	.....	
.....	.....	.....	.....	.....	.....	240	.....	.....	.....	240
.....	.....	.....	.....	6184t	6000t	.....	.....	.....	.....	
.....	.....	.....	.....	24736	24000	.....	.....	.....	.....	24368
.....	.....	.....	.....	.....	40t	.....	.....	.....	.....	
.....	.....	.....	.....	.....	160	.....	.....	.....	.....	260
.....	.....	.....	.....	.....	.....	30t	.....	.....	.....	
.....	.....	.....	.....	.....	.....	120	.....	.....	.....	120
.....	.....	.....	.....	.....	90t	.....	.....	.....	.....	
.....	.....	.....	.....	.....	360	.....	.....	.....	.....	360

OAXACA—(Concluded)

No.	Name	A	B	C	D	E	F	G
731	Yolotepec............	(1153)						
789	Yoloxnoquilla........	(1000)						
779	Yucuxaco.............	(616)						
279	Zacatepec............	550t						
		2200						
324	Zenzontepec..........	235t						
		940						
421	Zimatlan.............	910t	300p	593p		⎡2663p		
		3640	1200	2372		10652		
421	Tepezimatlan.........	952t		387p				
		3808		1548		⎣		
379	Caltitlan............	1205t						
		4820						
726	Estetla..............		219p	82p				
		(616)	876	328				
726	Totomachapa..........			55p				
		(238)		220				
253	Zultepec.............	150t	⎡360p					
		600	1440					
253	Zoquio...............							
253	Teotitlan............							
			⎣					
745	Tepitongo............							
		(92)						

OAXACA—CHONTALES

No.	Name	A	B	C	D	E	F	G
	Centecomaltepec......	80t						
		320						
	Colotepec............	(169)						
	Chontales Bravos [province]......	(4923)						
	Itacatepec...........	60t						
		240						
	Maxcaltepec..........	182t		60p		64p		
		728		240		256		
	Tecpa................	(308)						

Appendix I: Population in 1565

OAXACA—(Concluded)

H	I	J	K	L	M	N	O	P	Special items	Population
……	……	……	……	……	350t	400t	……	196t	……	
……	……	……	……	……	1400	1600	……	784	……	1500
……	……	……	……	……	350t	300t	……	……	……	
……	……	……	……	……	1400	1200	……	……	……	1300
……	……	……	……	……	200t	……	……	……	……	
……	……	……	……	……	800	……	……	……	……	800
……	……	……	……	923t	500t	……	……	366t	……	
……	……	……	……	3692	2000	……	……	1464	……	2846
……	……	……	……	……	200t	250t	……	533t	……	
……	……	……	……	……	800	1000	……	2132	……	900
……	……	……	……	……	350t	395t	……	……	……	
……	……	……	……	……	1400	1580	……	……	……	6802
……	……	……	……	……	700t	1714t	……	……	……	
……	……	……	……	……	2800	6856	……	……	……	……
……	……	……	……	……	……	546t	……	……	……	
……	……	……	……	……	……	2184	……	……	……	2184
……	……	……	……	……	200t	200t	……	……	……	
……	……	……	……	……	800	800	……	……	……	800
……	……	……	……	……	100t	……	……	……	……	
……	……	……	……	……	400	……	……	……	……	310
……	……	……	……	50t	……	……	……	……	……	
……	……	……	……	200	……	……	……	……	……	200
……	……	……	……	……	……	……	……	……	……	
……	……	……	……	……	……	……	……	……	……	
……	……	……	……	……	……	……	……	……	……	……
……	……	……	……	……	……	30t	……	……	……	
……	……	……	……	……	……	120	……	……	……	120

OAXACA—CHONTALES

H	I	J	K	L	M	N	O	P	Special items	Population
……	……	……	……	……	100t	……	……	……	……	
……	……	……	……	……	400	……	……	……	……	400
……	……	……	……	……	50t	60t	……	……	……	
……	……	……	……	……	200	240	……	……	……	220
……	……	……	……	……	……	1600t	……	……	……	
……	……	……	……	……	……	6400	……	……	……	6400
……	……	……	……	……	……	……	……	……	……	
……	……	……	……	……	……	……	……	……	……	240
……	……	……	……	……	……	……	……	……	……	
……	……	……	……	……	……	……	……	……	……	248
……	……	……	……	……	100t	……	……	……	……	
……	……	……	……	……	400	……	……	……	……	400

OAXACA—MIXTECAS

No.	Name	A	B	C	D	E	F	G
	Alupancingo	(616)						
	Comaltepec	130t						
		520						
	Cuatla	(277)						
	Cuautitlan	(92)						
	Cuautlatlahauca	(308)						
	Cuitepec	(142)	46p 184					
	Chiagualtepec	(769)						
	Icpatepec	(1015)				360p 1440		
	Ixtatepec	(616)	240p 960					
	Ixtepec	92t 368						
	Malinaltepec	44t 176						
	Michiapa	(308)						
	Moltepec	(215)						
	Nextepec	60t 240						
	Patanala	(769)						
	Paxtlahuaca	(1015)						
	Quitepec	(462)						
	Tequecistepec	50t 200						
	Tehuastepec	(1231)	⎰400p ⎱1600					
	Nanacatepec							
	Tuxtla	64t 256						
	Suchitepec	30t 120						
	Yeytepec	125t 500						
	Zuyutepec	(1231)	⎰400p 1600					
	Etepec		⎱					

Appendix I: Population in 1565

OAXACA—MIXTECAS

H	I	J	K	L	M	N	O	P	Special items	Population
.....	.....	.....	.....	.....	.....	200t	.....	.....	.....	
.....	.....	.....	.....	.....	.....	800	.....	.....	.....	800
.....	.....	.....	.....	.....	.....	.....	.....	.....	.....	
.....	.....	.....	.....	.....	.....	.....	.....	.....	.....	520
.....	.....	.....	.....	.....	.....	90t	.....	.....	.....	
.....	.....	.....	.....	.....	.....	360	.....	.....	.....	360
.....	.....	.....	.....	.....	.....	30t	.....	.....	.....	
.....	.....	.....	.....	.....	.....	120	.....	.....	.....	120
.....	.....	.....	.....	.....	100t	.....	.....	.....	.....	
.....	.....	.....	.....	.....	400	.....	.....	.....	.....	400
.....	.....	.....	.....	.....	.....	.....	.....	.....	.....	
.....	.....	.....	.....	.....	.....	.....	.....	.....	.....	184
.....	.....	.....	.....	.....	.....	250t	.....	.....	.....	
.....	.....	.....	.....	.....	.....	1000	.....	.....	.....	1000
.....	.....	.....	.....	.....	.....	300t	.....	.....	.....	
.....	.....	.....	.....	.....	.....	1200	.....	.....	.....	1320
.....	.....	.....	.....	.....	200t	.....	.....	.....	.....	
.....	.....	.....	.....	.....	800	.....	.....	.....	.....	800
.....	.....	.....	.....	.....	.....	.....	.....	.....	.....	
.....	.....	.....	.....	.....	.....	.....	.....	.....	.....	368
.....	.....	.....	.....	.....	.....	.....	.....	.....	.....	
.....	.....	.....	.....	.....	.....	.....	.....	.....	.....	176
.....	.....	.....	.....	.....	.....	100t	100t	.....	.....	
.....	.....	.....	.....	.....	.....	400	400	.....	.....	400
.....	.....	.....	.....	.....	.....	70t	.....	.....	.....	
.....	.....	.....	.....	.....	.....	280	.....	.....	.....	280
.....	.....	.....	.....	.....	80t	.....	.....	.....	.....	
.....	.....	.....	.....	.....	320	.....	.....	.....	.....	320
.....	.....	.....	.....	.....	.....	250t	250t	.....	.....	
.....	.....	.....	.....	.....	.....	1000	1000	.....	.....	1000
.....	.....	.....	.....	.....	360t	300t	.....	.....	.....	
.....	.....	.....	.....	.....	1440	1200	.....	.....	.....	1320
.....	.....	.....	.....	.....	150t	.....	.....	.....	.....	
.....	.....	.....	.....	.....	600	.....	.....	.....	.....	600
.....	.....	.....	.....	.....	.....	.....	.....	.....	.....	
.....	.....	.....	.....	.....	.....	.....	.....	.....	.....	200
.....	.....	.....	.....	.....	.....	.....	.....	.....	.....	
.....	.....	.....	.....	.....	.....	.....	.....	.....	.....	⎰ 1600
.....	.....	.....	.....	.....	.....	.....	.....	.....	.....	⎱ .....
.....	.....	.....	.....	.....	.....	.....	.....	.....	.....	
.....	.....	.....	.....	.....	.....	.....	.....	.....	.....	256
.....	.....	.....	.....	.....	.....	.....	.....	.....	.....	120
.....	.....	.....	.....	.....	200t	200t	.....	.....	.....	
.....	.....	.....	.....	.....	800	800	.....	.....	.....	800
.....	.....	.....	.....	.....	.....	.....	.....	.....	.....	
.....	.....	.....	.....	.....	.....	.....	.....	.....	.....	⎰ 1600
.....	.....	.....	.....	.....	.....	.....	.....	.....	.....	⎱ .....

OAXACA—ZAPOTECAS AND MIXES

No.	Name	A	B	C	D	E	F	G
	Ayotepec........................	(77)						
	Cacatepec.......................	(185)						
	Calajo...........................	(462)						
	Ciltaltepec......................	(800)	200p 800					
	Cuezcomaltepec.................	(616)						
	Eltianguillo.....................	(123)						
	Esuchicala......................	(308)						
	Huatenicamanes [pueblos]........	3000t 12000	760p 3040					
	Huazcomaltepec................	240t 960	400p 1600					
	Huayatepec.....................	⎰165t 660	⎰260p 1040					
	Lahoya.........................		⎱					
	Hucitepec.......................	(123)						
	Ixcocan.........................	300t 1200						
	Ixtactepec......................	(708)						
	Jolotepec.......................	(154)						
	Lavaylalana.....................	(920)	230p 920					
	Lomatlan.......................	(400)	100p 400					
	Madaxoya......................	(123)						
	Maltepec.......................	60t 240						
	Mexitlan........................	25t 100						
	Meyana.........................	(1538)	500p 2000					
	Nanacatepec....................	(538)	200p 800					
	Nobaan.........................	(430)						
	Paxosnan.......................	(123)						
	Pazolotepec.....................	(1231)	400p 1600					
	Santa Cruz.....................	(308)						

Appendix I: Population in 1565

OAXACA—ZAPOTECAS AND MIXES

H	I	J	K	L	M	N	O	P	Special items	Population
						25t				
						100				100
						60t				
						240				240
					150t					
					600					600
										800
						200t				
						800				800
						40t				
						160				160
						100t				
						400				400
										12000
										1600
						90t				
						360				680
						80t				
						320				......
						40t				
						160				160
										1200
				260t		200t				
				1040		800				920
					50t					
					200					200
										920
										400
						40t				
						160				160
										240
						30t				
						120				120
										2000
					200t	150t				
					800	600				700
						140t				
						560				560
						40t				
						160				160
										1600
						100t				
						400				400

OAXACA—ZAPOTECAS AND MIXES—(Continued)

No.	Name	A	B	C	D	E	F	G
	Sococho	340t						
		1360						
	Suchitepec	27t						
		108						
	Suchitepec							
		(462)						
	Taetz							
		(185)						
	Tava							
		(370)						
	Tecianzacualco							
		(154)						
	Tehuilotepec	62t	215p					
		248	860					
	Teotlacho							
		(185)						
	Tepequecagualco		150p					
		(462)	600					
	Ticatepec	145t						
		580						
	Tiquini							
		(185)						
	Titontepec		400p					
		(1231)	1600					
	Tlacolapacoya							
		(308)						
	Tlapalcatepec	160t		229p		260p		
		640		916		1040		
	Tlapanala	106t	280p					
		424	1120					
	Tlauciotepec		100p					
		(308)	400					
	Tlaxuca	493t						
		1972						
	Tlazoltepec	173t						
		692						
	Tonazayotepec							
		(185)						
	Totolinga	100t	350p					
		400	1400					
	Totontepec	145t						
		580						
	Tutlaco		150p					
		(462)	600					
	Tsaindan							
		(370)						
	Vichinaguia	⎡60t	⎡140p					
		240	560					
	Yatobe	⎣	⎣					

Appendix I: Population in 1565

OAXACA—ZAPOTECAS AND MIXES—(*Continued*)

H	I	J	K	L	M	N	O	P	Special items	Population
								73t		
								292		1360
										108
				150t						
				600						600
						60t				
						240				240
						120t				
						480				480
						50t				
						200				200
						90t				
						360				360
						60t				
						240				240
										600
					200t	120t				
					800	480				640
						60t				
						240				240
										1600
					100t					
					400					400
										978
				250t				139t		
				1000				556		1000
										400
										1972
										692
					60t					
					240					240
				50t		60t				
				200		240				220
										580
										600
						120p				
						480				480
										560

OAXACA—ZAPOTECAS AND MIXES—(Concluded)

No.	Name	A	B	C	D	E	F	G
	Xacobo	...... (185)	....	......	......	......	......	......
	Xareta	60t 240	360p 1440	......	......	......	......	......
	Xayatepec	...... (146)	....	......	......	......	......	......
	Xocochi	...... (154)	....	......	......	......	......	......
	Yacastla	125t 500	....	......	......	......	......	......
	Yachinicingo	...... (123)	....	......	......	......	......	......
	Yagavila	195t 780	300p 1200	......	......	......	......	......
	Yagayo	...... (924)	300p 1200	......	......	......	......	......
	Comultepec	180t 720	....	......	......	......	......	......
	Yao	...... (308)	....	......	......	......	......	......
	Yaquiza	...... (154)	....	......	......	......	......	......
	Yavago	53t 212	260p 1040	......	......	......	......	......
	Metepec	62t 248	....	......	......	......	......	......
	Yaxila	68t 272	120p 480	......	......	......	......	......
	Yotao	...... (185)	....	......	......	......	......	......
	Yotepec	...... (492)	....	......	......	......	......	......
	Lazagaya	40t 160	135p 540	......	......	......	......	......
	Zaiutepec	 924	300p 1200	......	......	......	......	......
	Zapotequilla	...... (370)	....	......	......	......	......	......
	Zoquio	...... (154)	....	......	......	......	......	......

OAXACA—BISHOPRIC

No.	Name	A	B	C	D	E	F	G
849	Amoltepec	...... (169)	60p 240	......	......	......	......	......
	Aticpac	63t 252	....	......	......	......	......	......
	Atiquipaque	52t 208	100p 400	......	......	......	......	......

Appendix I: Population in 1565

OAXACA—ZAPOTECAS AND MIXES—(Concluded)

H	I	J	K	L	M	N	O	P	Special items	Population
						60t				
						240				240
			100t			80t		45t		
			400			320		180		360
						80t				
						320				320
						50t				
						200				200
			350t							
			1400							1400
						40t				
						160				160
										1200
						60t				
						240				1200
						100t				
						400				400
						50t				
						200				200
						100t				
						400				400
						50t				
						200				200
						60t				
						240				240
						60t				
						240				240
						160t				
						640				640
			40t							
			160							160
										1200
						120t				
						480				480
						50t				
						200				200

OAXACA—BISHOPRIC

H	I	J	K	L	M	N	O	P	Special items	Population
					60t	50t				
					240	200				220
					60t		50t			
					240		200			220
										400

OAXACA—BISHOPRIC—(Continued)

No.	Name	A	B	C	D	E	F	G
	Cocantepec...................	(154)						
	Coculco.......................	40t 160						
	Cuytlaquiztlan................	(924)						
	Chichiapa.....................	(390)	130p 520					
	Elotepec......................	(225)	75p 300					
	Huautla......................	101t 404						
	Malinaltepec.................	(462)						
	Manalcatepec.................	(616)						
	Mixtepec.....................	(308)						
	Nanauticpac..................	30t 120						
	Pecalcatepec.................	(300)	100p 400					
	Petlaquistlavaca..............	(1170)	390p 1560					
	Suchiopan....................	30t 120						
	Tecaxic.......................	(480)		156p 624		156p 624		
	Tezhuatlan...................	(1538)						
	Tiquipa.......................	400t 1600						
	Tizatepec.....................	110t 440				100p 400		
	Tlacola.......................	(185)						
	Tonameca....................	40t 160						
	Tuulilapa.....................	161t 644						
	Utlanzingo...................	(62)						
	Uxitem.......................	(277)						
	Cachultenango................	(570)	190p 760					
	Petlacaltepec.................	400t 1600						
	Tequilanacoya................	(375)	125p 500					
	Toltepec......................	(431)						

Appendix I: Population in 1565

OAXACA—BISHOPRIC—(Continued)

H	I	J	K	L	M	N	O	P	Special items	Population
						50t				
						200				200
										160
					300t					
					1200					1200
										520
										300
										404
					150t					
					600					600
					200t					
					800					800
						100t				
						400				400
					70t					
					280					280
										400
								142t		
								568		1560
										120
										624
				500t						
				2000						2000
										1600
										400
						60t				
						240				240
					30t	40t				
					120	160				140
										644
					20t					
					80					80
					90t					
					360					360
										760
					400t					
					1600					1600
								60t		
								240		500
						140t				
						560				560

OAXACA—BISHOPRIC—(Concluded)

No.	Name	A	B	C	D	E	F	G
	Tonagayotepec	90t / 360		120p / 480				
	Xicaltepec	43t / 172						
	Xilotepec	70t / 280		48p / 192		47p / 188		
	Tanatepec	(308)						
847	Tlapancingo	(616)						
848	Tlacotepec	(1179)			300t / 1200			
848	Tepeji	(215)			70t / 280			
134	Jicayan	300t / 1200	400p / 1600					
134	Atoyac					150p / 600		
447	Tecomavaca	180t / 720				143p / 572		

SAN LUIS POTOSI

No.	Name	A	B	C	D	E	F	G
804	Axtla	(769)						
704	Coxcatlan	(1384)	800p / 3200					
663	Huehuetlan	(618)						
296	Macatlan	350t / 1400						
550	Ojitipa	180t / 720	1000p / 4000					
800	San Pedro	(618)						
143	Tamazunchale	102t / 408						
366	Tampamolon	450t / 1800						
526	Tamuin	376t / 1504	750p / 3000	525p / 2100		328p / 1312		
803	Tancanhuitz	49t / 196						
368	Tancuayalab	220t / 880						
264	Tanquian	(769)						
367	Temapache	307t / 1228						
703	Valles [villa]	(123)						
427	Xilitla	414t / 1656	750p / 3000					

Appendix I: Population in 1565
OAXACA—BISHOPRIC—(Concluded)

H	I	J	K	L	M	N	O	P	Special items	Population
.....	.....	.....	.....	.....	60t	.....	.....	.....	.....	
.....	.....	.....	.....	.....	240	.....	.....	.....	.....	360
.....	.....	.....	.....	.....	40t	.....	.....	.....	.....	
.....	.....	.....	.....	.....	160	.....	.....	.....	.....	160
.....	.....	.....	.....	.....	80t	.....	.....	.....	.....	
.....	.....	.....	.....	.....	320	.....	.....	.....	.....	266
.....	.....	.....	.....	.....	100t	.....	.....	.....	.....	
.....	.....	.....	.....	.....	400	.....	.....	.....	.....	400
.....	.....	.....	.....	.....	.....	.....	200t	.....	.....	
.....	.....	.....	.....	.....	.....	.....	800	.....	.....	800
.....	.....	.....	.....	450t	.....	400t	400t	.....	.....	
.....	.....	.....	.....	1800	.....	1600	1600	.....	.....	1533
.....	.....	.....	.....	.....	.....	80t	80t	.....	.....	
.....	.....	.....	.....	.....	.....	320	320	.....	.....	280
.....	.....	.....	.....	240t	300t	400t	100t	.....	.....	
.....	.....	.....	.....	960	1200	1600	400	.....	.....	1668
.....	.....	.....	.....	.....	150t	.....	.....	.....	.....	
.....	.....	.....	.....	.....	600	.....	.....	.....	.....	.....
.....	.....	.....	.....	.....	150t	.....	.....	.....	.....	
.....	.....	.....	.....	.....	600	.....	.....	.....	.....	586

SAN LUIS POTOSI

H	I	J	K	L	M	N	O	P	Special items	Population
.....	.....	.....	.....	.....	250t	.....	.....	.....	.....	
.....	.....	.....	.....	.....	1000	.....	.....	.....	.....	1000
.....	.....	.....	.....	600t	300t	(1800t)	400t	.....	.....	
.....	.....	.....	.....	2400	1200	.....	1600	.....	.....	1800
.....	.....	.....	.....	.....	200t	.....	.....	341t	.....	
.....	.....	.....	.....	.....	800	.....	.....	1364	.....	800
.....	.....	.....	.....	.....	.....	.....	100t	.....	.....	
.....	.....	.....	.....	.....	.....	.....	400	.....	.....	400
.....	.....	.....	.....	500t	.....	1200t	.....	.....	.....	
.....	.....	.....	.....	2000	.....	4800	.....	.....	.....	3400
.....	.....	.....	.....	.....	200t	.....	.....	.....	.....	
.....	.....	.....	.....	.....	800	.....	.....	.....	.....	800
.....	.....	.....	.....	.....	250t	.....	200t	510t	.....	
.....	.....	.....	.....	.....	1000	.....	800	2040	.....	1000
.....	.....	.....	.....	.....	.....	.....	.....	.....	.....	1800
.....	.....	.....	.....	.....	200t	.....	.....	.....	.....	
.....	.....	.....	.....	.....	800	.....	.....	.....	.....	1304
.....	.....	.....	.....	.....	250t	.....	.....	.....	.....	
.....	.....	.....	.....	.....	1000	.....	.....	.....	.....	1000
.....	.....	.....	.....	.....	.....	.....	.....	.....	.....	880
.....	.....	.....	.....	.....	250t	.....	.....	.....	.....	
.....	.....	.....	.....	.....	1000	.....	.....	.....	.....	1000
.....	.....	.....	.....	.....	300t	.....	.....	.....	.....	
.....	.....	.....	.....	.....	1200	.....	.....	.....	.....	1200
.....	.....	.....	.....	.....	40t	.....	.....	.....	.....	
.....	.....	.....	.....	.....	160	.....	.....	.....	.....	160
.....	800t	622t	.....	.....	300t	700t	622t	.....	.....	
.....	3200	2488	.....	.....	1200	2800	2488	.....	.....	2422

SAN LUIS POTOSI—VALLES

No.	Name	A	B	C	D	E	F	G
	Acatlan	42t 168						
	Amatlan	26t 104						
	Tamacolite	48t 192						
	Tamacuiche	54t 216						
	Tamahol	30t 120						
	Tamaholipa	176t 704						
	Tamahu	18t 72						
	Tamalaguaco	60t 240						
	Tameci	62t 248						
	Tampayal	34t 136						
	Tampucho	47t 188						
	Tancaxan	50t 200						
	Tancaxual	...... (86)						
	Tancojol	20t 80						
	Tancolon	40t 160						
	Tancoxual	116t 464						
	Tancuy	48t 192						
	Tanchaba	35t 140						
	Tanchilabe	16t 64						
	Tanchipa	...... (412)						
	Tanchipa	603t 2412						
	Tanlocuque	51t 204						
	Talecuen	...... (308)						
	Tantay	20t 80						

Appendix I: Population in 1565

SAN LUIS POTOSI—VALLES

H	I	J	K	L	M	N	O	P	Special items	Population
.....	......	......	......	......	......	......	......	.....	.....	
.....	......	......	......	......	......	......	......	.....	.....	168
.....	......	......	......	......	......	......	......	.....	.....	
.....	......	......	......	......	......	......	......	.....	.....	104
.....	......	......	......	......	......	......	......	.....	.....	
.....	......	......	......	......	......	......	......	.....	.....	192
.....	......	......	......	......	......	......	......	.....	.....	
.....	......	......	......	......	......	......	......	.....	.....	216
.....	......	......	......	......	......	......	......	.....	.....	
.....	......	......	......	......	......	......	......	.....	.....	120
.....	......	......	......	......	......	......	......	.....	.....	
.....	......	......	......	......	......	......	......	.....	.....	704
.....	......	......	......	......	......	......	......	.....	.....	
.....	......	......	......	......	......	......	......	.....	.....	72
.....	......	......	......	......	......	......	......	62t	.....	
.....	......	......	......	......	......	......	......	248	.....	240
.....	......	......	......	......	......	......	......	.....	.....	248
.....	......	......	......	......	......	......	......	.....	.....	
.....	......	......	......	......	......	......	......	.....	.....	136
.....	......	......	......	......	......	......	......	.....	.....	
.....	......	......	......	......	......	......	......	.....	.....	188
.....	......	......	......	......	......	......	......	32t	.....	
.....	......	......	......	......	......	......	......	128	.....	200
.....	......	......	......	......	28t	......	......	.....	.....	
.....	......	......	......	......	112	......	......	.....	.....	112
.....	......	......	......	......	......	......	......	.....	.....	80
.....	......	......	......	......	......	......	......	.....	.....	
.....	......	......	......	......	......	......	......	.....	.....	160
.....	......	......	......	......	......	......	......	.....	.....	
.....	......	......	......	......	......	......	......	.....	.....	464
.....	......	......	......	......	......	......	......	43t	.....	
.....	......	......	......	......	......	......	......	172	.....	192
.....	......	......	......	......	......	......	......	.....	.....	140
.....	......	......	......	......	......	......	......	.....	.....	
.....	......	......	......	......	......	......	......	.....	.....	64
.....	......	......	......	......	54t	......	......	.....	.....	
.....	......	......	......	......	216	......	......	.....	.....	216
.....	......	......	......	......	......	......	......	134t	.....	
.....	......	......	......	......	......	......	......	536	.....	2412
.....	......	......	......	......	⎛ 100t	......	......	.....	.....	
.....	......	......	......	......	400	......	......	.....	.....	400
.....	......	......	......	......	⎨	......	......	.....	.....	
.....	......	......	......	......	⎝	......	......	.....	.....	⎝......
.....	......	......	......	......	......	......	......	.....	.....	
.....	......	......	......	......	......	......	......	.....	.....	80

SAN LUIS POTOSI—VALLES—(Continued)

No.	Name	A	B	C	D	E	F	G
	Tantohox...	35t						
		140						
	Tamposque...	30t						
		120						
	Paquelan...							
		(308)						
	Tantoilan...							
	Tantoin...	40t						
		160						
	Tantolon...							
		(154)						
	Tantoyuca...	90t						
		360						
	Tantuana...	26t						
		104						
	Tanzacana...	40t						
		160						
	Tanzonomoco...	45t						
		180						
	Tanzumonoco...	72t						
		288						
	Taxiqui...							
		(92)						
	Tlacolula...	30t						
		120						

VERA CRUZ

No.	Name	A	B	C	D	E	F	G
720	Acatlan...				100t			
		(308)			400			
719	Actopan...				110t	52p		
		(253)			440	208		
89	Acultzingo...	204t	175p		300t			
		816	700		1200			
801	Alcececa...	74t	110p					
		296	440					
718	Almolonga...				20t			
		(63)			80			
487	Atzalan...							
		(5230)						
765	Atzitzintla...				50t			
		(154)			200			
554	Calpa...	40t						
		160						
554	Tamalol...							
		(308)						

Appendix I: Population in 1565

SAN LUIS POTOSI—VALLES—(Continued)

H	I	J	K	L	M	N	O	P	Special items	Population
.....	.....	.....	.....	.....	.....	.....	100t 400	.....	.....	400
.....	.....	.....	.....	.....	.....	.....	.....	.....	.....	......
.....	.....	.....	.....	.....	.....	.....	.....	.....	.....	
.....	.....	.....	.....	.....	.....	.....	.....	.....	.....	......
.....	.....	.....	.....	.....	.....	.....	.....	.....	.....	
.....	.....	.....	.....	.....	.....	.....	.....	.....	.....	......
.....	.....	.....	.....	.....	.....	.....	.....	.....	.....	160
.....	.....	.....	.....	.....	50t 200	.....	.....	.....	.....	200
.....	.....	.....	.....	.....	.....	.....	.....	.....	.....	360
.....	.....	.....	.....	.....	.....	.....	.....	.....	.....	104
.....	.....	.....	.....	.....	.....	.....	.....	.....	.....	160
.....	.....	.....	.....	.....	.....	.....	.....	.....	.....	180
.....	.....	.....	.....	.....	.....	.....	.....	.....	.....	288
.....	.....	.....	.....	.....	30t 120	.....	.....	.....	.....	120
.....	.....	.....	.....	.....	50t 200	.....	.....	.....	.....	200

VERA CRUZ

H	I	J	K	L	M	N	O	P	Special items	Population
.....	.....	.....	.....	.....	.....	100t 400	.....	.....	.....	400
.....	.....	.....	.....	.....	.....	85t 340	.....	.....	.....	329
.....	.....	.....	.....	.....	.....	300t 1200	.....	100t 400	.....	1200
.....	.....	.....	.....	.....	250t 1000	.....	.....	.....	.....	1000
.....	.....	.....	.....	.....	.....	21t 84	20t 80	.....	.....	82
.....	.....	.....	.....	.....	.....	1700t 6800	.....	.....	.....	6800
.....	.....	.....	.....	.....	.....	.....	.....	.....	.....	200
.....	.....	.....	50t 200	.....	.....	.....	40t 160	.....	.....	200
.....	.....	.....	.....	.....	.....	.....	100t 400	.....	.....	400

Population of Central Mexico

VERA CRUZ—(Continued)

No.	Name	A	B	C	D	E	F	G
554	Chila	53t						
		212						
759	Coacoazintla		100p		200t			
		(444)	400		800			
759	Chapultepec				140t	114p		
		(404)			560	456		
422	Cosamaloapan	77t			⎧850t			
		308			3400			
422	Tlaliscoyan							
		(2615)						
711	Amatlan							
					⎩			
187	Cotaxtla		500p					
		(1500)	2000					
283	Chiconamel	57t						
		228						
756	Chicontepec				700t			
		(2153)			2800			
162	Chichilintla	696t	1800p		1000t			
		2784	7200		4000			
255	Chilapa		300p					
		(708)	1200					
254	Chinameca		210p					
		(678)	840					
764	Chocaman		220p		200t			
		(622)	880		800			
762	Huatusco				⎧350t			
		(1307)			1400			
762	Coscomaltepec							
762	Alpatlahuaya							
					⎩			
102	Huatusco		60p					
		(185)	240					
229	Huayacocotla	11569tp	4100p					
		11569	16400					
31	Ilamatlan	634t	⎧2100p		⎧1500t			
		2536	8400		6000			
31	Atleucian	224t						
		896	⎩		⎩			
537	Ixhuatlan	41t						
		164						
625	Ixtepec		270p					
		(810)	1080					
623	Jalacingo		320p	1502p	800t	1403t		
		(3800)	1280	6008	3200	5612		
256	Jaltipan		1000p					
		(3076)	4000					
758	Jilotepec		300p		350t			
		(1148)	1200		1400			
505	Maltrata	158t	120p	311p	500t	311p		
		632	480	1244	2000	1244		

Appendix I: Population in 1565

VERA CRUZ—(Continued)

H	I	J	K	L	M	N	O	P	Special items	Population
										212
				60t		173t	163t	67t		
				240		692	652	268		577
						140t	150t			
						560	600			525
						100t	⌠165t			
						400	⎨ 660			3400
							⌡			
									34t	
								136		2000
							20t			
							80			80
										2800
				1500t			1200t	925t		
				6000			4800	3700		5000
				230t						
				920						920
				220t						
				880						880
				206t		200t	200t	93t		
				824		800	800	372		808
						⌠500t	⌠1000t			
						⎩ 2000	⎨ 4000			1700
							⌡			
										240
			2284t	4100t		2300t	2119t			
			9136	16400		9200	8476			11579
⌠1600t	1221t			⌠1550			⌠4034c			
⎨ 6400	4884			⎩ 6200			⎨ 5365			5697
	400t									
⌡	1600									
							200t			
							800			800
										1080
							400t			
							1600			4940
				1000t				303t		
				4000				1212		4000
				400t		360t	360t			
				1600		1440	1440			1493
							300t			
							1200			1496

VERA CRUZ—(Continued)

No.	Name	A	B	C	D	E	F	G
186	Metatepec	1110t	1200p	......	......	......	......	......
		4440	4800					
186	Tantoyuca	......	......	......	......	......	......	......
717	Miahuatlan	......	50p	......	150t	......	......	......
		(461)	200		600			
688	Minzapa	......	740p	......	......	......	......	......
		(1846)	2960					
626	Misantla	......	300p	......	600t	610p	......	......
		(2476)	1200		2400	2440		
369	Moyutla	54t	400p	......	......	......	......	......
		216	1600					
369	Ozuluama	181t	......	......	......	......	......	......
		724						
627	Naolingo	......	300p	......	230t	......	......	......
		(662)	1200		920			
192	Orizaba	132t	380p	......	250t	......	......	......
		528	1520		1000			
248	Otlatitlan	......	400p	......	......	......	......	......
		(1150)	1600					
802	Panuco [villa]	......	......	......	......	......	......	......
		(923)						
194	Papantla	421t	1720p	......	150t	......	......	......
		1684	6880		600			
194	Tuxpan	222t	......	......	150t	......	......	......
		888			600			
844	Jalapa	......	......	......	......	......	......	......
		(1966)						
840	Jalcomulco	......	......	......	......	......	......	......
		(308)						
841	Coatepec	......	......	......	......	......	......	......
		(616)						
842	El Chico (Xicochinilco)	......	......	395p	......	......	......	......
		(1069)		1580				
760	San Juan Ulua	......	......	......	160t	......	......	......
		(492)			640			
395	Tamiahua	30t	......	......	324t	......	......	......
		120			1296			
549	Tenixtepec	......	400p	......	......	......	......	......
			1600					
521	Tampico	150t	120p	......	......	......	......	......
		600	480					
212	Tempoal	245t	600p	......	......	192p	......	......
		980	2400			768		
716	Tepetlan	......	......	......	110t	......	......	......
		(328)			440			
763	Tepetlaxco	......	......	......	250t	......	......	......
		(769)			1000			
449	Tequila	250t	70p	406p	344t	344p	......	......
		1000	280	1624	1376	1376		

VERA CRUZ—(Continued)

H	I	J	K	L	M	N	O	P	Special items	Population
200p 4800	1200t 4800	.....	.....	1130t 4520	.....	1100t 4400	1063t 4252	.....	.....	4630
.....	.....	.....	.....	.....	100t 400	.....	.....	.....	.....	.....
.....	.....	.....	.....	.....	.....	150t 600	150t 600	.....	.....	600
.....	.....	.....	.....	600t 2400	.....	.....	.....	.....	.....	2400
.....	.....	.....	.....	.....	.....	905t 3620	585t 2340	.....	.....	3220
.....	.....	.....	.....	100t 400	.....	.....	.....	14t 56	.....	400
.....	.....	.....	.....	.....	70t 280	.....	.....	90t 360	.....	.....
.....	.....	.....	.....	.....	.....	200t 800	320t 1280	.....	.....	860
.....	.....	.....	.....	200t 800	.....	.....	105t 420	240t 960	.....	900
.....	.....	.....	.....	500t 2000	.....	248t 992	.....	168t 672	.....	1496
.....	.....	.....	.....	.....	300t 1200	.....	.....	.....	.....	1200
.....	.....	.....	.....	.....	.....	.....	.....	.....	.....	1200
.....	.....	.....	.....	.....	.....	.....	.....	.....	.....	.....
.....	.....	.....	.....	.....	.....	.....	639t 2556	.....	.....	2556
.....	.....	.....	.....	.....	.....	.....	100t 400	.....	.....	400
.....	.....	.....	.....	.....	.....	.....	200t 800	.....	.....	800
.....	.....	.....	.....	.....	.....	.....	300t 1200	.....	.....	1390
.....	.....	.....	.....	.....	.....	.....	.....	.....	.....	640
.....	.....	.....	.....	250t 1000	.....	.....	.....	.....	.....	1148
.....	.....	.....	.....	.....	.....	.....	.....	.....	.....	.....
.....	.....	.....	.....	.....	35t 140	226t 904	.....	.....	.....	522
.....	.....	.....	.....	.....	250t 1000	400t 1600	171t 684	.....	.....	1123
.....	.....	.....	.....	.....	.....	103t 412	103t 412	.....	.....	426
.....	.....	.....	.....	.....	.....	.....	.....	.....	.....	1000
.....	.....	.....	.....	.....	.....	408t 1632	.....	.....	.....	1502

VERA CRUZ—(Concluded)

No.	Name	A	B	C	D	E	F	G
294	Texhuacan	400p 1600						
715	Tlacolula	...... (2153)	100p 400		700t 2800			
628	Tlacotalpam	...... (796)	250p 1000	295p 1180		264p 1056		
58	Tuxtla	...... (3076)	1000p 4000					
315	Zongolica	805t 3220	650p 2600					

VERA CRUZ—PANUCO

No.	Name	A	B	C	D	E	F	G
	Apaztlan	30t 120						
	Cihuala	24t 96						
	Coyutla	152t 608	300p 1200					
	Chachapala	41t 164						
	Chacaual	66t 264	140p 560					
	Tampalache	80t 320						
	Chalchitlan	...... (2461)						
	Tantoin							
	Chachihuautla							
	Pizula							
	Guzahapa	78t 312						
	Huatzpaltepec	...... (30)	10p 40					
	Las Laxas	30t 120						
	Macolutla	70t 280						
	Mezuntlan	10t 40						
	Nanahuatla	95t 380						
	Nanahuatlan	93t 372						

Appendix I: Population in 1565

VERA CRUZ—(Concluded)

H	I	J	K	L	M	N	O	P	Special items	Population
								571t		
								2284		1600
						700t	700t			
						2800	2800			2800
						218t	218t			
						872	872			1036
					1000t	(400t)				
					4000					4000
								408t		
								1632		1632

VERA CRUZ—PANUCO

H	I	J	K	L	M	N	O	P	Special items	Population
										120
										96
				80t						
				320						320
										164
										560
				⎰800t						
				3200						3200
				⎱						
										312
										40
										120
										280
										40
										380
										372

VERA CRUZ—PANUCO—(Continued)

No.	Name	A	B	C	D	E	F	G
	Piaxtla	31t						
		124						
	Taculilla	27t						
		108						
	Tamacuil	102t						
		408						
	Tamalol	150t	⎰640p					
		600	⎱ 2560					
	Cuacaxo	107t						
		428						
	Tamalococuco	100t						
		400						
	Tamante		⎰200p					
			⎱ 800					
	Zayula	⎰84t						
		336						
	Tamos							
		⎱(616)						
	Tamatao	93t						
		372						
	Tamateque	60t						
		240						
	Tamazunchale	70t						
		280						
	Tamiutla	20t						
		80						
	Tamole	34t						
		136						
	Tamontao	30t						
		120						
	Tampacal		50p					
		(462)	⎰ 200					
	Tampuche	33t	⎱500p					
		132	2000					
	Huautla							
		(718)						
	Tampulen	20t						
		80						
	Tamu	23t						
		92						
	Tancazaeque	20t						
		80						
	Tancelete	32t						
		128						
	Tancetuco	91t						
		364						
	Tancolul	24t						
		96						
	Tancuche	42t						
		168						

Appendix I: Population in 1565

VERA CRUZ—PANUCO—(Continued)

H	I	J	K	L	M	N	O	P	Special items	Population
......	......	......	......	......	......	......	......	.....	.....	
......	......	......	......	......	......	......	......	.....	.....	124
......	......	......	......	......	......	......	......	.....	.....	
......	......	......	......	......	......	......	......	.....	.....	108
......	......	......	......	......	......	......	......	.....	.....	
......	......	......	......	......	......	......	......	.....	.....	408
......	......	......	......	120t	......	......	......	162t	.....	
......	......	......	......	480	......	......	......	648	.....	2560
......	......	......	......	......	......	......	......	.....	.....	
......	......	......	......	......	......	......	......	.....	.....	......
......	......	......	......	......	......	......	......	.....	.....	
......	......	......	......	......	......	......	......	.....	.....	400
......	......	......	......	......	......	......	......	.....	.....	800
......	......	......	......	......	......	......	......	.....	.....	......
......	......	......	......	......	......	......	......	.....	.....	
......	......	......	......	......	......	......	......	.....	.....	......
......	......	......	......	......	......	......	......	.....	.....	
......	......	......	......	......	......	......	......	.....	.....	372
......	......	......	......	......	......	......	......	.....	.....	240
......	......	......	......	......	......	......	30t	.....	.....	
......	......	......	......	......	......	......	120	.....	.....	120
......	......	......	......	......	......	......	......	.....	.....	80
......	......	......	......	......	......	......	......	.....	.....	
......	......	......	......	......	......	......	......	.....	.....	136
......	......	......	......	......	......	......	......	.....	.....	120
......	......	......	......	......	......	......	150t	.....	.....	
......	......	......	......	......	......	......	600	.....	.....	600
......	......	......	......	50t	......	......	......	.....	.....	
......	......	......	......	200	......	......	......	.....	.....	200
......	......	......	......	......	......	......	233t	.....	.....	
......	......	......	......	......	......	......	932	.....	.....	932
......	......	......	......	......	......	......	......	.....	.....	80
......	......	......	......	......	......	......	......	.....	.....	92
......	......	......	......	......	......	......	......	.....	.....	80
......	......	......	......	......	......	......	......	.....	.....	128
......	......	......	......	......	50t	......	300t	.....	.....	
......	......	......	......	......	200	......	1200	.....	.....	200
......	......	......	......	......	......	......	......	.....	.....	96
......	......	......	......	......	......	......	......	.....	.....	168

128 Population of Central Mexico

VERA CRUZ—PANUCO—(Concluded)

No.	Name	A	B	C	D	E	F	G
	Tancuiname...	32t						
			128					
	Tanchicuy...	27t						
			108					
	Tanchinamol...	100t						
			400					
	Tanchoy...	48t						
			192					
	Tanchicuy...	16t						
			64					
	Tanhuizin...							
			(178)					
	Tanistla...		400p					
			(366)	1600				
	Tanta...	32t						
			128					
	Tanta...		30p					
			(92)	120				
	Tantala...	260t	1600p					
			1040	6400				
	Tampacayal...	30t						
			120					
	Tantamol...	181t	220p					
			724	880				
	Tantoyeque...		40p					
			(115)	160				
	Tantoyetla...	12t						
			48					
	Tanxohol...	37t						
			148					
	Tanzaquila...	228t						
			912					
	Tanzulupe...	150t						
			600					
	Tenacusco...	400t	150p					
			1600	600				
	Tejupexpa...	22t						
			88					
	Tlacolula...	30t						
			120					
	Tlapahuautla...	47t						
			188					
	Topila...	18t						
			72					
	Topla...	100t						
			400					
	Xocutla...	50t						
			200					

Appendix I: Population in 1565

VERA CRUZ—PANUCO—(Concluded)

H	I	J	K	L	M	N	O	P	Special items	Population
										128
										108
										400
										192
										64
				58t						
				232						232
				119t						
				476						476
										128
				30t						
				120						120
				⎡600t						⎧
				2400						2400
								42t		
				⎣				168		⎨......
				50t						
				200						200
				30t						
				150						150
							30t			
							120			120
										148
										912
										600
				400t						
				1600						1600
										88
										120
										188
										72
							300t			
							1200			1200
										200

VERA CRUZ—COATZACOALCOS

No.	Name	A	B	C	D	E	F	G
	Coatzacoalcos [province]	......	......	......	......	......	......	......
	Cotatlan	......	460p	......	......	......	......	......
		(1538)	1840					
	Coatzacoalcos [pueblo]	......	1900p	......	......	......	......	......
		(5700)	7600					
	Huacaylapa	......	......	......	......	......	......	......
	Etlahualuco	......	......	......	......	......	......	......
	Huatzpaltepec	......	460p	......	......	......	......	......
		(1380)	1840					
	Huestepec	......	250p	......	......	......	......	......
		(1231)	1000					
	Jotlapa	......	110p	......	......	......	......	......
		(308)	440					
	Miahuatlan	......	34p	......	......	......	......	......
		(123)	136					
	Michoacan	......	180p	......	......	......	......	......
		(266)	720					
	Suchitatlan	......	340p	......	......	......	......	......
		(1076)	1360					
	Tacoltapa	......	223p	......	......	......	......	......
		(669)	892					
	Zapotitlan	......	200p	......	......	......	......	......
		(400)	800					
	Los Taquilpas	......	130p	......	......	......	......	......
		(390)	520					
	Atoco	......	400p	......	......	......	......	......
		(1200)	1600					
	Miahuatlan	......	100p	......	......	......	......	......
		(300)	400					
	Hueytlan	......	400p	......	......	......	......	......
		(1200)	1600					
281	Moloacan + Uliacan	......	60p	......	......	......	......	......
			240					
	Aguatoco	......	180p	......	......	......	......	......
			720					
	Chicuitlan	......	500p	......	......	......	......	......
			2000					
	Tapalan	......	150p	......	......	......	......	......
			600					
	Tonela	......	450p	......	......	......	......	......
			1800					

Appendix I: Population in 1565

VERA CRUZ—COATZACOALCOS

H	I	J	K	L	M	N	O	P	Special items	Population
......	......	......	......	......	3200t	......	......	......	......	
......	......	......	......	......	12800	......	......	......	......	......
......	......	......	......	500t	......	......	......	......	......	
......	......	......	......	2000	......	......	......	......	......	2000
......	......	......	......	......	......	......	......	......	......	
......	......	......	......	......	......	......	......	......	......	7600
......	......	......	......	......	......	......	......	......	......	
......	......	......	......	......	......	......	......	......	......	
......	......	......	......	......	......	......	......	......	......	......
......	......	......	......	......	350t	......	......	195t	......	
......	......	......	......	......	1400	......	......	780	......	1840
......	......	......	......	400t	......	......	......	......	......	
......	......	......	......	1600	......	......	......	......	......	1600
......	......	......	......	100t	......	......	......	......	......	
......	......	......	......	400	......	......	......	......	......	400
......	......	......	......	40t	......	......	......	......	......	
......	......	......	......	160	......	......	......	......	......	160
......	......	......	......	80t	......	......	......	19t	......	
......	......	......	......	320	......	......	......	76	......	320
......	......	......	......	350t	......	......	......	....•	......	
......	......	......	......	1400	......	......	......	......	......	1400
......	......	......	......	......	......	......	......	......	......	
......	......	......	......	......	......	......	......	......	......	892
......	......	......	......	130t	......	......	......	15t	......	
......	......	......	......	520	......	......	......	60	......	520
......	......	......	......	......	......	......	......	......	......	
......	......	......	......	......	......	......	......	......	......	520
......	......	......	......	......	......	......	......	......	......	
......	......	......	......	......	......	......	......	......	......	1600
......	......	......	......	......	......	......	......	......	......	
......	......	......	......	......	......	......	......	......	......	400
......	......	......	......	......	......	......	......	......	......	
......	......	......	......	......	......	......	......	......	......	1600
......	......	......	......	......	......	......	......	......	......	
......	......	......	......	......	......	......	......	......	......	240
......	......	......	......	......	......	......	......	......	......	
......	......	......	......	......	......	......	......	......	......	720
......	......	......	......	......	......	......	......	......	......	
......	......	......	......	......	......	......	......	......	......	2000
......	......	......	......	......	......	......	......	......	......	
......	......	......	......	......	......	......	......	......	......	600
......	......	......	......	......	......	......	......	......	......	
......	......	......	......	......	......	......	......	......	......	1800

Population of Central Mexico

VERA CRUZ—UNIDENTIFIED

No.	Name	A	B	C	D	E	F	G
	Atescac....................	(154)						
	Catusco....................	(74)	24p 96					
	Cuzumacernaca............	(924)	300p 1200					
	Chicocentepec..............	(142)	45p 180	45p 180	50t 200	45p 180		
	Icapacingo.................	(28)	9p 36					
	Ixcatlan...................	220t 880	445p 1780					
	Utlaquiquixtla..............	(2461)						
	Jicayan....................							
	Maxtlatlan.................	(108)						
	Mizcaoztoc.................	28t 112	40p 160					
	Ozpicha...................	(900)	300p 1200					
	Ozumacintla...............	(150)	50p 200					
	Pangololutla...............	(308)	170p 680					
	Puctla.....................	(591)			250t 1000			
	Quetzalcoatl...............	(180)	60p 240					
	Tecayuca...................	(180)	60p 240					
	Tecoautla..................	(185)	100p 400					
	Tenango...................	60t 240						
	Tlapacoya..................	(616)						
	Tlatlatelco.................	(185)	120p 480	60p 240		60p 240		
	Tonaya....................	(431)						
	Totutla....................	(120)	40p 160					
	Tuchitepec.................	(200)						
	Tustenec...................	(90)	30p 120					
	Xicaltepec.................	(154)	200p 800					

Appendix I: Population in 1565

VERA CRUZ—UNIDENTIFIED

H	I	J	K	L	M	N	O	P	Special items	Population
......	......	......	......	......	......	......	50t	......	......	
......	......	......	......	......	......	......	200	......	......	200
......	......	......	......	......	......	......	......	......	......	
......	......	......	......	......	......	......	......	......	......	96
......	......	......	......	300t	......	......	......	......	......	
......	......	......	......	1200	......	......	......	......	......	1200
......	......	......	......	45t	......	......	45t	......	......	
......	......	......	......	180	......	......	180	......	......	185
......	......	......	......	......	......	......	......	......	......	
......	......	......	......	......	......	......	......	......	......	36
......	......	......	......	⎡800t	......	......	......	......	......	
......	......	......	......	3200	......	......	......	......	......	3200
......	......	......	......	......	......	......	......	......	......	......
......	......	......	......	......	......	......	......	......	......	
......	......	......	......	⎣	......	......	......	......	......	⎣......
......	......	......	......	......	......	35t	15t	......	......	
......	......	......	......	......	......	140	60	......	......	140
......	......	......	......	......	......	......	......	20t	......	
......	......	......	......	......	......	......	......	80	......	160
......	......	......	......	......	......	......	......	......	......	1200
......	......	......	......	......	......	......	......	......	......	200
......	......	......	......	100t	......	......	......	......	......	
......	......	......	......	400	......	......	......	......	......	400
......	......	......	......	......	......	134t	134t	......	......	
......	......	......	......	......	......	536	536	......	......	768
......	......	......	......	......	......	......	......	......	......	240
......	......	......	......	......	......	......	......	......	......	240
......	......	......	......	......	......	......	60t	......	......	
......	......	......	......	......	......	......	240	......	......	240
......	......	......	......	......	100t	......	......	......	......	
......	......	......	......	......	400	......	......	......	......	400
......	......	......	......	......	......	......	200t	......	......	
......	......	......	......	......	......	......	800	......	......	800
......	......	......	......	......	......	......	......	......	......	240
......	......	......	......	......	......	......	140t	......	......	
......	......	......	......	......	......	......	560	......	......	560
......	......	......	......	......	......	......	......	......	......	160
......	......	......	......	......	50t	80t	......	......	......	
......	......	......	......	......	200	320	......	......	......	260
......	......	......	......	......	......	......	......	......	......	120
......	......	......	......	50t	......	......	......	......	......	
......	......	......	......	200	......	......	......	......	......	200

VERA CRUZ—UNIDENTIFIED—(Continued)

No.	Name	A	B	C	D	E	F	G
	Yahuatlan	(330)	110p 440	......	......	......	......	......
	Zempoal	(36)	12p 48	......	......	......	......	......
	Zihuacoatlan	(154)	......	......	......	......	......	......

TLAXCALA

No.	Name	A	B	C	D	E	F	G
600	Tlaxcala [province]	(307692)	......	......	......	......	......	......
706	Calpulalpan	(4000)	......	......	......	......	......	......
96	Sultepec	(6754)	500p 2000	......	......	......	......	......

QUERETARO

No.	Name	A	B	C	D	E	F	G
364	Jalpan	424t 1696	......	......	......	......	......	......
365	Tancoyol	90t 360	......	......	......	......	......	......

GUANAJUATO

No.	Name	A	B	C	D	E	F	G
7	Acambaro	(8307)	3000p 12000	......	......	......	......	......
653	Jerecuaro	110tp 110	......	......	......	......	......	......
538	Yuriria	10461tp 10461	......	......	......	1179p 4716	......	......
292	Xichu	(282)	......	......	......	94p 376	......	......

Appendix I: Population in 1565

VERA CRUZ—UNIDENTIFIED—(Continued)

H	I	J	K	L	M	N	O	P	Special items	Population
……	……	……	……	……	……	……	……	……	……	
……	……	……	……	……	……	……	……	……	……	440
……	……	……	……	……	……	……	……	……	……	
……	……	……	……	……	……	……	……	……	……	48
……	……	……	……	……	……	……	50t	……	……	
……	……	……	……	……	……	……	200	……	……	200

TLAXCALA

H	I	J	K	L	M	N	O	P	Special items	Population
……	……	……	……	……	……	……	……	……	100000t	
……	……	……	……	……	……	……	……	……	400000	400000
……	……	……	……	1300t	……	……	……	……	……	
……	……	……	……	5200	……	……	……	……	……	5200
……	……	……	……	[417t]	……	2000t	……	……	……	
……	……	……	……	……	……	8000	……	……	……	8000

QUERETARO

H	I	J	K	L	M	N	O	P	Special items	Population
……	……	……	……	……	……	……	……	……	……	
……	……	……	……	……	……	……	……	……	……	1696
……	……	……	……	……	……	……	……	……	……	
……	……	……	……	……	……	……	……	……	……	360

GUANAJUATO

H	I	J	K	L	M	N	O	P	Special items	Population
……	……	……	……	2800t	……	……	2600t	1557t	……	
……	……	……	……	11200	……	……	10400	6228	……	10800
……	……	……	……	……	……	……	……	……	……	
……	……	……	……	……	……	……	……	……	……	110
80t	2000t	……	……	……	……	……	900t	……	……	
4720	8000	……	……	……	……	……	3600	……	……	5612
……	……	……	……	……	……	……	……	……	……	
……	……	……	……	……	……	……	……	……	……	

ARCHBISHOPRIC OF MEXICO—UNIDENTIFIED

No.	Name	A	B	C	D	E	F	G
	Chicoloana	...... (861)	300p 1200	....	....	....	....	....

BISHOPRIC OF TLAXCALA—UNIDENTIFIED

No.	Name	A	B	C	D	E	F	G
	Anilicapa	...... (369)	....	......	......	......	......	......
	Atlan	...... (540)	180p 720	......	......	......	......	......
	Cayutepex	...... (1538)	....	......	......	......	......	......
	Ixiquitlan	...... (1692)	150p 600	......	......	......	......	......
	Jutlabuca	...... (710)	....	......	......	......	......	......
	Tepecicoapan	...... (215)	250p 1000	......	......	......	......	......
	Tequepilpa	...... (1270)	500p 2000	......	......	......	......	......
	Zacotlan	...... (3076)	660p 2640	......	......	......	......	......

MICHOACAN

No.	Name	A	B	C	D	E	F	G
536	Aquila	323t 1292	280p 1120	......	......	......	......	......
406	Araro	289tp 289	160p 640	......	......	......	......	......
415	Zinapecuaro	634tp 634	....	......	......	740p 2960	......	......
503	Ario	359t 1436	....	......	......	......	......	......
503	Iztaro	308t 1232	....	......	......	......	......	......
569	Atlan	145t 580	50p 200	......	......	28p 112	......	......
664	Bocaneo	...... (618)	....	......	......	......	......	......
567	Borona	110t 440	100p 400	......	......	50p 200	......	......
494	Capula	1375tp 1375	200p 800	800p 3200	......	873p 3492	......	......
565	Cihuatlan	110t 440	100p 400	......	......	......	......	......

Appendix I: Population in 1565

ARCHBISHOPRIC OF MEXICO—UNIDENTIFIED

H	I	J	K	L	M	N	O	P	Special items	Population
......	......	......	......	280t	......	......	......	......	......	
......	......	......	......	1120	......	......	......	......	......	1120

BISHOPRIC OF TLAXCALA—UNIDENTIFIED

H	I	J	K	L	M	N	O	P	Special items	Population
......	......	......	......	......	......	120t	......	......	......	
......	......	......	......	......	......	480	......	......	......	480
......	......	......	......	......	......	......	......	......	......	
......	......	......	......	......	......	......	......	......	......	720
......	......	......	......	500t	......	......	......	......	......	
......	......	......	......	2000	......	......	......	......	......	2000
......	......	......	......	550t	......	......	......	......	......	
......	......	......	......	2200	......	......	......	......	......	2200
......	......	......	......	231t	......	......	......	......	......	
......	......	......	......	924	......	......	......	......	......	924
......	......	......	......	70t	......	......	......	......	......	
......	......	......	......	280	......	......	......	......	......	280
......	......	......	......	413t	......	......	......	......	......	
......	......	......	......	1652	......	......	......	......	......	1652
......	......	......	......	1000t	......	......	......	......	......	
......	......	......	......	4000	......	......	......	......	......	4000

MICHOACAN

H	I	J	K	L	M	N	O	P	Special items	Population
......	......	......	......	......	......	......	......	......	......	
......	......	......	......	......	......	......	......	......	......	1292
......	......	......	......	......	......	......	......	......	......	
......	......	......	......	......	......	......	......	......	......	289
......	......	......	......	......	......	......	......	......	......	
......	......	......	......	......	......	......	......	......	......	2960
......	......	......	......	......	......	1200t	......	......	......	
......	......	......	......	......	......	4800	......	......	......	4800
......	......	......	......	......	......	250t	......	......	......	
......	......	......	......	......	......	1000	......	......	......	1000
......	......	......	......	......	......	......	......	......	......	
......	......	......	......	......	......	......	......	......	......	112
......	......	......	......	......	......	......	......	......	800tp	
......	......	......	......	......	......	......	......	......	800	800
......	......	......	......	......	......	......	......	......	......	
......	......	......	......	......	......	......	......	......	......	200
......	......	......	......	......	......	750t	......	......	......	
......	......	......	......	......	......	3000	......	......	......	3231
......	......	......	......	......	......	......	......	......	......	
......	......	......	......	......	......	......	......	......	......	400

Population of Central Mexico

MICHOACAN—(Continued)

No.	Name	A	B	C	D	E	F	G
572	Ciutlan	103t 412	60p 240					
510	Coalcoman	480t 1920		400p 1600				
169	Coeneo	 (3261)	1060p 4240					
169	Carandacho							
19	Comanja	2400t 9600	1540p 6160					
19	Naranja							
570	Cuacuatlan	60t 240	40p 160					
77	Cuitzeo	5926tp 5926	1000p 4000	931p 3724		2072p 8288		
77	Cupandaro	 (6305)						
285	Cutzco	1524t 6096	1600p 6400	2696p 10784		931p 3724		
564	Chacala	106t 424	50p 200			31p 124		
416	Chilchota	971t 3884	570p 2280	972p 3888		593p 2372		
175	Chucandiro	456tp 456	420p 1680					
473	Chiguimitio	407tp 407						
291	Erongaricuaro	2495tp 2495						
115	Huacana	240t 960	600p 2400					
108	Huango	1171t 4684	1000p 4000					
429	Huaniqueo	1484tp 1484	300p 1200	489p 1956		489p 1956		
113	Indaparapeo	717tp 717	400p 1600					
576	Ixtapa	53t 212						
481	Jacona	4361t 17444	1000p 4000	1184p 4736	631p 2524			
850	Sahuayo							
851	Guaracha							
852	Ixtlan				800p 3200			
853	Tangamandapio							
539	Charapaco							
507	Pajacuaran							

Appendix I: Population in 1565

MICHOACAN—(Continued)

H	I	J	K	L	M	N	O	P	Special items	Population
......	......	......	......	......	......	......	......	.....	.....	
......	......	......	......	......	......	......	......	.....	.....	412
......	......	......	......	......	......	......	200t	......	.....	
......	......	......	......	......	......	......	800	.....	.....	1600
......	......	......	......	......	......	450t	......	.....	.....	
......	......	......	......	......	......	1800	......	.....	.....	4240
......	......	......	......	......	......	......	......	.....	.....	
......	......	......	......	......	......	......	......	.....	.....	6160
......	......	......	......	......	......	......	......	.....	.....	
......	......	......	......	......	......	800t	......	.....	.....	
......	......	......	......	......	......	3200	......	.....	.....	......
......	......	......	......	......	......	......	......	.....	.....	
......	......	......	......	......	......	......	......	.....	.....	240
:076t	1500t	......	......	......	......	1000t	1900t	.....	.....	
8304	6000	......	......	......	......	4000	7600	.....	.....	8197
......	......	......	......	......	......	1000t	......	.....	.....	
......	......	......	......	......	......	4000	......	.....	.....	......
......	......	......	......	......	......	600t	1100t	.....	.....	
......	......	......	......	......	......	2400	4400	.....	.....	5636
......	......	......	......	......	......	......	......	.....	.....	124
......	......	......	......	......	......	800t	......	.....	.....	
......	......	......	......	......	......	3200	......	.....	.....	3153
......	......	......	......	400t	......	600t	460t	.....	.....	
......	......	......	......	1600	......	2400	1840	......	.....	2000
......	......	......	......	......	......	......	......	.....	.....	
......	......	......	......	......	......	......	......	.....	.....	407
......	......	......	......	......	......	......	......	.....	.....	
......	......	......	......	......	......	......	......	.....	.....	2495
......	......	......	......	500t	......	240t	......	.....	.....	
......	......	......	......	2000	......	960	......	.....	.....	1480
34t	800t	......	......	845t	......	......	......	.....	.....	
2936	3200	......	......	3380	......	......	......	.....	.....	3172
......	......	......	......	......	......	......	......	.....	.....	
......	......	......	......	......	......	......	......	.....	.....	1956
......	......	......	......	370t	......	300t	......	.....	.....	
......	......	......	......	1480	......	1200	......	.....	.....	1480
......	......	......	......	60t	......	......	......	.....	.....	
......	......	......	......	240	......	......	......	.....	.....	240
)00t	1200t	......	......	......	......	1000t	......	.....	.....	
4000	4800	......	......	......	......	4000	......	.....	.....	17444
......	......	......	......	......	......	......	......	.....	.....	......
......	......	......	......	......	......	......	......	.....	.....	
......	......	......	......	......	......	......	......	.....	.....	
......	......	......	......	......	......	......	......	.....	.....	......
......	......	......	......	......	......	......	......	.....	.....	
......	......	......	......	......	......	......	......	.....	.....	
......	......	......	......	......	......	......	......	.....	.....	......
......	......	......	......	......	......	......	......	.....	.....	
......	......	......	......	......	......	......	......	.....	.....	......

MICHOACAN—(Continued)

No.	Name	A	B	C	D	E	F	G
482	Jiquilpan	(1203)	380p 1520	401p 1604	......	401p 1604	......	......
561	Lacoaba	500t 2000	......	......	......	......	......	......
790	Maquili	(231)	......	......	......	......	......	......
297	Marabatio	569t 2276	400p 1600	841p 3364	......	1070p 4280	......	......
823	Matalcingo	1083tp 1083	270p 1080	......	......	......	......	......
578	Metlapan	19t 76	40p 160	......	......	......	......	......
571	Mexcaloacan	60t 240	80p 320	......	......	......	......	......
265	Mezaa	166t 664	60p 240	......	......	42p 168	......	......
562	Nexpa	32t 128	50p 200	......	......	......	......	......
332	Patzcuaro	2652tp 2652	......	......	......	......	......	......
147	Periban	1995tp 1995	1250p 5000	......	......	......	......	......
577	Piquitla	100t 400	80p 320	......	......	......	......	......
508	Pomaro	593t 2372	......	......	......	......	......	......
195	Pomucuaran	2530tp 2530	430p 1720	......	......	......	......	......
290	Puruandiro	629t 2516	......	......	......	......	......	......
752	Sevina	(2769)	......	......	......	......	......	......
132	Tacambaro	1942tp 1942	750p 3000	......	......	......	......	......
65	Tancitaro	(2853)	1000p 4000	1100p 4400	......	755p 3020	......	......
307	Tarecuato	843tp 843	......	......	......	......	......	......
67	Tarimbaro	1589t 6356	2000p 8000	......	......	......	......	......
67	Acareno	120p 480	......	......	......	......	......	......
66	Taximaroa	2559t 10236	2000p 8000	......	......	......	......	......
201	Taymeo	1129t 4516	1000p 4000	......	......	727p 2908	......	......
616	Tepalcatepec	4516tp 4516	450p 1800	......	......	......	......	......
656	Teremendo	(1126)	340p 1360	547p 2188	......	365p 1460	......	......
656	Jasso	......	......	......	......	......	......	......
467	Tinguindin	1209tp 1209	500p 2000	608p 2432	......	608p 2432	......	......

Appendix I: Population in 1565

MICHOACAN—(Continued)

H	I	J	K	L	M	N	O	P	Special items	Population
										1604
										2000
							75t			
							300			300
						800t				
						3200				3615
	600t					700t				
	2400					2800				2600
										160
										320
										168
										200
										2652
			1400t				1200t			
			5600				4800			5600
										400
										2372
								2164t		
								8656		2530
						600t		282t		
						2400		1128		2400
						900t				
						3600				3600
	800t	800t				800t				
	3200	3200				3200				3200
										3710
							465t	350t		
							1860	1400		1860
								383t		
								1582		8000
										480
					3000t	3000t				
					12000	12000				12000
						700t	500t			
						2800	2000			2908
						400t				
						1600				1800
						437t				
						1748				1465
										......
										2432

MICHOACAN—(Concluded)

No.	Name	A	B	C	D	E	F	G
306	Tiripitio...	4132tp	1000p	......	......	1105p	......	......
		4132	4000	......	......	4420	......	......
545	Tisupan...	556t	180p	......	......	187p	......	......
		2224	720	......	......	748	......	......
637	Tlacavanas...	......	60p	......	......	......	......	......
		(180)	240	......	......	......	......	......
466	Tlazazalca...	1736tp	450p	806p	......	530p	......	......
		1736	1800	3224	......	2120	......	......
563	Topetina...	103t	70p	......	......	......	......	......
		412	280	......	......	......	......	......
148	Turicato...	1474tp	600p	850p	......	741p	......	......
		1474	2400	3420	......	2964	......	......
477	Ucareo...	2409tp	700p	1160p	......	1160p	......	......
		2409	2800	4640	......	4640	......	......
670	Uchichila (Tzintzuntzan)...	......	1400p	13839p	......	11696p	......	......
		(30548)	5600	55356	......	46784	......	......
694	Undameo...	......	......	......	......	......	......	......
		(1846)	......	......	......	......	......	......
70	Uruapan...	2462tp	870p	......	......	......	......	......
		2462	3480	......	......	......	......	......
18	Sirosto...	3423tp	......	......	......	......	......	......
		3423	......	......	......	......	......	......
548	Jicalan...	145tp	350p	......	......	......	......	......
		145	1400	......	......	......	......	......
214	Zacapu...	1665tp	1000p	......	......	......	......	......
		1665	4000	......	......	......	......	......
214	Tescalco...	......	......	......	......	......	......	......
		......	......	......	......	......	......	......
568	Zoyotlan...	......	130p	......	......	......	......	......
		(390)	520	......	......	......	......	......
	Arimao...	......	400p	194p	......	......	......	......
		(597)	1600	776	......	......	......	......
	Capulalcomulco...	1685tp	......	221p	......	221p	......	......
		1685	......	884	......	884	......	......
	Cinagua...	570t	400p	400p	......	......	......	......
		2280	1600	1600	......	......	......	......
	Guayangareo...	......	......	......	......	......	......	......
		(462)	......	......	......	......	......	......
	Huanajo...	......	250p	304p	......	304p	......	......
		(935)	1000	1216	......	1216	......	......
	Mutzantla...	......	......	......	......	......	......	......
		(1071)	......	......	......	......	......	......
	Necotlan...	222t	100p	200p	......	246p	......	......
		888	400	800	......	984	......	......
	Pusenquia...	......	90p	......	......	......	......	......
		(240)	360	......	......	......	......	......
	Tacacala...	......	......	......	......	......	......	......
		(787)	......	......	......	......	......	......
	Tanataro...	......	......	......	......	......	......	......
		(1160)	......	......	......	......	......	......
819	Ostula...	182t	......	......	......	......	......	......
		728	......	......	......	......	......	......

Appendix I: Population in 1565

MICHOACAN—(Concluded)

H	I	J	K	L	M	N	O	P	Special items	Population
.....	1500t	1200t	.....	.....	.....	1200t	.....	.....	.....	
.....	6000	4800	.....	.....	.....	4800	.....	.....	.....	5073
.....	.....	.....	.....	.....	.....	.....	.....	.....	.....	
.....	.....	.....	.....	.....	.....	.....	.....	.....	.....	748
.....	.....	.....	.....	.....	.....	.....	.....	.....	.....	
.....	.....	.....	.....	.....	.....	.....	.....	.....	.....	240
.....	.....	.....	.....	.....	.....	.....	.....	.....	.....	
.....	.....	.....	.....	.....	.....	.....	.....	.....	.....	2672
.....	.....	.....	.....	.....	.....	.....	.....	.....	.....	
.....	.....	.....	.....	.....	.....	.....	.....	.....	.....	412
.....	.....	.....	.....	850t	600t	758t	.....	.....	.....	
.....	.....	.....	.....	3400	2400	3032	.....	.....	.....	3809
.....	1500t	.....	.....	.....	.....	1359t	.....	.....	.....	
.....	6000	.....	.....	.....	.....	5436	.....	.....	.....	5179
.....	.....	.....	.....	.....	.....	4000t	.....	.....	.....	
.....	.....	.....	.....	.....	.....	16000	.....	.....	.....	39713
.....	600t	.....	.....	.....	.....	.....	.....	.....	.....	
.....	2400	.....	.....	.....	.....	.....	.....	.....	.....	2400
.....	.....	.....	.....	⎧4200t	.....	.....	.....	.....	.....	⎧
.....	.....	.....	.....	⎪16800	.....	.....	.....	.....	.....	⎪16800
.....	.....	.....	.....	⎪.....	.....	2100t	.....	.....	.....	⎪
.....	.....	.....	.....	⎪.....	.....	8400	.....	.....	.....	⎪.....
.....	.....	.....	.....	⎪.....	.....	.....	.....	.....	.....	⎬
.....	.....	.....	.....	⎪.....	.....	.....	.....	.....	.....	⎪.....
.....	.....	.....	.....	⎪1000t	.....	.....	.....	263t	.....	⎪
.....	.....	.....	.....	⎪4000	.....	.....	.....	1052	.....	⎪4000
.....	.....	.....	.....	⎪.....	.....	.....	.....	.....	.....	⎪
.....	.....	.....	.....	⎩.....	.....	.....	.....	.....	.....	⎩.....
.....	.....	.....	.....	.....	.....	.....	.....	.....	.....	520
.....	.....	.....	.....	.....	.....	.....	.....	.....	.....	776
.....	.....	.....	.....	.....	.....	.....	.....	.....	.....	884
.....	.....	.....	.....	.....	.....	270t	.....	.....	.....	
.....	.....	.....	.....	.....	.....	1080	.....	.....	.....	1335
.....	.....	.....	.....	.....	.....	150t	.....	.....	.....	
.....	.....	.....	.....	.....	.....	600	.....	.....	.....	600
.....	.....	.....	.....	.....	.....	.....	.....	.....	.....	1216
.....	.....	.....	.....	.....	.....	348t	.....	.....	.....	
.....	.....	.....	.....	.....	.....	1392	.....	.....	.....	1392
.....	.....	.....	.....	.....	.....	.....	80t	.....	.....	
.....	.....	.....	.....	.....	.....	.....	320	.....	.....	892
.....	.....	.....	.....	.....	.....	.....	.....	.....	.....	360
.....	.....	.....	.....	.....	.....	256t	.....	.....	.....	
.....	.....	.....	.....	.....	.....	1024	.....	.....	.....	1024
.....	.....	.....	.....	377t	.....	.....	.....	.....	.....	
.....	.....	.....	.....	1508	.....	.....	.....	.....	.....	1508
.....	.....	.....	.....	160t	.....	.....	.....	.....	.....	
.....	.....	.....	.....	640	.....	.....	.....	.....	.....	640

Population of Central Mexico

JALISCO

No.	Name	A	B	C	D	E	F	G
331	Ocotic....................	854tp						
		854						
393	Ahuacapan................	206t						
		824						
651	Ahuacatlan................	23t	400p					
		112	1600					
661	Ahualulco.................	440t						
		1760						
403	Ameca....................	800t		272p		277p		
		3200		1088		1108		
535	Amula....................	129t	1800p					
		516	7200					
417	Cuzalapa..................	433t						
		1732						
517	Tuxcacuesco...............	233t						
		932						
805	Analco....................							
		(4297)						
408	Atemajac..................	505tp						
		505						
384	Atengo....................	488t						
		1952						
387	Atiztac...................	639tp						
		639						
78	Atoyac...................	1414t	10378p	2082p		833p		
		5656	41512	8328		3332		
207	Ajijic.....................	598t		1188p		295p		
		2392		4752		1180		
80	Amacueca.................	888t				551p		
		3552				2204		
84	Cocula....................	621t				651p		
		2484				2604		
86	Chapala...................	825t				290p		
		3300				1160		
85	Jocotepec.................	224t				147p		
		896				588		
79	Sayula....................	952t		1772p		1180p		
		3808		7088		4720		
81	Techalutla................	939t				738p		
		3756				2952		
82	Teocuitatlan...............	551t				358p		
		2204				1432		
338	Tepec.....................	250t				190p		
		1000				760		
83	Zacualco..................	1172t		1882p		1176p		
		4688		7528		4704		
159	Autlan....................	713t	1100p					
		2852	4400					
376	Ciutlán...................	222t						
		888						
321	Contla....................	1117tp						
		1117						

Appendix I: Population in 1565

JALISCO

H	I	J	K	L	M	N	O	P
							373t	
							1492	
							125t	
							500	
							[40t]	
				7286t				
				29144				307t
								1228
				682t				
				2728				

JALISCO—(Continued)

No.	Name	A	B	C	D	E	F	G
418	Copala...................	86t						
		344						
495	Cuyutlan................	326t						
		1304						
793	Chimaltitlan.............							
662	Etzatlan.................	1636t	1100p					
		6544	4400					
792	Hostotipaquillo..........	(1336)						
796	Huachinango.............	120t						
		480						
391	Ixcatan..................	736tp						
		736						
479	Jilotlan..................	638t	700p					
		2552	2800					
118	Jocotlan.................	(3986)						
333	Juchitlan................	416tp						
		416						
795	Mascota.................	(438)						
488	Matatlan................	324tp						
		324						
525	Matatlan................	1136tp						
		1136						
648	Mazatlan................	11t						
		44						
327	Mexticacan..............	552tp						
		552						
649	Miahuatlan..............	20t						
		80						
798	Mitic....................	(1175)						
647	Moxuma.................	(2400)	600p					
			2400					
559	Oconahua...............	1484t						
		5936						
330	Ocotlan.................	1360tp						
		1360						
497	Poncitlan................	6937tp						
		6937						
497	Cuitzeo.................	2787tp						
		2787						
420	Sihuatlan................	72t						
		288						
359	Tala.....................	408tp						
		408						
459	Tamazula................	1146t				425p		
		4584				1700		
799	Tecualtitlan.............	(1163)						

Appendix I: Population in 1565

JALISCO—(Continued)

H	I	J	K	L	M	N	O	P
							122t	
							488	
							33t	
							132	
							116t	
							464	
						300t		
						1200		
							346t	
							1384	
							25t	
							100	
							38t	
							152	
							48t	
							192	
							130t	
							520	
							102t	
							408	
							679t	
							2716	
							200t	
							800	
							101t	
							404	

JALISCO—(Continued)

No.	Name	A	B	C	D	E	F	G
339	Tenamaxtlan	(5580)						
339	Tecolotlan							
339	Atengo							
339	Ayutitlan							
339	Ayutla							
339	Istlahuaca							
797	Teocaltiche							
349	Teponahuasco	762tp 762						
361	Tequepaca	524tp 524						
791	Tequila	(1152)						
360	Tesixtan	624tp 624						
659	Tetlan	312t 1248						
659	Utitlan	127tp 127						
516	Teutlan	63t 252						
362	Tlacotan	1398tp 1398						
660	Tlajomulco	1748t 6992						
358	Tomatlan	400t 1600						
658	Tonala	2550tp 2550						
458	Tuxpan	986t 3944				916p 3664		
634	Xiquitlan	(80)	20p 80					
642	Xonacatlan	36t 144						
320	Yahualica	334tp 334						
496	Zalatitlan	186tp 186						
419	Zapotitlan	374t 1496				404p 1616		
489	Zapotlan	870t 3480						
	Acatachime	646tp 646						

Appendix I: Population in 1565

JALISCO—(Continued)

H	I	J	K	L	M	N	O	P
				930t				
				3720				
							281t	
							1124	
							100t	
							400	
							502t	
							2008	
							271t	
							1084	

JALISCO—(Continued)

No.	Name	A	B	C	D	E	F	G
	Acatitlan	140t						
		560						
	Ahuesculco							
		(368)						
	Apamila	29t						
		116						
	Ayuquila	78t						
		312						
	Tecolutlan	130t						
		520						
	La Barranca	303tp						
		303						
	Calatitlan							
		(472)						
	Camotlan							
		(484)						
	Copala	312tp						
		312						
	Coyna	348tp						
		348						
	Coyutlan	26t						
		104						
	Cuistlan	371tp						
		371						
	Cuistlan	615tp						
		615						
	Cuyupustlan	749tp						
		749						
	Cuyutlan							
		(461)						
	Cuyutlan	88t						
		352						
	Cuzpaltan	196tp						
		196						
	Chipiltitlan	102t						
		408						
	Ixtlan	186tp						
		186						
	Ixtlan	90t						
		360						
	El Judio	100t						
		400						
	Matitlan	214tp						
		214						
	Maxcala	322tp						
		322						
	Mazatlan	175t						
		700						
	Mechinango	340t						
		1360						
	Melagua	103t						
		412						

Appendix I: Population in 1565

JALISCO—(Continued)

H	I	J	K	L	M	N	O	P
							32t	
							128	
							41t	
							164	
							42t	
							168	
							34t	
							136	
							40t	
							160	
								23t
								92

JALISCO—(Concluded)

No.	Name	A	B	C	D	E	F	G
	Mexpan	180t						
		720						
	Milpa	200t	200p					
		800	800					
	Matlan	130t						
		520						
	Mizquitlan	781tp						
		781						
	Nochistlan	386tp						
		386						
	Opono	360t						
		1440						
	Orita	103t						
		412						
	Otomitlan	70t						
		280						
	Oztoticpac	452tp						
		452						
	Pampuchin	440t						
		1760						
	Pauhela	146t						
		584						
	Piloto							
		(876)						
	Tene	654t						
		2616						
	Tepetichan	449tp						
		449						
	Tetitlan	189t						
		756						
	Tlapuma	48t						
		192						
	Tozuquilla							
		(3237)						
	Tuycan	67tp						
		67						
	Xiquian	33t						
		132						
	Xirosto	118t						
		472						
	Xocotepec	644t						
		2576						
	Xocotlan	120t						
		480						
	Xochimilco	71t						
		284						
	Yauquila	54t						
		216						
	Yetla	34t						
		136						
	Zacapila	57t						
		228						
	Compostela	72t						
		288						

Appendix I: Population in 1565

JALISCO—(Concluded)

H	I	J	K	L	M	N	O	P
				344t				
				1376				
							35t	
							140	
							53t	
							212	
							55t	
							220	
							76t	
							304	
							281t	
							1124	

NAYARIT

No.	Name	A	B	C	D	E	F	G
386	Acaponeta..................	30t	......	......	......	......	......	......
		120	......	......	......	......	......	......
381	Ahuacatlan.................	2066tp	......	......	......	......	......	......
		2066	......	......	......	......	......	......
382	Amajaque...................	290t	......	......	......	......	......	......
		1160	......	......	......	......	......	......
383	Amatlan....................	168t	......	......	......	......	......	......
		672	......	......	......	......	......	......
380	Apetatuca..................	235t	......	......	......	......	......	......
		940	......	......	......	......	......	......
389	Chacala....................	31t	......	......	......	......	......	......
		124	......	......	......	......	......	......
250	Huaynamota................	500t	......	......	......	......	......	......
		2000	......	......	......	......	......	......
390	Ixtapa.....................	56t	......	......	......	......	......	......
		224	......	......	......	......	......	......
399	Jala.......................	1030tp	......	......	......	......	......	......
		1030	......	......	......	......	......	......
397	Jalcocotlan................	50t	......	......	......	......	......	......
		200	......	......	......	......	......	......
396	Jalisco....................	436t	......	......	......	......	......	......
		1744	......	......	......	......	......	......
398	Jaltempa...................	53t	......	......	......	......	......	......
		212	......	......	......	......	......	......
534	Sentispac..................	556t	......	......	......	......	......	......
		2224	......	......	......	......	......	......
353	Tepatitlan.................	794t	......	......	......	......	......	......
		3176	......	......	......	......	......	......
357	Tepetlahuaca...............	168t	......	......	......	......	......	......
		672	......	......	......	......	......	......
524	Tepic......................	147t	......	......	......	......	......	......
		588	......	......	......	......	......	......
356	Tepuzhuacan................	122t	......	......	......	......	......	......
		488	......	......	......	......	......	......
354	Tequepespan................	94t	......	......	......	......	......	......
		376	......	......	......	......	......	......
354	Camotlan...................	232tp	......	......	......	......	......	......
		232	......	......	......	......	......	......
354	Tepitlan...................	......	......	......	......	......	......	......
		(841)	......	......	......	......	......	......
354	San Pedro..................	......	......	......	......	......	......	......
		(207)	......	......	......	......	......	......
355	Tetitlan...................	636t	......	......	......	......	......	......
		2544	......	......	......	......	......	......
388	Zacualpan..................	332tp	......	......	......	......	......	......
		332	......	......	......	......	......	......
377	Zanatlan...................	60t	......	......	......	......	......	......
		240	......	......	......	......	......	......
375	Zapotan....................	143t	......	......	......	......	......	......
		572	......	......	......	......	......	......
	Acasucheles................	117tp	......	......	......	......	......	......
		117	......	......	......	......	......	......

Appendix I: Population in 1565

NAYARIT

H	I	J	K	L	M	N	O	P
....	....	....	....	....	....	....	332t	......
....	....	....	....	....	....	....	1328	......
....	....	....	....	....	....	....	179t	......
....	....	....	....	....	....	....	716	......
....	....	....	....	....	....	....	39t	......
....	....	....	....	....	....	....	156	......
....	....	....	....	....	....	....	54t	......
....	....	....	....	....	....	....	216	......
....	....	....	....	....	....	....	....	......
....	....	....	....	....	....	....	....	......
....	....	....	....	....	....	....	....	......
....	....	....	....	....	....	....	....	......
....	....	....	....	....	....	....	....	......
....	....	....	....	....	....	....	....	......
....	....	....	....	....	....	....	296t	......
....	....	....	....	....	....	....	1184	......
....	....	....	....	....	....	....	114t	......
....	....	....	....	....	....	....	456	......
....	....	....	....	....	....	....	177t	......
....	....	....	....	....	....	....	708	......
....	....	....	....	....	....	....	....	......
....	....	....	....	....	....	....	....	......
....	....	....	....	....	....	....	....	......
....	....	....	....	....	....	....	....	......
....	....	....	....	....	....	....	....	......
....	....	....	....	....	....	....	....	......
....	....	....	....	....	....	....	112t	......
....	....	....	....	....	....	....	448	......
....	....	....	....	....	....	....	....	......
....	....	....	....	....	....	....	38t	......
....	....	....	....	....	....	....	152	......
....	....	....	....	....	....	....	47t	......
....	....	....	....	....	....	....	188	......
....	....	....	....	....	....	....	73t	......
....	....	....	....	....	....	....	292	......
....	....	....	....	....	....	....	18t	......
....	....	....	....	....	....	....	72	......
....	....	....	....	....	....	....	....	......
....	....	....	....	....	....	....	....	......
....	....	....	....	....	....	....	....	......
....	....	....	....	....	....	....	....	......
....	....	....	....	....	....	....	....	......
....	....	....	....	....	....	....	....	......
....	....	....	....	....	....	....	....	......

NAYARIT—(Continued)

No.	Name	A	B	C	D	E	F	G
	Apazan	229t						
			916					
	Astatlan	162t						
			648					
	Caliacapan	92t						
			368					
	Cotlapil	120t						
			480					
	Nochistlan	95t						
			380					
	Cuyacan	33t						
			132					
	Huacel	1198tp						
			1198					
	Huamoltipac	15t						
			60					
	Iztimiztique	68t						
			272					
	Matacticpac	35t						
			140					
397	Mecatlan	38t						
			152					
	Pontoque	99t						
			396					
	Tecomatlan	15t						
			60					
	Tecoxquines	274t						
			1096					
	Tepehuapa	60t						
			240					
	Timichoc	106t						
			424					
	Tintococ	112t						
			448					
	Xalacingo	40t						
			160					
	Zacatlan	365t						
			1460					
684	Culiacan [province]	4407t						
			17628					
794	Compostela							

COLIMA

No.	Name	A	B	C	D	E	F	G
639	Acatlan	60t	40p					
		240	160					
822	Alcozaue							
	+ Mixtanejo	(6048)						
824	Alima	71t	120p					
		284	480					

Appendix I: Population in 1565 157

NAYARIT—(*Continued*)

H	I	J	K	L	M	N	O	P
							876t	
							3504	
							72t	
							288	

COLIMA

H	I	J	K	L	M	N	O	P
				1008t				
				4032				

COLIMA—(Continued)

No.	Name	A	B	C	D	E	F	G
176	Cinamacatitlan	...... (3600)	500p 2000	......	......	......	......	......
176	Cholo	......	......	......	......	......	......	......
641	Coatlan	58t 232	40p 160	......	......	......	......	......
604	Colima [villa]	...... (12000)	3000p 12000	......	......	......	......	......
286	Comala	167t 668	......	......	......	......	......	......
646	Cuzcatlan	...... (1110)	50p 200	......	......	240p 960	......	......
825	Chiametla	74t 296	......	......	......	......	......	......
346	Chiapan	...... (18000)	......	......	......	......	......	......
346	Tecocitlan	189t 756	......	......	......	......	......	......
346	Coxiutlan	......	......	......	......	......	......	......
346	Amatlan	80t 320	......	......	......	......	......	......
346	Tezontlan	......	......	......	......	......	......	......
633	Ixtapa	...... (280)	70p 280	......	......	......	......	......
665	Ixtlahuacan	159t 636	......	..•..	......	......	......	......
645	Juluapa	...... (774)	250p 1000	......	......	129p 516	......	......
640	Malacatlan	40t 160	......	.. ..	......	......	......	......
650	Maloastla	40t 160	......	......	......	......	......	......
258	Petatlan	45t 180	40p 160	......	......	......	......	......
638	Petlayuneca	...... (600)	150p 600	......	......	......	......	......
635	Tamala	...... (200)	50p 200	......	......	......	......	......
344	Tecociapa	170t 680	......	......	......	......	......	......
257	Tecociapa	...... (600)	150p 600	......	......	......	......	......
347	Tecolapa	120t 480	......	......	......	......	......	......
520	Tecoman	163t 652	400p 1600	......	......	......	......	......
343	Tecuxuacan	121t 484	......	......	......	......	......	......
345	Temcatepan	75t 300	......	......	......	......	......	......

Appendix I: Population in 1565

COLIMA—(Continued)

H	I	J	K	L	M	N	O	P
				600t 2400				
				150t 600				
				3000t 12000				
				40t 160				

COLIMA—(*Continued*)

No.	Name	A	B	C	D	E	F	G
348	Tepehuacan	39t						
		156						
519	Tepetitango	141t	350p					
		564	1400					
518	Tequepa	123t	150p					
		492	600					
341	Tlacoloaxtla	103t						
		412						
342	Totolmoloya	26t						
		104						
643	Xicotlan	150t	70p					
		600	280					
644	Xiloteupam	70t	60p					
		280	240					
636	Xocotlan	116t						
		464						
	Ahuatitlan	101t						
		404						
	Ameca		40p					
		(160)	160					
	Apapatlan	71t						
		284						
	Apatlan	231t						
		924						
	Alimanci							
	Cacalutla		40p					
		(160)	160					
	Calagua		45p					
		(180)	180					
	Cayamaca		70p					
		(280)	280					
	Cihuatlan	72t						
		288						
	Coatlan	244t						
		976						
	Contlan	20t						
		80						
	Coyutlan	84t						
		336						
	Chalatipam		100p					
		(400)	400					
	Ecatlan	114t						
		456						
	Escayamoza	40t						
		160						
	Estapa	24t						
		96						
	Mahuala		80p					
		(922)	320					
	Naopala	34t						
		136						

Appendix I: Population in 1565

COLIMA—(Continued)

H	I	J	K	L	M	N	O	P
				30t				
				120				
				100t				
				400				
				80t				
				320				

COLIMA—(*Concluded*)

No.	Name	A	B	C	E	E	F	G
	Ocotlan	......	150p	......	......	......	......	......
		(2534)	600	......	......	......	......	......
	Piroma	......	......	......	......	......	......	......
		......	......	......	......	......	......	......
	Oclitanabasta	......	......	......	......	......	......	......
		......	......	......	......	......	......	......
	Pomayagua	46t	......	......	......	......	......	......
		184	......	......	......	......	......	......
	Popoyutla	27t	......	......	......	......	......	......
		108	......	......	......	......	......	......
	Puchititlan	......	300p	......	......	......	......	......
		(1200)	1200	......	......	......	......	......
	Teutitlan	63t	......	......	......	......	......	......
		252	......	......	......	......	......	......
	Zaligua	187t	......	......	......	......	......	......
		748	......	......	......	......	......	......
	Zaliguacan	432t	......	......	......	......	......	......
		1728	......	......	......	......	......	......
	Zumpamanique	286t	......	......	......	......	......	......
		1144	......	......	......	......	......	......
	Zautlan	......	30p	......	......	......	......	......
		(120)	120	......	......	......	......	......
	Zayula	......	90p	......	......	......	......	......
		(360)	360	......	......	......	......	......
509	Quezalapa	211t	......	......	......	......	......	......
		844	......	......	......	......	......	......

ZACATECAS

No.	Name	A	B	C	D	E	F	G
438	Nochistlan	2804tp	......	......	......	......	......	......
		2804	......	......	......	......	......	......
328	Jalpa	2553tp	......	......	......	......	......	......
		2553	......	......	......	......	......	......
329	Moyahua	1097tp	......	......	......	......	......	......
		1097	......	......	......	......	......	......
329	Mezquitatlan	......	......	......	......	......	......	......
		......	......	......	......	......	......	......
329	Tracache	......	......	......	......	......	......	......
		......	......	......	......	......	......	......
334	Juchipilla	1141tp	......	......	......	......	......	......
		1141	......	......	......	......	......	......
385	Apasol	363tp	......	......	......	......	......	......
		363	......	......	......	......	......	......
350	Teul	976tp	......	......	......	......	......	......
		976	......	......	......	......	......	......
352	Tepechitlan	1296tp	......	......	......	......	......	......
		1296	......	......	......	......	......	......

Appendix I: Population in 1565

COLIMA—(Concluded)

H	I	J	K	L	M	N	O	P
				220t 880				
				20t 80				15t 60

ZACATECAS

H	I	J	K	L	M	N	O	P
							280t 1120	
							82t 328	

ZACATECAS—(Continued)

No.	Name	A	B	C	D	E	F	G
351	Tlaltenango [pueblo]	704tp						
		704						
351	Cicacalco							
		(9648)						
351	Tocatique							
351	Momax							
351	Huejucar							
	Teteuque	79tp						
		79						

GENERAL—UNIDENTIFIED

No.	Name	A	B	C	D	E	F	G
	Acacula					117p		
						468		
	Ahuatitlanapa			180p		188p		
				720		752		
	Ahuehuepan					540p		
						2160		
	Atengo		135p					
			540					
	Chiconanatengo							
	Cuauquilpa					302p		
						1208		
	Huautla			364p		208p		
				1456		832		
	Hueyapa					657p		
						2628		
	Icoatlan		60p					
			240					
	Tacatepec			40p				
				160				
	Tochenacuche			50p				
				200				
	Tuchitlapilco					88p		
						352		
	Xalitla			112p				
				448				
	Xulapa		100p					
			400					
	Yztitlan			67p				
				268				
	Zoatlan					1000p		
						4000		

Appendix I: Population in 1565

ZACATECAS—(Continued)

H	I	J	K	L	M	N	O	P
...	...	...	...	...	3350tp	...	379t	...
...	...	...	...	...	3350	...	1516	...

GENERAL—UNIDENTIFIED

H	I	J	K	L	M	N	O	P	Population
									468
									736
									2160
									540
									1208
				200t					
					800				1146
									2628
									240
									160
									200
									352
									448
									400
									268
									4000

APPENDIX II

Alphabetical List of Indian Communities of Central Mexico in the Sixteenth Century

(Note: The modern states in which communities lie are given in the second column, or, if a community is unidentified, the bishopric or other information. Identified places are indicated by numbers in the third column which refer to the Sketch Map. The fourth column gives the holders, Crown or encomendero, ca. 1565. Spelling follows the 1920 Mexican census and official maps.)

Acacula	?		Crown
Acaguapisca	Guerrero	259	Antón Sánchez
Acalpica	Guerrero	583	Crown
Acaltepec	Oaxaca	786	Crown
Acaluacán	México	546	Diego Arias Sotelo
Acámbaro	Michoacán	7	Hernán Pérez de Bocanegra
Acamixtlavaca	Guerrero	161	Alonso Pérez
Acaponeta	Nayarit	386	Antón de la Puebla
Acapulco	Guerrero	126	Aldonza de Villafuerte
Acapuzalco	Guerrero	284	Juan de Caraballar
Acasucheles	Nayarit		Alonso Valiente
			Martín Sánchez
Acatachima	Nueva Galicia		Pedro Cuadrado
Acatitlán	Jalisco		Francisco de Estrada
Acatlán	San Luis Potosí		Francisco Barrón
Acatlán	Guerrero	480	Crown
Acatlán	Colima	639	Crown
Acatlán	Vera Cruz	720	Martín de Mafra
Acatlán	Puebla	401	Crown
Acatlán	Hidalgo	273	Pedro de Paz
Acatzingo	Puebla	554	Crown
Acaxuchitlán	México	87	Andrés de Rosas
Acaxuchitlán	Hidalgo	149	Luisa de Acuña
Acayuca	Hidalgo	152	García de Navarrete
Acayuca	Vera Cruz	256	Francisco Marín
Acolman	México	38	Pedro de Solís

Appendix II: List of Communities 167

Actopan	Hidalgo	156	Juan Guerrero
Actopan	Vera Cruz	719	?
Acualilco	Vera Cruz (Coatzacoalcos)		Crown
Acuimantla	Hidalgo	47	Alonso Ortiz de Zúñiga Jerónimo de Medina
Acuitlapan	Guerrero	772	Juan Cermeño
Acultzingo	Vera Cruz	89	Diego de Montalvo
Achichipico	Morelos	5	Marqués del Valle
Achiotepec	Hidalgo	204	Pedro de Meneses Diego de Coria
Achiotla	Jalisco	647	Crown
Achiutla	Oaxaca	154	Tristán de Arellano
Aguandero	Michoacán	477	Crown
Aguatepec	Oaxaca	154	Tristán de Arellano
Aguatoco	Vera Cruz (Coatzacoalcos)		Crown
Ahuacapan	Jalisco	393	Crown Hernán Ruiz de la Peña
Ahuacara	Nayarit		Juan de Santiago Herrero
Ahuacatitlán	Colima	257	Ginesa López
Ahuacatlán	Jalisco	651	Crown
Ahuacatlán	Nayarit	381	Crown Alvaro de Bracamonte
Ahualulco	Jalisco	661	Crown
Ahuatipán	Hidalgo	541	Crown
Ahuatitlán	Colima		Juana de Medina
Ahuatitlanapa	?		Crown
Ahuatlán	Puebla	405	Crown
Ahuehuepan	?		Crown
Ahuesculco	Jalisco		?
Ajijic	Jalisco	270	Crown Alonso de Avalos
Ajuchitlán	Guerrero	491	Crown
Alahuixtlán	Guerrero	227	Juan de Aguila
Alcececa	Vera Cruz	801	Crown
Alcozaue	Colima	822	Juan Jiménez
Alima	Colima	824	Crown
Aljojuca	Puebla	710	?

Almería	Vera Cruz	627	Crown
Almolonga	Vera Cruz	718	Crown
Almolonga	Oaxaca	22	Mateo de Monjaraz Diego de Loaisa
Alotepec	Oaxaca	742	?
Alpatlahuac	Puebla	552	?
Alpatlahuaya	Vera Cruz	762	?
Alpoyeca	Guerrero	809	Crown Bernardino Vázquez de Tapia Beatriz de Estrada
Alupancingo	Oaxaca		?
Amacueca	Jalisco	80	Crown Alonso de Avalos
Amacuitlapilco	Morelos	676	Marqués del Valle
Amajaque	Nayarit	382	Crown Alvaro de Bracamonte
Amaltepec	Oaxaca	163	Juan de Bonilla
Amascalapa	Vera Cruz (Coatzacoalcos)		Crown
Amatepec	México	407	Crown
Amatlán	Vera Cruz		Pedro Moreno
Amatlán	Michoacán	346	Jorge Carrillo
Amatlán	San Luis Potosí		Francisco Barrón
Amatlán	Oaxaca	22	Mateo de Monjaraz Diego de Loaisa
Amatlán	Oaxaca	200	García de Contreras Juan de Valdivieso
Amatlán	Vera Cruz	711	?
Amatlán	Oaxaca	624	Crown
Amatlán de Cañas	Nayarit	383	Crown Alvaro de Bracamonte
Amayuca	Morelos	673	Marqués del Valle
Ambuma	Jalisco	647	Crown
Ameca	Colima		Crown
Ameca	Jalisco	403	Crown
Amecameca	México	423	Crown
Ameluca	Puebla	754	?
Amoltepec	Oaxaca	849	Crown

Appendix II: List of Communities 169

Amula	Jalisco	535	Crown
Amusgos	Oaxaca	6	Hernando de Avila
Anacuilco	Costa del Sur		Crown
Analco	Jalisco	805	?
Andaama	Oaxaca		Díaz Carballar
Anilicapa	Bish. of Tlaxcala		?
Apam	Hidalgo	705	Crown
Apamila	Jalisco		?
Apapatlán	Colima		Alonso de Arévalo
Apasco	Oaxaca	90	Gonzalo de Robles
Apatlán	Colima		Francisco Preciado
Apaxco	México	4	Cristóbal Hernández
Apazán	Nayarit		Jerónimo Pérez
Apaztlán	Vera Cruz (Pánuco)		Crown
Apetatuca	Nayarit	380	Alonso de Castañeda Pero Ruiz de Haro
Apoala	Oaxaca	90	Gonzalo de Robles
Apozol	Zacatecas	385	Francisco Delgado
Aquila	Michoacán	536	Crown
Aquilpa	Guerrero	808	Crown Bernardino Vázquez de Tapia Beatriz de Estrada
Araro	Michoacán	406	Crown
Arimao	Michoacán		Crown Juan Gómez de Herrera
Ario	Michoacán	503	Crown
Astata	Oaxaca	155	Gil González
Astatlán	Nueva Galicia		Tomás Gil
Atemajac	Jalisco	408	Crown
Atempa	Guerrero	295	Crown Bernardino Vázquez de Tapia
Atempan	Puebla	404	Crown
Atenango	Guerrero	409	Crown
Atenchancaleca	Guerrero	260	Crown
Atengo	?		Marqués del Valle
Atengo	Hidalgo	272	Diego Ramírez

170   *Population of Central Mexico*

Atengoychán	Jalisco	384	Crown
			Alvaro de Bracamonte
Atepec	Oaxaca	463	Crown
Atescac	Vera Cruz		Crown
Atiquipaque	Oaxaca (Tehuantepec)		Francisco de Rosales
Atitlaquia	Hidalgo	402	Crown
Atiztac	Jalisco	387	Francisco Delgadillo
Atlacahualoya	Morelos	682	Marqués del Valle
Atlacomulco	México	164	Manuel de Villegas
Atlahuaca	Oaxaca	278	Crown
			Juan Gallego
Atlamamulco	Morelos	5	Marqués del Valle
Atlán	Bish. of Tlaxcala		Crown
Atlán	Michoacán	569	Crown
Atlapulco	México	2	Catalina de Zárate
Atlatlauca	México	607	Crown
Atleucián	Vera Cruz	31	Juan de Cervantes
Atlimaxacingo del Monte	Guerrero	810	Crown Bernardino Vázquez de Tapia Beatriz de Estrada
Atlimaxacingo del Río	Guerrero	275	Same
Atlixtac	Guerrero	277	Same
Atoco	Vera Cruz (Coatzacoalcos)		Crown
Atotonilco	Morelos	677	Marqués del Valle
Atotonilco el Grande	Hidalgo	157	Pedro de Paz
Atotonilco	Hidalgo	1	Melchor Pedraza
Atoyac	Jalisco	78	Crown
			Alonso de Avalos
Atoyac	Oaxaca	134	Crown
			Pedro Nieto
Atoyac	Oaxaca	133	Francisco Vázquez
Atoyaquillo	Oaxaca	91	Juan Griego
Atzala	Puebla	815	?
Atzala	Guerrero	468	Crown

Appendix II: List of Communities 171

Atzalan	Bish. of Tlaxcala		?
Atzcapotzalco	Distrito Federal	158	Alvaro Maldonado
Atzitzintla	Vera Cruz	765	?
Autepec	Guerrero (Zacatula)		Crown
Autlán	Jalisco	159	Crown Hernán Ruiz de la Peña
Axacuba	Hidalgo	3	Jerónimo López
Axapusco	México	167	Alvaro de Santa Cruz
Axochiapan	Morelos	812	Marqués del Valle
Axochitlán	Puebla	271	?
Axomulco	Oaxaca	200	García de Contreras Juan de Valdivieso
Axtla	San Luis Potosí	804	?
Ayacastepec	Oaxaca	150	Juan Becerra
Ayautla	Oaxaca	630	Crown
Ayoquezco	Oaxaca	751	Crown
Ayotepec	Oaxaca (Mixes)		?
Ayotzinapa	Guerrero	732	Baltasar Mejía Salmerón
Ayucan	México	233	Juan Cano
Ayuquila	Jalisco (Valle de Milpa)		Martín Sánchez
Ayutla de los Libres	Guerrero	88	Alonso Lozano
Ayutla	Guerrero (Zacatula)	580	Crown
Ayutla	Oaxaca (Costa del Sur)		Crown
Ayutla	Oaxaca	274	Crown Pedro Nieto
Azoyú	Guerrero	276	Crown Bernardino Vázquez de Tapia Beatriz de Estrada
Azuntepec	Oaxaca	153	Francisco Flores
La Barranca	Jalisco (Guadalajara)		Crown
Bocaneo	Michoacán	664	?
Borona	Michoacán	242	Crown

172   *Population of Central Mexico*

Cacahuatepec	Guerrero	242	Diego Prado
Cacalango	Vera Cruz		
	(Coatzacoalcos)		Crown
Cacalotepec	Guerrero		Pedro Pantoja
Cacalotepec	Oaxaca	499	Crown
Cacalotepec	Oaxaca	141	Antón Miguel
Cacalutla	Colima		Crown
Cacaotepec	Oaxaca	200	García de Contreras
			Juan de Valdivieso
Cacatepec	Oaxaca		
	(Zapotecas)		?
Cachultenango	Oaxaca		Crown
Cahuitlán	Oaxaca	816	Crown
Calagua	Colima		Crown
Calajo	Oaxaca		
	(Zapotecas)		?
Calatitlán	Jalisco		?
Calcoyuca	México	206	Luisa de Estrada
Calcuautla	Vera Cruz	255	Juan López Frías
Caliacapan	Nayarit		Domingo de Arteaga
Calihuala	Oaxaca	714	?
Calimaya	México	13	Hernán Gutiérrez Altamirano
Calmeca	Puebla	722	?
Calpa	Vera Cruz	160	Benito de Cuenca
Calpulalpan	Tlaxcala	706	?
Calpulalpan	Oaxaca	202	Pero Nuñez Sedeño
Calticán	Puebla	16	Gaspar de Garnica
			Francisco de Montaño
Caltitlán	Oaxaca	379	?
Camotlán	Jalisco		
	(Guadalajara)		?
Camotlán	Oaxaca	835	Crown
Camotlán	Oaxaca (Mixe)	834	?
Camotlán	Nayarit	354	Juan de Samaniego
Camutla	Guerrero	584	Crown
Capotancingo	Vera Cruz		
	(Coatzacoalcos)		Crown
Capula	Michoacán	494	Crown

Appendix II: List of Communities 173

Capulalcolulco	Michoacán (Zacatula)		Crown
Capulhuac	México	233	Juan Cano
Caquete	México	233	Juan Cano
Carandacho	Michoacán	169	Alonso de Avila
Caroque	Nueva Galicia		Alonso Alvarez
Castilblanco (Temoxtitlán)	Puebla	203	Hernando de Nava Juan de Arriaga
Catusco	Vera Cruz		Crown
Caxitlantongo	Puebla	755	?
Cayaco	Guerrero	597	Crown
Cayamaca	Colima		Crown
Cayutepex	Bish. of Tlaxcala or México		Pedro Calderón
Cempoala	Vera Cruz (Coatzacoalcos)		Bartolomé Sánchez
Centayuca	Puebla	216	Crown Ruy González
Centecomaltepec	Oaxaca (Chontales)		Diego de Leyva
Cetusco	Oaxaca	829	Crown
Cicacalco	Zacatecas	351	Toribio de Bolaños
Cihuala	Vera Cruz (Pánuco)		Crown
Cihuatlán	Colima		Crown
Cihuatlán	Michoacán	565	Crown
Cihuatlán	Guerrero	593	Francisco de Salcedo
Cinagua	Michoacán		Crown
Cinamacatitlán	Colima	176	Diego de Velasco
Citlaltepec	Oaxaca (Zapotecas)		Crown
Ciutlán	Michoacán	572	Crown
Ciutlán	Jalisco	376	Juan de Villalba Marcos de Carmona
Coacoazintla	Vera Cruz	759	Domingo Gallego
Coahuayutla	Guerrero	262	Diego Ruiz
Coalcomán	Michoacán	510	Crown
Coatepec	Puebla	723	?
Coatepec	Vera Cruz	841	Crown

Population of Central Mexico

Coatepec	Oaxaca	217	Pedro de Avila
Coatepec de las Beatas	México	770	Antonio de la Torre
Coatepec	México(Texcoco)	605	Crown
Coatitlán	México	546	Diego Arias Sotelo
Coatlán	Guerrero	772	Juan Cermeño
Coatlán	Oaxaca	22	Mateo de Monjaraz / Diego de Loaisa
Coatlán	Colima		Juan Fernández
Coatlán–Santa María	Oaxaca	738	?
Coatlán	Colima	641	Crown
Coatzacoalcos (Province)	Vera Cruz	683	Various encomenderos
Coatzacoalcos	Vera Cruz		Crown
Coatzingo	Puebla	282	Diego Quixada
Cocantepec	Oaxaca		?
Cocula	Guerrero	199	Gonzalo de Cerezo
Cocula	Jalisco	84	Crown / Alonso de Avalos
Coculco	Vera Cruz		Crown
Coeneo	Michoacán	169	Alonso de Avila
Cohetzala	Puebla	424	Crown
Coixtlavaca	Oaxaca	104	Bartolomé Sotomayor / Alonso de Bazán
Colima (Villa)	Colima	604	Crown
Colipa	Vera Cruz	627	Crown
Colotepec	Oaxaca (Chontales)		?
Colucán	Puebla	410	Crown
Colutla	Guerrero		Crown
Comala	Colima	286	Alonso Carrillo
Comaltepec	Oaxaca		Luis de Castilla
Comaltepec	Oaxaca	500	Crown
Comanja	Michoacán	19	Juan Infante
Compostela	Nayarit	794	?
Comultepec	Oaxaca (Zapotecas)		Crown
Contla	Jalisco	321	Pedro de Placencia

Appendix II: List of Communities 175

Contlán	Colima		Pedro de Santa Cruz
Conzozotla	Puebla	610	Crown
Copala	Jalisco		
	(Guadalajara)		Francisco de la Mota
Copala	Guerrero	522	?
Copala	Jalisco		Crown
Copalillo	Guerrero	61	Crown
			Lorenzo de Porcallo
Cosamaloapan	Vera Cruz	422	Crown
Coscomaltepec	Vera Cruz	762	?
Cotahuistla	Oaxaca	821	?
Cotatlán	Vera Cruz		
	(Coatzacoalcos)		Bartolomé Sánchez
Cotaxtla	Vera Cruz	187	Marqués del Valle
Cotlapil	Nayarit		Domingo de Artiaga
Coxcatlán	Puebla	414	Crown
Coxcatlán	San Luis Potosí	704	Juan Sánchez
Coxiutlán	Colima	346	Jorge Carrillo
Coyna	Jalisco		Andrés de Villanueva
Coyoacán	D. F.	95	Marqués del Valle
Coyotepec	México	777	?
Coyotepec	Oaxaca	103	Bartolomé Sánchez
Coyuca	Guerrero		Crown
	(Zacatula)		Diego Ruiz
Coyuca	Guerrero	146	Pedro de Meneses
Coyuquilla	Guerrero	168	Crown
			Diego Ruiz
Coyutla	Vera Cruz		
	(Pánuco)		Juan Romero
Coyutlán	Colima		Martín Monje
Coyutlán	Jalisco		Pedro de Simancas
Cozoaltepec	Oaxaca	624	Crown
Cuacuatlán	Michoacán	570	Crown
Cuahualulco	Puebla (Chal-		
	chicomula)		?
Cuapan	Puebla	222	Diego de Ordaz
Cuapanoya	México		
	(Capulhuac)		?
Cuaranchán	Michoacán	481	Crown

176   Population of Central Mexico

Cuatinchán	Puebla	28	Crown
			Juan Pérez de Artiaga
Cuatla	Oaxaca	?	
Cuauquilpa	?		Crown
Cuautitlán	Oaxaca (Mixteca)		?
Cuautitlán	México	166	Alonso de Avila
Cuautlatlahauca	Oaxaca (Mixteca)		?
Cuernavaca	Morelos	11	Marqués del Valle
Cuetzala	Guerrero	707	?
Cuevas (Cuitlavaca)	México	10	Juan de Cuevas
Cuezcomaltepec	Oaxaca (Mixes)		?
Cuicatlán	Oaxaca	501	Crown
Cuilapan	Oaxaca	20	Marqués del Valle
Cuistlán	Jalisco (Guadalajara)		Juan de Zaldívar
Cuistlán	Jalisco		Crown
Cuitepec	Oaxaca (Ixcuintepec)		Crown
Cuitlapa	Guerrero	287	Crown
			Bernardino Vázquez de Tapia
			Beatriz de Estrada
Cuitlatenamic	Costa del Sur		?
Cuitzeo	Michoacán	77	Juana de Torres
Cuitzeo	Jalisco	497	Crown
Cuixtlán	Oaxaca	22	Mateo de Monjaraz
			Diego de Loaisa
Culhuacán	México	8	Cristóbal de Oñate
Culiacán (Province)	Sinaloa	684	Various encomenderos
Cupándaro	Michoacán	77	Juana de Torres
Cuquila	Oaxaca (Mixteca)		?
Cusmiquila	Oaxaca	224	Juan Rodríguez de Salas
Cutzamala	Guerrero	172	Bernardino de Bocanegra
Cutzco	Michoacán	285	Gonzalo Ruiz
Cuyacán	Nayarit		Alonso Alvarez
Cuyotepexi	Oaxaca	727	?
Cuytlaguiztlán	Oaxaca		?

Appendix II: List of Communities 177

Cuyuca	Guerrero (Zacatula)		Crown
Cuyupustlán	Jalisco (Guadalajara)		Melchor Pérez
Cuyutlán	Jalisco (Guadalajara)		?
Cuyutlán	Jalisco	495	Crown
Cuyutlán	Jalisco (Purificación)		Pedro Moreno
Cuzalapa	Jalisco	417	Crown
Cúzaro	Michoacán	332	Juan Infante
Cuzcatlán	Colima	646	Crown
Cuzpaltán	Jalisco (Guadalajara)		Diego Hurtado
Cuzumacernaca	Vera Cruz		Pedro Moreno
Chacaual	Vera Cruz (Pánuco)		Alonso Ginovés
Chacala	Michoacán	564	Crown
Chacala	Nayarit	389	Alonso Valiente Martín Sánchez
Chacalapa	Vera Cruz	256	Francisco Marín
Chachapala	Vera Cruz (Pánuco)		Crown
Chachoapam	Oaxaca	246	Juan de Benavides
Chalatipam	Colima		Crown
Chalcacingo	Morelos	680	Marqués del Valle
Chalcatongo	Oaxaca	730	Tristán de Arellano
Chalco	México	423	Crown
Chalchicomula	Puebla	700	?
Chalchitlán	Vera Cruz (Pánuco)		Francisco de Torres
Chalcholoacán	Vera Cruz (Coatzacoalcos)		Crown
Chalma	Puebla	721	?
Chapa de Mota	México	702	?
Chapala	Jalisco	86	Crown Alonso de Avalos
Chapantongo	Hidalgo	171	Leonor Vázquez
Chapulco	Puebla	98	Esteban de Carbajal

Chapultepec	Vera Cruz	759	Crown
Charapaco	Michoacán	539	Crown
Chayuco	Oaxaca	280	Luis de Castilla
Chazumba	Oaxaca	533	Crown
Chiagualtepec	Oaxaca (Mixteca)		?
Chiametla	Colima	825	Crown
Chiapa	Puebla	12	Jerónimo Ruiz de la Mota
Chiapan	Colima	346	Jorge Carrillo
Chiautla	Puebla	424	Crown
Chicahuaxtla	Oaxaca	323	Francisco Vázquez
Chicaloacán	Vera Cruz (Coatzacoalcos)		Crown
Chicarapo	Michoacán	481	Crown
El Chico (Xicochimilco)	Vera Cruz	842	Crown
Chicoacán	Vera Cruz (Coatzacoalcos)		Crown
Chicocentepec	Vera Cruz (Naolingo)		Crown
Chicoloana	Archbish. of México		Gaspar López
Chicome	Oaxaca	154	Tristán de Arellano
Chicomezuchil	Oaxaca	21	Diego de Vargas
Chiconamel	Vera Cruz	283	Alonso de Audelo
Chiconautla	México	425	Crown
Chicontepec	Vera Cruz	756	?
Chicuitlán	Vera Cruz (Coatzacoalcos)		Crown
Chichatlán	Hidalgo	238	Francisco de Torres
Chichiapa	Oaxaca (Nejapa)		Crown
Chichicapa	Oaxaca	543	Crown
Chichicastepec	Oaxaca	322	Hernando Alonso
Chichicaxtla	Hidalgo	701	?
Chichilintla	Vera Cruz	162	Juan de Cuenca
Chichiquila	Puebla	107	?
Chiepetlán	Guerrero	378	Crown Bernardino Vázquez de Tapia Beatriz de Estrada

Appendix II: List of Communities 179

Chietla	Puebla	411	Crown
Chila	Vera Cruz	160	Benito de Cuenca
Chila	Puebla	99	Lorenzo Marroquino
Chila	Puebla	174	Alvaro Maldonado
Chila de la Sal	Puebla	424	Crown
Chilapa	Guerrero	17	Diego de Ordaz
Chilapa	Vera Cruz	255	Juan López Frías
Chilcuautla	Hidalgo	94	Juan de Avila
Chilchota	Michoacán	416	Crown
Chilpopocatlán	Hidalgo	553	Crown
Chiltoyac	Bish. of Tlaxcala		Gonzalo Rodríguez de Villafuerte
Chimalhuacán	México	9	Blas de Bustamante
Chimalhuacán	México (Chalco)	423	Crown
Chimaltitlán	Jalisco	793	?
Chinameca-Mixteca	Vera Cruz	254	Cristóbal de Herrera
Chinantla	Puebla	609	Crown
Chipila	Guerrero	261	Crown Francisco Gutiérrez
Chipiltitlán	Jalisco (Purificación)		Bartolomé Chavarín
Chiquimitío	Michoacán	493	Crown
Chisme	Oaxaca	744	?
Choapan	Oaxaca	498	Crown
Chocamán	Vera Cruz	764	María de Villanueva
Cholo	Colima	176	Diego de Velasco
Cholula	Puebla	412	Crown
Chontales bravos (Province)	Oaxaca	311	?
Chucándiro	Michoacán	175	Gonzalo Galván
Churubusco	D. F.	119	Bernardino Vázquez de Tapia
Ecatepec	México	546	Diego Arias Sotelo
Ecatlán	Colima		Crown
Ejutla	Oaxaca	22	Diego de Loaisa Mateo de Monjaraz
Elotepec	Oaxaca	685	Crown

180   Population of Central Mexico

Eloxochitlán	Puebla	25	Juan Durán
Eltianguillo	Oaxaca (Mixes)	?	
Epatlán	Puebla	178	Crown
			Juan Pérez de Herrera
Epazoyuca	Hidalgo	24	Francisca del Rincón
Erongarícuaro	Michoacán	291	Juan Infante
Esayameco	Puebla	610	Crown
Escayamoza	Colima		Crown
Estapa	Colima		Alonso López
Estetla	Oaxaca	726	?
Esuchi	Michoacán		Crown
Esuchicala	Oaxaca (Zapotecas)		?
Etepec	Oaxaca (Mixteca)		Tello de Medina
Etla	Oaxaca	26	Marqués del Valle
Etlagón	Oaxaca	310	Crown
			Francisco Franco
Etlahualuco	Vera Cruz (Coatzacoalcos)		Gonzalo Hernández
Etlatongo	Oaxaca	136	Juan de Valdivieso
Etzatlán	Jalisco	662	Crown
Guaracha	Michoacán	851	Crown
Guaríscaro	Guanajuato	538	Crown
Guayangareo	Michoacán (Cuitzeo)		?
Guzahapa	Vera Cruz (Pánuco)		Diego Corzo
Hinhitlán	Guerrero (Zacatula)		?
Hostotipaquillo	Jalisco	792	?
Huacana	Michoacán	115	Juan Pantoja
Huacaylapa	Vera Cruz (Coatzacoalcos)		Gonzalo Hernández
Huacel	Nayarit		?
Huachapa	Vera Cruz (Coatzacoalcos)		Crown
Huachinango	Jalisco	796	?

Appendix II: List of Communities 181

Huachinango	Puebla	106	Agustín de Villanueva
Huajolotitlán	Oaxaca	782	Crown
Huajolotitlán	Oaxaca	431	?
Huajuapan	Oaxaca	725	Juan de Arriaga
Huamelula	Oaxaca	430	Crown
Huamolticpac	Nayarit		Bartolomé Pérez
Huamuxtitlán	Guerrero	301	Bernardino Vázquez de Tapia
Huanajo	Michoacán (Uruápam)		Crown
Huandacareo	Michoacán	77	Juana de Torres
Huango	Michoacán	108	Juan de Villaseñor
Huanimeo	Michoacán	332	Juan Infante
Huaniqueo	Michoacán	429	Crown
Huapanapa	Oaxaca	529	Crown
Huaquechula	Puebla	29	Jorge de Alvarado
Huaquilpa	Vera Cruz (Coatzacoalcos)		Crown
Huaricata	Nayarit		Alonso de Toro
Huatenicamanes	Oaxaca (Zapotecas)		Crown Juan Antonio
Huatlavaca	Puebla	426	Crown
Huatulco	Oaxaca	316	Diego Gutiérrez
Huatusco	Vera Cruz	762	?
Huatusco-Santiago	Vera Cruz	102	Crown
Huatzpaltepec	Vera Cruz (Pánuco)		Hernán García
Huatzpaltepec	Vera Cruz (Coatzacoalcos)		Crown Jorge de Alvarado
Huauclilla	Oaxaca	818	?
Huautla	Oaxaca		?
Huautla	Vera Cruz (Pánuco)		Cristóbal de Frías
Huautla	?		Crown
Huautla	Oaxaca	177	Melchor de Castañón
Huautla	Oaxaca	136	Juan de Valdivieso
Huautla	Hidalgo	289	Cristóbal Bezos
Huayacocotla	Vera Cruz	229	Julián de la Loa Gómez de Alvarado

182 Population of Central Mexico

Huayatepec	Oaxaca (Zapotecas)		Díaz Carballar
Huayatepec	Oaxaca (Villa Alta)		Crown
Huaynamota	Nayarit	250	Juan de Arce
Huazalingo	Hidalgo	27	Gabriel de Aguilera
Huazamota	Nayarit		Gonzalo Martín
Huazcomaltepec	Oaxaca (Zapotecas)		Juan de Aracena
Huazulco	Morelos	124	Miguel de Solís
Hucitepec	Oaxaca (Mixe)		?
Huehuetlán	Puebla	424	Crown
Huehuetlán	Puebla	111	Juan de Carbajal
Huehuetlán	San Luis Potosí	663	Francisco Barrón
Huehuetoca	México	776	?
Huejotzingo	Puebla	599	Crown
Huejuca	México	233	Juan Cano
Huejúcar	Zacatecas	351	Toribio de Bolaños
Huejutla	Hidalgo	428	Crown
Hueoquilpa	Hidalgo (Teutlalpa)		Crown
Huestepec	Vera Cruz (Coatzacoalcos)		Luis Alvarez
Huestepec	Vera Cruz (Coatzacoalcos)		Gaspar de Hita
Huexotla	México	697	?
Hueyapa	?		Crown
Hueypoxtla	México	179	Antón Bravo / Dr. Frías
Hueytlalpan	Puebla	610	Crown
Hueytlán	Vera Cruz (Coatzacoalcos)		Crown
Hueytlán	Guerrero	584	Crown
Huichapan	Hidalgo	696	?
Huiltepec	Oaxaca	783	?
Huiramángaro	Michoacán	291	Juan Infante
Huitepec	Oaxaca	832	Crown
Huitlalotla	Guerrero	262	Crown / Diego Ruiz
Huitzila	Puebla	755	?

Appendix II: List of Communities 183

Huitzilapan	México	476	Crown
Huitziltepec	Guerrero	769	?
Huitzizilapan	México	843	Crown
Huixquilucan	México	611	Crown
Huixtac	Guerrero	555	Crown
Huiztlán	Guerrero	263	Ana de Porras
Huizuco	Guerrero	109	Bernardino de Casasola
Icapacingo	Vera Cruz		Crown
Icitecomal	Hidalgo (Teutlalpa)		Crown
Icoatlán	?		Crown
Icpatepec	Oaxaca		?
Iguala	Guerrero	436	Crown
Igualán	Guerrero	60	Crown Bernardino Vázquez de Tapia Beatriz de Estrada
Igualapa	Guerrero	138	Bernardino del Castillo
Igualtepec	Oaxaca	32	Francisco de Terrazas García de Aguilar
Igualtepec	Oaxaca	724	?
Ilamatlán	Vera Cruz	31	Juan de Cervantes
Indaparapeo	Michoacán	113	Gaspar Morcillo
Irechato	Michoacán	477	Crown
Itacatepec	Oaxaca (Chontales)		?
Ixcamilpa	Puebla	424	Crown
Ixcatán	Jalisco	391	Diego de Colio
Ixcateopan	Guerrero	557	Crown
Ixcatlán	Vera Cruz		Juan López de Ximena
Ixcatlán	Oaxaca	181	Rodrigo de Segura
Ixcatlán	Oaxaca	728	Melchor de Castañón
Ixcatoya	Oaxaca	182	Piérrez Gómez
Ixcocán	Oaxaca (Zapotecas)		Gonzalo Ximénez
Ixcuinquitlapilco	Hidalgo	612	Crown
Ixcuintepec	Oaxaca	685	Crown
Ixcuintepec-Santiago	Oaxaca	392	Juan de Aldaz

184 Population of Central Mexico

Ixhuatlán	Guerrero (Mochtitlán)		Crown
Ixhuatlán	Vera Cruz	537	Crown
Ixhuatlán	Vera Cruz (Tepetlaxco)	763	?
Ixiquitlán	Bish. of Tlaxcala		Francisco Velázquez de Lara
Ixmiquilpan	Hidalgo	183	Crown Gil González
Ixpuchtepec	Oaxaca	153	Francisca de la Cueva
Ixquilpa	Hidalgo (Teutlalpa)		?
Ixtacamaxtitlán	Pucbla	512	?
Ixtapa	Guerrero (Taxco)		Crown
Ixtapa	Guerrero	574	Crown
Ixtapa	Michoacán	576	Antón Sánchez
Ixtapa	Colima	633	Crown
Ixtapa	México	165	Gonzalo Gómez
Ixtapa	Nayarit	390	Juan de Villalba
Ixtapalapa	D. F.	699	Juan Martín de Cuellar
Ixtapaluca	D. F.	110	Same
Ixtatepec	Oaxaca (Mixteca)		Alonso Morcillo
Ixtayuca	Puebla	686	Rodrigo de Castañeda
Ixtayucan	Puebla	598	?
Ixtayutla	Oaxaca	556	Cristóbal López de Solís
Ixtepec	Oaxaca (Tututepec)		Luis de Castilla
Ixtepec	Oaxaca	435	Crown
Ixtepec	Puebla (Hueytlalpan)		?
Ixtepec	Vera Cruz	625	Crown
Ixtepexi	Oaxaca	325	Juan de Aragón
Ixtlahuaca	México	433	Crown
Ixtlahuacan	Colima	665	Crown
Ixtlán	Nueva Galicia		Sabina de Esquivel
Ixtlán	Jalisco		Francisco Cornejo
Ixtlán	Michoacán	852	Crown
Ixtlán de Juárez	Oaxaca	114	Alonso Martín Muñoz
Iztaro	Michoacán	503	Crown
Iztimiztique	Nayarit		Crown Alvaro de Bracamonte
Izúcar	Puebla	432	Crown

Appendix II: List of Communities 185

Jacona	Michoacán	481	Crown
Jala	Nayarit	399	Crown
			Alvaro de Bracamonte
Jalacingo	Vera Cruz	623	Crown
Jalahui	Oaxaca	749	?
Jalapa	Vera Cruz	844	Crown
Jalapa	Guerrero	480	Crown
Jalapa	Oaxaca	363	Juan Coronel
Jalapa	Vera Cruz	192	Macías Coronel
Jalapa	Oaxaca	76	Marqués del Valle
Jalcocotlán	Nayarit	397	Juan de Villalba
Jalcomulco	Vera Cruz	840	Crown
Jalisco	Nayarit	396	Cristóbal de Oñate
Jalpa	Zacatecas	328	Diego de Proaño
Jalpan	Puebla	753	?
Jalpan	Querétaro	364	Francisco Barrón
Jaltempa	Nayarit	398	Antón Pérez
Jaltepec	Oaxaca	483	Crown
Jaltepetongo	Oaxaca	184	Jerónimo de Salinas
Jaltianguis	Oaxaca	463	Crown
Jaltipan	Vera Cruz	256	Francisco Marín
Jamiltepec	Oaxaca	314	Luis de Castilla
Jantetelco	Morelos	671	Marqués del Valle
Japutica	Guerrero	269	Sebastián de Ebora
Jasso	Michoacán	656	Crown
Jasso(Xipacoya)	Hidalgo	71	Juan Jaso
Jerécuaro	Guanajuato	653	Juan Infante
Jicalán	Michoacán	548	Pedro de Villegas
Jicayán	Oaxaca	134	Crown
			Pedro Nieto
Jicayán	Oaxaca	140	Juan de Tovar
			Francisco Guillén
Jicotepec	Puebla	531	Crown
Jilotepec	Vera Cruz	758	Alonso de Castellanos
Jilotlán	Jalisco	479	Crown
Jiquilpan	Michoacán	482	Crown
Jocotepec	Jalisco	85	Crown
			Alonso de Avalos
Jocotipac	Oaxaca	90	Gonzalo de Robles

186 Population of Central Mexico

Jocotlán	Jalisco	118	?
Jojupango	Puebla	75	Diego de Villapadierna
			Gonzalo de Salazar
Jolalpan	Puebla	243	Gómez de Hoyos
Jolotepec	Oaxaca		
	(Zapotecas)		?
Jonacatepec	Morelos	667	Marqués del Valle
Jonacatlán	Puebla (Coxcatlán)		Martín de Olivares
Jonotla	Puebla	485	Crown
Jotlapa	Vera Cruz		
	(Coatzacoalcos)		Juan Martín
Juchipila	Zacatecas	334	Hernando Flores
Juchitán	Jalisco	333	Juan Miguel
Juchitlán	Guerrero	522	?
Juchitlán	Guerrero	551	Crown
Judío (Estancia del)	Jalisco		Hernando del Valle
Juluapan	Colima	645	Crown
Juluchuga	Guerrero	591	Crown
Jumiltepec	Morelos	231	Antonio Velázquez
Justepec	Oaxaca	448	Crown
Justlavaca	Oaxaca	154	Crown
			Tristán de Arellano
Jutlabuca	Bish. of Tlaxcala		Francisco Valadés
Lacoaba	Michoacán	561	Pedro Ruiz
Lachichivia	Oaxaca	827	Francisco de Tarifa
Laguancoyula	Guerrero		
	(Zacatula)		Francisco Castejón
Lahoya	Oaxaca		
	(Zapotecas)		Crown
Lalopa	Oaxaca	837	Crown
Lapaguia	Oaxaca	734	Juan Gallego
Lavaylalana	Oaxaca		
	(Zapotecas)		Crown
Las Laxas	Vera Cruz		
	(Pánuco)		Alonso García
Lazagaya	Oaxaca		
	(Zapotecas)		Francisco Franco

Appendix II: List of Communities 187

Lomatlán	Oaxaca (Zapotecas)		Crown
Macatlán	San Luis Potosí	296	Crown Francisco de Saldaña
Macolutla	Vera Cruz (Pánuco)		Crown
Macuiltianguis	Oaxaca	224	Juan Rodríguez de Salas
Macuilxcóhitl	Hidalgo	236	Juna Cano
Macuilxóchitl	Oaxaca	504	Crown
Macuyapa	Vera Cruz (Coatzacoalcos)		Crown
Madaxoya	Oaxaca (Mixes)		?
Mahuala	Colima		Martín Monjaraz
Malacatepec	México	46	Antonio de Avila
Malacatlán	Colima	640	Crown
Malila	Hidalgo	492	Crown
Malinalcingo	Vera Cruz	627	Crown
Malinalco	México	117	Crown Sebastián Rodríguez
Malinaltepec	Oaxaca		?
Malinaltepec	Oaxaca		Luis de Castilla
Malinaltepec	Oaxaca	189	Bartolomé Tofiño
Maloastla	Colima	650	Crown
Maltrata	Vera Cruz	505	Crown
Manalcatepec	Oaxaca		?
Maninaltepec	Oaxaca (Zapotecas)	687	Francisco de Aguilar
Maquili	Michoacán	790	?
Marabatío	Michoacán	297	Pedro Xuárez
Mascota	Jalisco	795	?
Matacticpac	Nayarit		Alonso de Castañeda
Matalcingo	Michoacán	823	Crown
Matatlán	Jalisco	525	Crown
Matatlán	Jalisco	488	Crown
Matitlán	Jalisco		Juan Delgado
Matlán	Nueva Galicia		Pedro de Santa Cruz Rodrigo Guipuzcoano
Matlaque	Puebla	75	Diego de Villapadierna Gonzalo de Salazar

188 Population of Central Mexico

Matlayac	Morelos (Jantetelco)		Marqués del Valle
Maxcala	Jalisco		Bartolomé García
Maxcaltepec	Oaxaca (Chontales)		Crown
Maxtlatlán	Vera Cruz (Naolingo)		Crown
Mayanala	Guerrero	225	Mateo Vázquez
Mazaltajola	Bish. of Tlaxcala		Gonzalo Rodríguez de Villafuerte
Mazatlán	Jalisco		Juan de Almesto
Mazatlán	Oaxaca	247	Alonso de Zamora
Mazatlán	Oaxaca	448	Crown
Mazatlán	Vera Cruz	255	Juan López Frías
Mazatlán	Jalisco	648	Francisco de Cifuentes
Mecatixpam	Colima	257	Ginesa López
Mecatlán	Nayarit	397	Juan de Villalba
Mecatlán	Puebla	174	Cristóbal de Maldonado
Mechinango	Nueva Galicia		Francisco de Estrada
Melagua	Jalisco (Purificación)		Melchor Alvarez
Metatepec	Vera Cruz	186	Pedro de Fuentes
Metepec	Oaxaca (Zapotecas)		Crown
Metepec	México	34	Juan de Altamirano
Metlaltepec	Oaxaca	743	?
Metlaltoyuca	Puebla	151	Crown
Metlapan	Michoacán	578	Crown
Metztitlán	Hidalgo	35	Francisco de Mérida Diego de Guevara
Mexcalcingo	Puebla	326	Andrés Dorantes
Mexcaloacan	Michoacán	571	Crown
Mexicalcingo	D. F.	613	Crown
México (City)	D. F.	601	Crown
Mexitlán	Oaxaca (Mixes)		Crown
Mexpan	Nueva Galicia		Alonso López
Mexquitlán	Guerrero	61	Crown Lorenzo de Porcallo
Mexticacán	Jalisco	327	Juan de Zubia

Appendix II: List of Communities

Meyana	Oaxaca (Zapotecas)		Alonso Díaz
Mezaa	Michoacán	265	Alonso Berdejo
Mezquitlán	Guerrero	614	Crown
Mezquituta	Zacatecas	329	Diego Orozco
Mezuntlán	Vera Cruz (Pánuco)		Pedro de Fuentes
Miahuatlán	Vera Cruz (Coatzacoalcos)		Crown
Miahuatlán	Vera Cruz (Coatzacoalcos)		Teresa Méndez
Miahuatlán	Jalisco	649	Pedro de Arévalo
Miahuatlán	Vera Cruz	717	Juan Valiente
Miahuatlán	Oaxaca	439	Crown
Miahuatlán	Oaxaca	22	Diego de Loaisa Mateo de Monjaraz
Michiapa	Oaxaca		?
Michimaloya	México	116	Alonso Velázquez
Michoacán	Vera Cruz (Coatzacoalcos)		Bernal Díaz del Castillo
Mila	Guerrero	266	Diego Correa
Milpa	Nueva Galicia		Pedro de Santa Cruz Rodrigo Guipuzcoano
Milpa Alta	D. F.	708	Crown
Milpazingo	Vera Cruz (Coatzacoalcos)		Catalina de Hita
Mimiapan	México	299	Catalina de Peralta
Minzapa	Vera Cruz	688	Gonzalo Rodríguez de Villafuerte Juan de España
Miquitla	Guerrero (Zacatula)		Crown
Misantla	Vera Cruz	626	Crown
Mispam	Colima		Martín Monjaraz
Mitepec	Puebla	689	Alonso García Bravo
Mitic	Jalisco	798	?
Mitla	Oaxaca	668	Crown
Mitla	Oaxaca	154	Tristán de Arellano
Mitlancingo	Guerrero	61	Crown Lorenzo de Porcallo

Population of Central Mexico

Mitlantongo	Oaxaca	188	Jerónimo Ruiz de la Mota
Mixquic	México	36	Gil Ramírez de Avalos
Mixtanejo	Colima	822	Juan Jiménez
Mixtepec	Oaxaca (Huautla)		?
Mixtepec	Oaxaca	312	Luis de Castilla
Mixtepec	Oaxaca	185	Juan Martínez
Mixtepec	Oaxaca	472	Melchor Juárez
Mixtlán	Jalisco	393	Crown
Mizcaoztoc	Vera Cruz (Río de Alvarado)		Hernán Ruiz de la Peña Antón Martín Breva
Mizquiahuala	Hidalgo	230	Crown
Mizquitlán	Nueva Galicia		Pablo de Retamales Juan Sánchez
Moctún	Oaxaca	740	?
Mochtitlán	Guerrero	767	?
Molango	Hidalgo	437	Crown
Maloacan	Vera Cruz	281	Crown
Moltepec	Oaxaca (Mixteca)		?
Momax	Zacatecas	351	Toribio de Bolaños
Monzapa	Vera Cruz	255	Juan López Frías
Moxuma	Jalisco	647	Crown
Moyahua	Zacatecas	329	Diego Orozco
Moyutla	Vera Cruz	369	María de Saldaña
Mutzantla	Michoacán		?
Nanacatepec	Oaxaca (Mixteca)		Melchor de San Miguel
Nanacatepec	Oaxaca (Zapotecas)		Crown
Nanahuatla	Vera Cruz (Pánuco)		Crown
Nanahuatlán	Vera Cruz (Pánuco)		Joanes de Aspetia
Nanatiquipac	Oaxaca	177	Melchor de Castañón
Nanauticpac	Oaxaca		Juan Navarro
Naolingo	Vera Cruz	627	Crown
Naopala	Colima		Martín Ruiz de Monjaraz
Naranja	Michoacán	19	Juan Infante

Appendix II: List of Communities

Nauzontla	Puebla	757	?
Necotepec	Oaxaca	153	Francisco de la Cueva
Necotlán	Michoacán		Crown
Necoxtla	Puebla	486	Crown
Nejapa	Oaxaca	441	Crown
Nexpa	Hidalgo	394	Alonso Navarrete
Nexpa	Guerrero	298	Gutierre de Badajoz
Nexpa	Michoacán	562	Crown
Nextepec	Oaxaca (Mixteca)		Crown
Nextlalpan	México	37	Pedro de Moreno
			Juan Galindo
Nexuca	Guerrero		
	(Zacatula)		Crown
Nobaan	Oaxaca (Mixes)		?
Nochistlán	Jalisco		
	(Guadalajara)		Crown
Nochistlán	Oaxaca	440	Crown
Nochistlán	Zacatecas	438	Crown
Nopala	Oaxaca	57	Luis de Castilla
Nopalucan	Puebla	690	Crown
Noxtepe	Guerrero	193	Juan de Cabra
Nuxco	Guerrero	592	Crown
Oapan	Guerrero	39	Martín de Ircio
Oaxaca (Villa)	Oaxaca	30	Marqués del Valle
Oaxaca Viejo	Oaxaca	223	Crown
			Juan de Arriaga
Oaxtepec	Morelos	228	Marqués del Valle
Ocelotepec	Vera Cruz		
	(Coatzacoalcos)		Crown
Ociloaque	?		Agustina de Meneses
Oconahua	Jalisco	559	Crown
Ocotepec	Oaxaca	736	?
Ocotepec	Oaxaca	144	Diego Gutiérrez
Ocotepec	Oaxaca	145	Juan Bautista
Ocotic	Jalisco	331	Andrés de Villanueva
Ocotlán	Colima		Juan Fernández
Ocotlán	Puebla	424	Crown
Ocotlán	Oaxaca	40	Pedro Zamorano

Ocotlán	Oaxaca	442	Crown
Ocotlán	Jalisco	330	Alonso Martín
Ocucuapa	Vera Cruz (Coatzacoalcos)		Crown
Ocuilan	México	190	Pedro Zamorano Antonio de Torre
Ocuituco	Morelos	506	Crown
Ojitipa	San Luis Potosí	550	Francisco Barrón
Ojitlán	Oaxaca	558	Crown
Olinalá	Guerrero	191	Baltasar de Aguilar
Olintepec	Oaxaca	153	Francisca de la Cueva
Oluta	Vera Cruz	256	Francisco Marín
Ometepec	Guerrero	138	Francisco de Herrera Bernardino del Castillo
Opono	Jalisco (Purificación)		Crown
Oquilabuhe	Oaxaca (Zapotecas)		Crown
Orita	Nueva Galicia		Juan Durán
Orizaba	Vera Cruz	192	Macías Coronel
Ostopa	Vera Cruz (Coatzacoalcos)		Crown
Ostuacán	Vera Cruz (Coatzacoalcos)		Crown
Ostula	Michoacán	819	Rodrigo Devia
Ostuma	Guerrero	227	Juan de Aguila
Otlatitlán	Vera Cruz	248	Juan de Limpias
Otomitlán	Nueva Galicia		Pedro Ruiz de Haro
Otumba	México	615	Crown
Otzolotepec	México	299	Alonso de Villanueva
Otzolotepec	Puebla	106	Agustín de Villanueva
Oxtotipac	México	288	Juan Velázquez Rodríguez
Oxtutla	Guerrero	61	Crown Lorenzo de Porcallo
Ozolotepec	Oaxaca	120	Alonso Ruiz Portero
Ozpicha	Vera Cruz		Crown
Oztatlahuauca	Hidalgo		?
Oztoticpac	Nueva Galicia		Andrés Lorenzo
Ozuluama	Vera Cruz	369	María de Saldaña
Ozumacintla	Vera Cruz		Juan de Miranda

Appendix II: List of Communities 193

Pachuca	Hidalgo	121	Antonio de la Cadena
Pahuatlán	Puebla	149	Luis de la Torre
Pajacuarán	Michoacán	507	Crown
Pampuchín	Jalisco (Purificación)		Diego Téllez
Pamutla	Guerrero	594	Crown
Pangololutla	Bish. of Tlaxcala		Gonzalo Ruiz de Villafuerte
Pantepec	Puebla	337	?
Pantla	Guerrero	573	Crown
Pánuco (Villa)	Vera Cruz	802	Crown
Papalotepec	Oaxaca	443	Crown
Papalocticpa	Puebla	41	Juan de la Torre
Papalutla	Guerrero	61	Crown Lorenzo de Porcallo
Papalutla	Guerrero	191	Baltasar de Aguilar
Papantla	Vera Cruz	194	Andrés de Tapia
Paquelán	San Luis Potosí		Pero Hernández
Patanala	Oaxaca		?
Pátzcuaro	Michoacán	332	Juan Infante
Pauhela	Jalisco (Purificación)		Juan de Castañeda
Paxalo	Guerrero	586	Crown
Paxosnan	Oaxaca (Mixes)		?
Paxtlahuaca	Oaxaca		?
Pazulco	Morelos	5	Marqués del Valle
Pazoltepec	Oaxaca (Zapotecas)		Crown
Pecalcatepec	Oaxaca		Crown
Pechucalco	Vera Cruz (Coatzacoalcos)		Bartolomé Sánchez
Penjema	Jalisco	647	Crown
Peñoles	Oaxaca	632	Crown
Peribán	Michoacán	147	Francisco de Chaves
Petatlán	Guerrero	589	Crown
Petatlán	Colima	258	Hernando de Gamboa
Petlacala	Oaxaca	300	Bernardino Vázquez de Tapia Crown Beatriz de Estrada

Petlacaltepec	Oaxaca		
	(Chontales)		Pedro Martín de Coria
Petlalcingo	Puebla	766	Santos Hernández
Petlaquistlavaca	Oaxaca		Francisco de Alavés
Petlayuneca	Colima	638	Crown
Piaxtla	Vera Cruz		
	(Pánuco)		Crown
Piaxtla	Puebla	137	Crown
			Francisco de Olmos
Pichátoro	Michoacán	291	Juan Infante
Pichique	Guerrero	579	Crown
Pilcintepec	Oaxaca	734	Juan Gallego
Piloto	Jalisco		
	(Purificación)		?
Piltlán	Guerrero		
	(Zacatula)		Crown
Pinotepa	Oaxaca	560	Crown
Piquitla	Michoacán	577	Crown
Piroma	Colima		Juan Fernández
Pizcaya	Guerrero	771	?
Pochotitlán	Guerrero	532	Crown
Pochutla	Oaxaca	511	Crown
Pómaro	Michoacán	508	Crown
Pomayagua	Colima		Juan Guriezo
Pomucuarán	Michoacán	195	Juan Infante
Poncitlán	Jalisco	497	Crown
Pontoque	Nayarit		Juan Durán
Popoyutla	Colima		Juan de Almesto
Potuctla	Oaxaca		
	(Costa del Sur)		Crown
Puctla	Vera Cruz		
	(Río de Alvarado)		?
Puctla	Oaxaca	196	Antonio Asnal
Puctla	Puebla	686	Rodrigo de Castañeda
Puchititlán	Colima		Crown
Puchutlán	Guerrero	267	Francisco Gutiérrez
Puebla	Puebla	693	Crown
Pungarabato	Guerrero	197	Hernando de Bazán
Purenxícuaro	Michoacán	332	Juan Infante

Appendix II: List of Communities 195

Puruándiro	Michoacán	290	Juan de Villaseñor
Puscatlán	Vera Cruz (Coatzacoalcos)		Crown
Pusenquia	Michoacán		Crown
Pustlán	Bish. of Tlaxcala		Crown
Pustlán	Guerrero	581	Crown
Putlancingo	Oaxaca	630	Crown
Quecholac	Puebla	100	Pedro de Villanueva Antón Rodríguez de la Madalena
Quetzalcoatl	Vera Cruz (Costa del Norte)		Crown
Quezala	México	173	Juan Enríquez Magariño
Quezalapa	Oaxaca	788	Diego de Leiva
Quezalapa	Oaxaca (Zapotecas)		Crown
Quezalapa	Colima	509	Crown
Quezalatengo	Hidalgo	35	Francisco de Mérida Diego de Guevara
Quezaltepec	Vera Cruz (Coatzacoalcos)		Luis Alvarez
Quimixtlán	Puebla	107	Crown
Quiotepec	Oaxaca	444	Crown
Quitatán	Vera Cruz (Coatzacoalcos)		Crown
Quitepec	Oaxaca (Mixteca)		?
La Rinconada (Ixcalpa)	Puebla	112	Marqués del Valle
Río Hondo	Oaxaca	733	Diego de Loaisa Mateo de Monjaraz
Sahuayo	Michoacán	850	Crown
Salipa	Jalisco	647	Crown
San Juan de Ulúa	Vera Cruz	760	?
San Miguel el Grande (Ixcatlán)	Oaxaca	735	?

San Miguel	Guanajuato	538	Crown
San Pedro	San Luis Potosí	800	?
Santa Cruz	Oaxaca (Zapotecas)		?
Sayula	Jalisco	79	Crown Alonso de Avalos
Sayula	Hidalgo	502	Crown
El Seco (San Salvador)	Puebla	698	?
Sentispac	Nayarit	534	Crown
Serandaguacho	Michoacán	332	Juan Infante
Sevina	Michoacán	752	Juan Infante
Sihuatlán	Jalisco	420	Crown
Silacayoapan	Oaxaca	713	?
Sirosto	Michoacán	18	Francisco de Villegas
Soacango	México	219	Alonso de la Serna
Sococho	Oaxaca (Zapotecas)		Juan Martínez
Sola	Oaxaca	23	Ramón López
Sosola	Oaxaca	105	Sebastián de Grijalva
Soyaltepec	Oaxaca	631	Crown
Soyaltepec	Oaxaca	490	Crown
Soyanaquilpan	México	241	Juan Bautista Marín
Suchiopan	Oaxaca		Luis de Castilla
Suchipil	Nayarit	381	Crown Alvaro de Bracamonte
Suchiquizala	Oaxaca	32	Francisco de Terrazas García de Aguilar
Suchitatlán	Vera Cruz (Coatzacoalcos)		Gaspar de Hita
Suchitepec	Oaxaca (Zapotecas)		Díaz Carballar
Suchitepec	Oaxaca (Zapotecas)		Crown
Suchitepec	Oaxaca	22	Mateo de Monjaraz Diego de Loaisa
Suchitepec	Oaxaca	316	Diego Gutiérrez
Suchitepec	Oaxaca	200	García de Contreras Juan de Valdivieso

Appendix II: List of Communities 197

Suchitonalá	Guerrero	88	Crown
Suchixtepec	Oaxaca	180	Juan de Morales
Sultepec	Tlaxcala	96	Francisco Calvo
Tacacala	Michoacán		?
Tacámbaro	Michoacán	132	Cristóbal de Oñate
Tacatepec	?		Crown
Tacoltapa	Vera Cruz (Coatzacoalcos)		Alonso García
Tacuázcuaro	Michoacán	467	Crown
Tacuba	D. F.	43	Juan Cano
Tacubaya	D. F.	95	Marqués del Valle
Taculilla	Vera Cruz (Pánuco)		Crown
Taetz	Oaxaca (Mixes)		?
Tagni	Oaxaca	838	Crown
Tala	Jalisco	359	Juan Sánchez Olea
Talchicua	Hidalgo	238	Francisco de Torres
Talea	Oaxaca	527	Crown
Talhuacpa	Hidalgo		Crown
Talistaca	Oaxaca	544	Crown
Talistaca	México	49	Juan Velázquez Rodríguez Ramiro de Arellano
Tamacasapa	Guerrero	468	Crown
Tamacolite	San Luis Potosí		Crown
Tamacuiche	San Luis Potosí		Diego de Castañeda
Tamacuil	Vera Cruz (Pánuco)		Cristóbal de Frías
Tamahol	San Luis Potosí		Gonzalo Bernal
Tamaholipa	San Luis Potosí		Crown
Tamahu	San Luis Potosí		Antonio González
Tamala	Colima	635	Crown
Tamalaguaco	San Luis Potosí		Diego de Rivera
Tamalocuco	Vera Cruz (Pánuco)		Lázaro Martín
Tamalol	San Luis Potosí(?)		Rodrigo de Navarrete
Tamalol	Vera Cruz	160	Benito de Cuenca
Tamamolo	Vera Cruz	627	Crown
Tamandagapeo	Michoacán	481	Crown

Tamante	Vera Cruz (Pánuco)		Francisco Corzo
Tamasulapa	Oaxaca	69	Luis Xuárez
Tamatao	Vera Cruz (Pánuco)		Juan Muñoz de Zayas
Tamateque	Vera Cruz (Pánuco)		Crown
Tamazola	Oaxaca	200	García de Contreras Juan de Valdivieso
Tamazula	Jalisco	459	Crown
Tamazunchale	Vera Cruz (Pánuco)		Juan Acedo
Tamazunchale	San Luis Potosí	143	Juan de Cervantes
Tamecí	San Luis Potosí		Benito el Negro
Tamiahua	Vera Cruz	395	Juan de Villagómez
Tamiutla	Vera Cruz (Pánuco)		Crown
Tamole	Vera Cruz (Pánuco)		Benito de Cuenca
Tamontao	Vera Cruz (Pánuco)		Crown
Tamos	Vera Cruz (Pánuco)		Francisco Corzo
Tampacal	Vera Cruz (Pánuco)		Juan Rodríguez
Tampacayal	Vera Cruz (Pánuco)		Diego de Torres
Tampalache	Vera Cruz (Pánuco)		Alonso Ginovés
Tampamolón	San Luis Potosí	366	Francisco Barrón
Tampayal	San Luis Potosí		Gonzalo Bernal
Tampico	Vera Cruz	521	Crown
Tamposque	San Luis Potosí		Pero Hernández
Tampuche	Vera Cruz (Pánuco)		Cristóbal de Frías
Tampucho	San Luis Potosí		Juan Gallegos
Tampulen	Vera Cruz (Pánuco)		Crown
Tamu	Vera Cruz (Pánuco)		Martín de San Juan

Appendix II: List of Communities 199

Tamuín	San Luis Potosí	526	Crown
Tanátaro	Michoacán		Diego de Ma
Tanatepec	Oaxaca		?
Tancamalnonco	San Luis Potosí		Hernán García
Tancanhuitz	San Luis Potosí	803	Juan el Negro
Tancaxan	San Luis Potosí		Francisco Barrón
Tancaxual	San Luis Potosí		Antonio Paita
Tancazneque	Vera Cruz (Pánuco)		Telmo de Maeda
Tancelete	Vera Cruz (Pánuco)		Juan Romero
Tancetuco	Vera Cruz (Pánuco)		Juan de Busto
Tancítaro	Michoacán	65	Crown Domingo de Medina
Tancojol	San Luis Potosí		Francisco Barrón
Tancolón	San Luis Potosí		Francisco Barrón
Tancolul	Vera Cruz (Pánuco)		Francisco de las Roelas
Tancoxual	San Luis Potosí		Jorge Vela
Tancoyol	Querétaro	365	Francisco Barrón
Tancuayalab	San Luis Potosí	368	Licenciado Alemán
Tancuche	Vera Cruz (Pánuco)		Crown
Tancuiname	Vera Cruz (Pánuco)		Crown
Tancuy	San Luis Potosí		Ana Vázquez
Tanchaba	San Luis Potosí		Diego de Castañeda
Tanchicuy	Vera Cruz (Pánuco)		Alonso Ginovés
Tanchicuy	Vera Cruz (Pánuco)		Crown
Tanchilabe	San Luis Potosí		Crown
Tanchinamol	Vera Cruz (Pánuco)		Crown
Tanchipa	San Luis Potosí		Cristóbal Maldonado
Tanchipa	San Luis Potosí		Antonio González Alvaro de Rivera
Tanchoy	Vera Cruz (Pánuco)		Crown

200 Population of Central Mexico

Tangamandapio	Michoacán	853	Crown
Tanguatepec	Vera Cruz (Coatzacoalcos)		Teresa Méndez
Tanhuizín	Vera Cruz (Pánuco)		Juan de Villanueva
Tanistla	Vera Cruz (Pánuco)		Licenciado Alemán
Tanlocuque	San Luis Potosí		Alvaro de Rivera
Tanquián	San Luis Potosí	264 ?	
Tanta	Vera Cruz (Pánuco)		Alonso Audelo
Tantala	Vera Cruz (Pánuco)		Diego de Torres
Tantamol	Vera Cruz (Pánuco)		Gonzalo de Avila
Tantay	San Luis Potosí		Antonio González
Tantohox	San Luis Potosí		Pero Hernández
Tantoilán	San Luis Potosí		Pero Hernández
Tantoín	San Luis Potosí		Francisco Barrón
Tantolón	San Luis Potosí		Hernán García
Tantoyeque	Vera Cruz (Pánuco)		Melchor Rodríguez
Tantoyetla	Vera Cruz (Pánuco)		Cristóbal de la Cuesta
Tantoyuca	Vera Cruz	186	Pedro de Fuentes
Tantoyuca	San Luis Potosí		Camacho
Tantui	Vera Cruz (Pánuco)		Juan de Villanueva
Tantuana	San Luis Potosí		Catalina de Herrera
Tanxohol	Vera Cruz (Pánuco)		Juan Acedo
Tanzacana	San Luis Potosí		Teodor Griego
Tanzacuila	Vera Cruz (Pánuco)		Vicencio Corzo
Tanzonomoco	San Luis Potosí		Camacho
Tanzui	Vera Cruz (Pánuco)		Juan de Villanueva
Tanzulupe	Vera Cruz (Pánuco)		Juan Sánchez

Appendix II: List of Communities 201

Tanzumonoco	San Luis Potosí		Pero Hernández
Tapacoya	Vera Cruz	627	Crown
Tapalán	Vera Cruz (Coatzacoalcos)		Crown
Los Taquilpas	Vera Cruz (Coatzacoalcos)		Crown
Tarecuato	Michoacán	307	Francisco de Chaves
Tarímbaro	Michoacán	67	Diego Arias Sotelo
Tataltepec	Oaxaca	780	?
Tatetla	Puebla	655	Crown
Tauzán	Hidalgo	394	Alonso de Navarrete
Tava	Oaxaca (Mixes)		?
Taveluca	?		Crown
Taxco	Guerrero	468	Crown
Taxicui	San Luis Potosí		Alonso de Alvarado
Taximaroa	Michoacán	66	Juan Velázquez de Salazar
Taymeo	Michoacán	201	Crown
			Pedro de Avila
Teacalco	México	335	Caciques of México
Tecajec	Morelos	5	Marqués del Valle
Tecali	Puebla	205	Josepe de Orduña
Tecama	México	303	Juan Ponce de León
Tecamachalco	Puebla	59	Alonso Valiente
Tecaxic	Oaxaca		Crown
Tecayuca	Vera Cruz		Crown
Tecianzacualco	Oaxaca (Mixes)		?
Tecoautla	Vera Cruz		Crown
Tecociapa	Colima	344	Juan Pinzón
Tecociapa	Colima	257	Ginesa López
Tecocitlán	Colima	346	Jorge Carrillo
Tecolapa	Colima	347	Juan Martel
Tecoloapan	México	206	Luisa de Estrada
Tecolotlán	Jalisco	339	Martín Monje
			Pero Gómez
Tecomaltepec	Oaxaca	788	Diego de Leiva
Tecomán	Colima	520	Crown
Tecomatlán	Nayarit		Cristóbal de Oñate
Tecomatlán	Jalisco	393	Crown
			Hernán Ruiz de la Peña

Tecomatlán	Guerrero	575	Crown
Tecomavaca	Oaxaca	447	Crown
Tecomaxtlavaca	Oaxaca	154	Tristán de Luna
Tecoxquines	Nayarit		Luis Alonso
Tecpa	Oaxaca (Chontales)		?
Tecpan	Guerrero	595	Alonso de Vargas
Tecualtitlán	Jalisco	799	?
Tecuxuacán	Colima	343	Francisco de Cifuentes
Techalutla	Jalisco	81	Crown
Tehuacán	Puebla	209	Alonso de Avalos Crown Antonio Ruiz de Castañeda
Tehuantepec	Oaxaca	210	Marqués del Valle
Tehuastepec	Oaxaca (Mixteca)		Melchor de San Miguel
Tehuilotepec	Oaxaca (Zapotecas)		León Sánchez
Teiticpac	Oaxaca	829	Crown
Teiticpac	Oaxaca	830	Crown
Tejaluca	Puebla	450	Crown
Tejupan	Oaxaca	465	Crown
Telecuen	San Luis Potosí		Alvaro de Rivera
Telistac	Morelos	674	Marqués del Valle
Telitlazingo	Puebla	698	?
Teloloapan	Guerrero	454	Crown
Temalacazingo	Guerrero	61	Crown Lorenzo de Porcallo
Temalhuacán	Guerrero	585	Francisco Salcedo
Temacatepán	Colima	345	Juan Pinzón
Temapache	San Luis Potosí	367	Diego de Castañeda
Temascalapa	Oaxaca	747	Alonso Cano
Temascaltepec	Oaxaca	313	Luis de Castilla
Temascaltepec	México	129	Francisco de Chaves
Temaxcalapa	México	768	Jerónimo de Medina
Temoac	Morelos	813	Marqués del Valle
Temoac	Morelos	124	Miguel de Solís
Tempoal	Vera Cruz	212	Isabel de Escobar
Tenacusco	Vera Cruz (Pánuco)		Rodrigo Bezos

Appendix II: List of Communities 203

Tenamaxtlán	Jalisco	339	Martín Monje
			Pero Gómez
Tenampulco	Puebla	131	Diego de Valadés
Tenancingo	Guerrero	61	Crown
			Lorenzo de Porcallo
Tenancingo	México	97	Pedro de Salcedo
Tenango	Vera Cruz		Francisco de Rosales
Tenango del Valle	México	53	Crown
			Bernardino de Bocanegra
Tenango	Hidalgo	35	Francisco de Mérida
			Diego de Guevara
Tenango	Guerrero	515	Crown
Tenango del Aire	México	423	Crown
Tenango	Oaxaca	374	Francisco de Rosales
Tenango-Tepexi	Guerrero	309	Crown
			Bernardino Vázquez de Tapia
			Beatriz de Estrada
Tenantitlán	Vera Cruz (Coatzacoalcos)		Crown
Tenayuca	D. F.	528	Crown
Tene	Jalisco (Purificación)		Iñigo Ortiz de Zúñiga
Tenixtepec	Vera Cruz	549	Juan de Villagómez
Tenexpa	Oaxaca	785	Gil de Robles
Teocaltiche	Jalisco	797	?
Teococuilco	Oaxaca	463	Crown
Teocuitatlán	Jalisco	82	Crown
			Alonso de Avalos
Teoloyucan	México	778	?
Teopantlán	Puebla	244	Crown
			Alonso González
Teotalcingo	Oaxaca	310	Crown
			Francisco Franco
Teotalco	Vera Cruz (Coatzacoalcos)		Luis Alvarez
Teotihuacán	México	42	Alonso de Bazán
Teotitlán del Camino	Oaxaca	448	Crown

Teotitlán del Valle	Oaxaca	504	Crown
Teotlalcingo	Puebla	846	?
Teotlalco	Puebla	216	Crown
Teotlalpa	Hidalgo		Ruy González Crown
Teotlaxco	Oaxaca	471	Crown
Teozacualco	Oaxaca	318	Crown
Teozapotlán	Oaxaca	523	Juan Ochoa de Lexalde Crown
Teozatlán	Oaxaca	249	Martín de Peralta
Tepalcatepec	Michoacán	616	Crown
Tepaltzingo	Morelos	672	Marqués del Valle
Tepanco	Puebla	547	?
Tepantepec	Bish. of Tlaxcala		Crown
Tepanzacualco	Oaxaca	371	Alvaro Manzano
Tepapayeca	Puebla	63	Jorge de Alvarado
Tepatepec	Hidalgo	514	Crown
Tepatitlán	Nayarit	353	Juan Pascal
Tepeaca	Puebla	452	Crown
Tepeapa	Oaxaca	630	Crown
Tepeapulco	Hidalgo	652	Crown
Tepec	Jalisco	338	Crown
Tepecicoapan	Bish. of Tlaxcala		Alonso de Avalos Andrés Tello
Tepecuacuilco	Guerrero	213	Luis de Godoy
Tepécuaro	Guanajuato	538	Crown
Tepechitlán	Zacatecas	352	Francisco de Bobadilla
Tepehuacán	Michoacán	147	Francisco de Chaves
Tepehuacán	Nayarit	353	Juan Pascal
Tepehuacán	Colima	348	Mateo Sánchez
Tepehuapa	Nayarit		Pero Ruiz
Tepeitic	Hidalgo	514	Crown
Tepeji	Oaxaca	848	Juan Bosque
Tepemachalco	México	34	Juan Altamirano
Tepeojuma	Puebla	62	Martín de Calahorra
Tepequecagualco	Oaxaca (Zapotecas)		Alvaro Manzano
Teptichán	Nueva Galicia		Francisco de Bobadilla

Appendix II: List of Communities 205

Tepitango	Colima	519	Crown
Tepetitlán	Hidalgo	232	Bartolomé Gómez
Tepetlahuaca	Nayarit	357	Cristóbal de Oñate
			Diego de Villegas
Tepetlán	Vera Cruz	716	?
Tepetlaoxtoc	México	127	Juan Velázquez de Salazar
Tepetlaxco	Vera Cruz	763	?
Tepetlolutla	Oaxaca	68	Francisco de Reinoso
Tepeucila	Oaxaca	530	Crown
Tepexco	Puebla	675	Crown
Tepexi	Puebla	566	Crown
Tepexi	Oaxaca	472	Melchor Juárez
Tepexi del Río	México	123	Juan de Moscoso
Tepexistepec	Oaxaca	153	Francisco de la Cueva
Tepexoxuca	México	233	Juan Cano
Tepexpan	México	50	Juan Baeza de Herrera
Tepezimatlán	Oaxaca	421	Crown
Tepic	Nayarit	524	Crown
Tepitongo	Oaxaca	745	?
Teponahuasco	Jalisco	349	Diego Velázquez
Teposcolula	Oaxaca	464	Crown
Tepotzotlán	México	617	Crown
Tepozotlán	Vera Cruz		
	(Coatzacoalcos)		Crown
Tepoztlán	Morelos	142	Marqués del Valle
Tepuxtepec	Oaxaca	831	?
Tepuzhuacán	Nayarit	356	Alvaro de Bracamonte
Tequecistepec	Oaxaca		Luis de Castilla
Tequepa	Colima	518	Crown
Tequepaca	Jalisco	361	Cristóbal Romero
Tequepespan	Nayarit	354	Juan de Samaniego
Tequepila	Jalisco	647	Crown
Tequepila	Bish. of Tlaxcala		Pedro de Meneses
Tequila	Jalisco	791	Crown
Tequila	Vera Cruz	449	Crown
Tequilanacoya	Oaxaca		Marqués del Valle
Tequisistlán	México	51	Crown
			Juan de Tovar
Tequistepec	Puebla	16	Gaspar de Garnica
			Francisco de Montaño

206 Population of Central Mexico

Tequistepec	Vera Cruz	256	Francisco Marín
Tequixistlán	Oaxaca	311	María Ramírez
Tequixquiac	México	44	Martín López
			Gonzalo Portillo
Tequixtepec	Oaxaca	373	Melchor de San Miguel
Tequixtepec	Oaxaca	618	Crown
Teremendo	Michoacán	656	Crown
Tescalco	Michoacán	214	Gonzalo de Avalos
Tesixtán	Jalisco	360	Cristóbal Romero
Tetela	Puebla	235	María Escudero
Tetela del Río	Guerrero	215	Francisco Rodríguez de Guadalcanal
Tetela de Ocampo	Puebla	461	Crown
Tetela	Morelos	681	Marqués del Valle
Tetepango	Hidalgo	456	Crown
Tetepec	Oaxaca	317	Crown
			Pedro Nieto
Teteuque	Zacatecas		Andrés de Villanueva
Tetipac	Guerrero	226	Juan de la Peña Vallejo
Tetitlán	Jalisco (Purificación)		Antonio de Aguayo
Tetitlán	Nayarit	355	Juan de Samaniego
Tetlán	Jalisco	659	Crown
Teul	Zacatecas	350	Juan Delgado
Teutila	Oaxaca	473	Crown
Teutitlán	Colima		Crown
Teutlán	Jalisco	516	Crown
Texaquique	México	208	Juan de Olivera
Texcala	Morelos	5	Marqués del Valle
Texcaltitlán	México	129	Francisco de Chaves
Texcatepec	Hidalgo	55	Cristóbal Cabezón
			Juan de Estrada
Texcoco	México	475	Crown
Texhuacán	Vera Cruz	294	Francisco de Reinoso
Texmelucán	Puebla	814	?
Texupexpa	Vera Cruz (Pánuco)		Crown
Texupilco	México	129	Francisco de Chaves

Appendix II: List of Communities

Tezapotitlán	Hidalgo (Huasteca)		Crown
Texhuatlán	Oaxaca		Beatriz de Zayas
Teziutlán	Puebla	654	Crown
Tezontepec	Hidalgo	336	Baltasar de Obregón
Tezontepec	Hidalgo	130	Alonso Pérez
Tezontlán	Jalisco		Jorge Carrillo
Tianguistengo	Hidalgo	52	Francisco de Tremiño
Ticatepque	Oaxaca (Zapotecas)		Pedro Durán
Tilapa	Puebla	453	Crown
Tilcuautla	Hidalgo	775	Cristóbal Cabezón
Tiltepec	Oaxaca	370	Crown Alonso de Ojeda
Tiltepec	Oaxaca	184	Jerónimo de Salinas
Tilzapuapa	Vera Cruz (Coatzacoalcos)		Crown
Timichoc	Nayarit		Alonso Rodríguez
Tingüindín	Michoacán	467	Crown
Tintococ	Nayarit		Alonso Alvarez
Tiquini	Oaxaca (Zapotecas)		?
Tiquipa	Oaxaca (Huatulco)		Crown
Tiquiquipa	Vera Cruz	256	Francisco Marín
Tiripitío	Michoacán	306	Juan de Alvarado
Tisupan	Michoacán	545	Crown
Titicapa	Oaxaca	542	Crown
Titontepec	Oaxaca (Zapotecas)		Crown
Tixtla	Guerrero	64	Martín de Ircio
Tizatepec	Oaxaca		Juan Gallego
Tizayuca	Hidalgo	125	Crown Alonso Pérez de Zamora
Tlacachique	Hidalgo		?
Tlacamama	Oaxaca	207	Alvaro de Santa Cruz
Tlacavanas	Michoacán	637	Crown
Tlacintla	Hidalgo	183	Crown Gil González

208 *Population of Central Mexico*

Tlacochahuayl	Oaxaca	340	Rodrigo Pacheco
Tlacolapacoya	Oaxaca (Zapotecas)	?	
Tlacola	Oaxaca (Center)	?	
Tlacoloaxtla	Colima	341	Francisco Santos
Tlacolula	Oaxaca	462	Crown
Tlacolula	Vera Cruz	715	Crown
Tlacolula	Vera Cruz (Pánuco)		Juan de Busto
Tlacolula	San Luis Potosí	?	
Tlacolula	Guerrero	298	Gutierre de Badajoz
Tlacolultepec	Puebla	41	Juan de la Torre
Tlacotalpan	Vera Cruz	628	Crown
Tlacotán	Jalisco	362	Juan de Zaldívar
Tlacotepec	Oaxaca	848	Juan Bosque
Tlacotepec	Guerrero	446	?
Tlacotepec	México	54	Alonso de la Serna
			Gaspar de Garnica
Tlacotepec	México	173	Juan Enríquez Magariño
Tlacotepec	Morelos	124	Miguel de Solís
Tlacotepec	Oaxaca	319	Francisco Vázquez
Tlacotepec	Oaxaca	472	Melchor Juárez
Tlacotepec	Puebla	761	Crown
Tlacotlapilco	Hidalgo	457	Crown
Tlacozautitlán	Guerrero	61	Crown
			Lorenzo de Porcallo
Tlacuatzintepec	Oaxaca	788	Diego de Leiva
Tlacuilotepec	Puebla	128	Juan de la Torre
Tlacuiltenango	Morelos	709	?
Tlacustepec	Hidalgo	402	Crown
Tlachichilpa	México	46	Antonio de Avila
Tlachinola	Guerrero	60	Crown
			Bernardino Vázquez de Tapia
			Beatriz de Estrada
Tlahuelilpa	Hidalgo	460	Crown
Tlahuilotepec	Oaxaca	741	Juan Gómez
Tlajomulco	Jalisco	660	Crown
Tlaliscoyán	Vera Cruz	712	Crown

Tlalnepantla	México	666	Angel de Villafañe
Tlaltenango	Zacatecas	351	Toribio de Bolaños
Tlamaco	Hidalgo	122	Jerónimo Tría
Tlamanalco	México	423	Crown
Tlanacopán	Hidalgo	240	Gaspar Juárez
Tlanalapa	México	49	Juan Velázquez Rodríguez Ramiro de Arrellano
Tlanchinol	Hidalgo	47	Alonso Ortiz de Zúñiga Jerónimo de Medina
Tlapa	Guerrero	60	Crown Bernardino Vázquez de Tapia Beatriz de Estrada
Tlapacoya	Vera Cruz		?
Tlapahuautla	Vera Cruz (Pánuco)		Francisco de Torres
Tlapalcatepec	Oaxaca (Mixes)		Crown
Tlapanala	Oaxaca (Zapotecas)		Bartolomé de Alcántara
Tlapanaloyan	México	305	Lope Vázquez de Acuña
Tlapancingo	Oaxaca	847	?
Tlapaxala	Puebla	606	?
Tlapotongo	Puebla	603	Jorge González
Tlapuma	Jalisco (Purificación)		Crown
Tlaquepaque	Jalisco	657	Crown
Tlaquilpa	Hidalgo	293	Manuel y Diego Téllez
Tlateca	Vera Cruz		Juan de Miranda
Tlatlatetelco	Vera Cruz (Río de Alvarado)		Juan Velázquez Rodríguez Ramiro de Arellano
Tlatlauquitepec	Puebla	451	Crown
Tlauciotepec	Oaxaca (Zapotecas)		Crown
Tlaxcala	Tlaxcala	600	Crown
Tlaxco	Puebla	692	Crown
Tlaxcoapan	Puebla	845	?
Tlaxiaco	Oaxaca	133	Francisco Vázquez
Tlaxmalac	Guerrero	225	Mateo Vázquez
Tlaxuca	Oaxaca (Zapotecas)		Crown

Population of Central Mexico

Tlayacapan	Morelos	806	?
Tlayecac	Morelos	679	Marqués del Valle
Tlazazalca	Michoacán	466	Crown
Tlazoltepec	Oaxaca (Zapotecas)		Alonso Días Carballar
Tliztaca	Guerrero	619	Crown
Tochenacuche	?		Crown
Tochimilco (Ocopetlayuca)	Puebla	93	Crown
Tolcayuca	Hidalgo	125	Crown Alonzo Pérez de Zamora
Tolimán	Guerrero	268	Alonso Martín
Toltepec	Oaxaca (Pochutla)		?
Toluca	México	45	Marqués del Valle
Tomatlán	Jalisco	358	Juan Fernández de Ixar
Tonagayotepec	Oaxaca (Mixes)		Crown
Tonaguia	Oaxaca	469	Crown
Tonalá	Puebla	432	Crown
Tonalá	Jalisco	658	Crown
Tonalá	Oaxaca	669	Crown
Tonaltepec	Oaxaca	820	Crown
Tonameca	Oaxaca (Pochutla)		Crown
Tonatico	Puebla	602	Crown
Tonatla	Guerrero (Huamuxtitlán)		?
Tonaya	Vera Cruz		?
Tonela	Vera Cruz (Coatzacoalcos)		Crown
Topa	Vera Cruz (Coatzacoalcos)		Crown
Topetina	Michoacán	563	Crown
Topila	Vera Cruz (Pánuco)		Crown
Topiltepec	Oaxaca	787	?
Topla	Vera Cruz (Pánuco)		Diego de Torres
Tornacustla	Hidalgo	211	Gonzalo Hernández de Mosquero

Appendix II: List of Communities

Totatiche	Zacatecas	351	Toribio de Bolaños
Totimehuacán	Puebla	218	Alonso Galeote
Totolapa	Guerrero	826	Crown
Totolapan	Oaxaca	135	Antonio de Villaroel
Totolapan	Morelos	621	Crown
Totolapilla	Oaxaca	372	Tristán de Arellano
Totolcingo	México	51	Crown
			Juan de Tovar
Totolinga	Oaxaca		
	(Zapotecas)		Francisco de Saldaña
Totolmoloya	Colima	342	Juan Bautista
Totoltepec	Guerrero	455	Crown
Totomistla-huacan	Guerrero	308	Crown
			Bernardino Vázquez de Tapia
			Beatriz de Estrada
Totontepec	Oaxaca		
	(Zapotecas)		Crown
Totututla	Vera Cruz (Río de Alvarado)		Crown
Tozuquilla	Jalisco (Guadalajara)		?
Tracache	Zacatecas	329	Diego Orozco
Tuchitepec	Vera Cruz		?
Tuchitlán	Puebla (Coxcotlán)		?
Tuchitlapilco	?		Crown
Tula	Hidalgo	474	Crown
Tulancingo	Hidalgo	48	Hernando de Avila
			Francisco de Terrazas
Tulantongo	Oaxaca	251	Alonso de Estrada
Tulimán	Guerrero	61	Crown
			Lorenzo de Porcallo
Tultepec	Guerrero	88	Crown
Tultitlán	México	56	Juan de Moscoso
Tupetongo	Oaxaca	469	Crown
Turicato	Michoacán	148	Antonio de Olivera
			Diego Hernández Nieto
Tustenec	Vera Cruz		Crown

Population of Central Mexico

Tutepetongo	Oaxaca	443	Juan Ochoa de Lejalde
Tutla	Oaxaca	737	?
Tutlaco	Oaxaca (Zapotecas)		Crown
Tutotepec	Oaxaca	57	Luis de Castilla
Tututepec	Hidalgo	245	Diego Rodríguez de Orozco
Tututepec	Guerrero	620	Crown Bernardino Vázquez de Tapia Beatriz de Estrada
Tuulilapa	Oaxaca		Alonso Martín Muñoz
Tuxcacuesco	Jalisco	517	Crown
Tuxpan	Jalisco	458	Crown
Tuxpan	Vera Cruz	194	Andrés de Tapia
Tuxtepec	Oaxaca	470	Crown
Tuxtla	Oaxaca		Luis de Castilla
Tuxtla	Vera Cruz	58	Marqués del Valle
Tuycán	Nueva Galicia		Hernando Flores
Tuzantalpa	Hidalgo	55	Cristóbal Cabezón Juan de Estrada
Tuzantla	Guerrero	622	Crown
Tuzapan	Puebla	304	Andrés de Tapia
Tzaindán	Oaxaca (Mixes)		?
Ucareo	Michoacán	477	Crown
Uchichila (Tzintzuntzan)	Michoacán	670	Crown
Uliacán	Vera Cruz (Coatzacoalcos)		Crown
Undameo	Michoacán		?
Uricho	Michoacán	291	Juan Infante
Uriparao	Michoacán	77	Juana de Torres
Uruápam	Michoacán	70	Pedro de Villegas
Usila	Oaxaca	478	Crown
Utlanzingo	Oaxaca (Río de Alvarado)		?
Utlapicula	Hidalgo	238	Francisco de Torres
Utlaquiquixtla	Vera Cruz		Juan López de Jimena
Utlaspa (San Jerónimo)	México	400	Sebastián de Moscoso

Appendix II: List of Communities 213

Utlatlán	Guerrero	109	Bernardino de Casasola
Uxitem	Oaxaca		?
Valles	San Luis Potosí	703	Crown
El Verde (San Salvador)	Puebla	817	?
Vichinaguia	Oaxaca (Zapotecas)		Crown
Villa Alta	Oaxaca	739	López de Velasco
Villanueva	Puebla	100	Pedro de Villanueva
Vistique	Jalisco	339	Martín Monje
Xacobo	Oaxaca (Mixes)		?
Xalacingo	Nayarit		Crown Alvaro de Bracamonte
Xalatlaco	México	239	Leonor de Andrada
Xalitla	?		Crown
Xalostoc	Morelos	678	Marqués del Valle
Xaltepec	Oaxaca	252	Angel de Villafañe
Xaltocan	México	198	Alonso de Avila
Xaputigua	Guerrero (Zacatula)		Crown
Xareta	Oaxaca (Zapotecas)		Hernando de Lorita
Xayatepec	Oaxaca (Mixes)		?
Xerveo	Michoacán	77	Juana de Torres
Xicaltepec	Oaxaca		Pedro Castellar
Xicotlán	Puebla	424	Crown
Xicotlán	Colima	643	Crown
Xichu	Guanajuato	292	Crown
Xihuacán	Guerrero	588	Crown
Xilitla	San Luis Potosí	427	Crown
Xilocingo	México	299	Catalina de Peralta
Xilotepec	Oaxaca (Mixes)		Crown
Xilotepec	México	73	Francisco de Velasco Luis de Quesada
Xiloteupa	Colima	644	Crown
Xilotzingo	México	72	Francisco Vázquez
Ximalcota	Guerrero	590	Crown

214 Population of Central Mexico

Xipacoya(Jasso)	Hidalgo	71	Juan Jasso
Xiquián	Nueva Galicia		Alonso Alvarez
Xiquipilco	México	74	Pedro de Roa
Xiquitlán	Jalisco	634	Crown
Xirosto	Jalisco (Purificación)		Alonso de Toro
Xiutetelco	Puebla	139	?
Xocochi	Oaxaca (Mixes)		?
Xocotepec	Jalisco (Purificación)		Francisco Pilo
Xocotitlán	México	220	Manuel de Villegas
Xocotlán	Jalisco (Purificación)		Francisco Cornejo
Xocotlán	Colima	636	Crown
Xocoyolo	Puebla		?
Xocutla	Vera Cruz (Pánuco)		Crown
Xocutla	Guerrero	532	Crown Cristóbal Manrecín
Xochiac	México	607	Crown
Xochicoatlán	Hidalgo	513	Crown
Xochicuatla	México	173	Juan Enríquez Magariño
Xochimilco	Nueva Galicia		Crown
Xochimilco	D. F.	445	Crown
Xochistlavaca	Guerrero	138	Francisco de Herrera
Xochitepec	Guerrero	532	Crown Cristóbal Manrecín
Xochitlán	Morelos	5	Marqués del Valle
Xonacatlán	Jalisco	642	Pedro de Simancas
Xoquicingo	México	773	?
Xuchitepec	Costa del Sur		Crown
Xulapa	?		Gómez de Hoyos
Xuma	Jalisco	647	Crown
Xuquila	Oaxaca	828	?
Yacapul	Guerrero (Acapulco)		Juana de Zúñiga
Yacastla	Oaxaca (Zapotecas)		Gonzalo Jiménez

Appendix II: List of Communities 215

Yacoche	Oaxaca	839	Crown
Yachinicingo	Oaxaca (Mixes)		?
Yagavila	Oaxaca (Zapotecas)		Crown
Yagayo	Oaxaca (Zapotecas)		Crown
Yagoni	Oaxaca	748	?
Yahualica	Hidalgo	629	Crown
Yahualica	Jalisco	320	Cristóbal Romero
Yahuatlán	Vera Cruz		Gregorio de Villalobos
Yalalag	Oaxaca	750	?
Yanhuitlán	Oaxaca	33	Gonzalo de Las Casas
Yao	Oaxaca (Mixes)		?
Yaquiza	Oaxaca (Mixes)		?
Yatobe	Oaxaca (Zapotecas)		Crown
Yauqila	Jalisco (Purificación)		Antón de Ortega
Yautepec	Oaxaca	434	Crown
Yautepec	Morelos	142	Marqués del Valle
Yavago	Oaxaca (Zapotecas)		Crown
Yaviche	Oaxaca	746	?
Yaxila	Oaxaca (Zapotecas)		Crown
Yecapixtla	Morelos	5	Marqués del Valle
Yetecomac	Hidalgo	456	Crown
Yetla	Jalisco (Purificación)		Bartolomé Chavarín
Yetoixtlahuaca	Puebla	424	Crown
Yeytepec	Oaxaca (Mixteca)		Tello de Medina
Yococui	Oaxaca	781	?
Yolotepec	Oaxaca	731	Alonso de Castellanos
Yoloxnoquilla	Oaxaca	789	?
Yotao	Oaxaca (Mixes)		?
Yotepec	Oaxaca (or Vera Cruz)		?
Yoveo	Oaxaca	833	?
Yucuxaco	Oaxaca	779	?

Population of Central Mexico

Yuriria	Guanajuato	538	Crown
Yztitlán	?		Crown
Zacalutla	Guerrero	596	Crown
Zacamal	Hidalgo	1	Melchor Pedraza
Zacango	México	770	Diego de Ocampo
Zacapila	Jalisco (Purificación)		Antón de Ortega
Zacapoaxtla	Puebla	757	?
Zacapu	Michoacán	214	Gonzalo de Avalos
Zacatepec	Oaxaca	279	Rafael de Trexo
Zacatitlán	Jalisco	647	Crown
Zacatlán	Nayarit		Crown
Zacatlán	Puebla	15	Antonio de Carbajal
Zacatula	Guerrero	582	Crown
Zacoalco	Jalisco	83	Crown Alonso de Avalos
Zacotlán	Bish. of Tlaxcala		Francisco de Oliveros
Zacualco	Morelos	124	Miguel de Solís
Zacualpa	Guerrero	61	Crown Lorenzo de Porcallo
Zacualpan	México	167	Alvaro de Santa Cruz
Zacualpan	México	97	Pedro de Salcedo
Zacualpan	Nayarit	388	Various encomenderos
Zahuatlán	Guerrero (Zacatula)		Crown
Zahuatlán	Morelos	5	Marqués del Valle
Zaiutepec	Oaxaca (Zapotecas)		Juan de Aldaza
Zalatitlán	Jalisco	496	Crown
Zaligua	Colima		Crown
Zaliguacán	Colima		Manuel de Cáceres
Zanatlán	Nayarit	377	Juan Sánchez Herrador
Zanguayo	Michoacán	481	Crown
Zapotán	Nayarit	375	Bartolomé Pérez
Zapotequilla	Oaxaca (Zapotecas)		?
Zapotitlán	Vera Cruz (Coatzacoalcos)		Diego de Lizama

Appendix II: List of Communities 217

Zapotitlán	Puebla	16	Gaspar de Garnica
			Francisco de Montaño
Zapotitlán	Guerrero	260	Crown
Zapotitlán	Jalisco	419	Crown
Zapotlán	Hidalgo	413	Crown
Zapotlán	Jalisco	489	Crown
Zautlán	Colima		Crown
Zayula	Colima		Crown
Zayula	Vera Cruz		
	(Pánuco)		Francisco Corzo
Zayultepec	Vera Cruz	256	Francisco Marín
Zempoal	Vera Cruz		Crown
Zempoala	Hidalgo	92	Crown
			Rodrigo de Sandoval
Zenzontepec	Oaxaca	324	García de Contreras
			Juan de Valdivieso
Zihuacoatlán	Vera Cruz (Jalapa)		Crown
Zihuatanejo	Guerrero	587	Crown
Zimapan	Hidalgo	811	?
Zimatlán	Guerrero		
	(Acapulco)		Pedro Pantoja
Zimatlán	Oaxaca	421	Crown
Zinacamastoc	Oaxaca	630	Crown
Zinacantepec	México	14	Juan de Sámano
Zinapécuaro	Michoacán	415	Crown
Zinguilucan	Hidalgo	807	Crown
Ziotepec	México	774	?
Zirándaro	Guerrero	302	Benavides
Zitlaltepec	México	608	Crown
Zitlaltomagua	Guerrero		
	(Acapulco)		Cecilia Lucero
Zoatlán	?		Crown
Zochila	Oaxaca	836	?
Zolcoacoa	Guerrero		
	(Zacatula)		Crown
Zongolica	Vera Cruz	315	Crown
			Martín de Sepúlveda
Zoquiapan	Oaxaca	463	Crown
Zoquío	Oaxaca (Mixes)		?

Zoquitlán	Oaxaca	153	Francisco Flores
Zoquitlán	Puebla	101	Crown
			Francisco de Montalvo
Zoyatitlanapa	Puebla	484	Crown
Zoyatlán	Oaxaca	631	Crown
Zoyatlán	Michoacán	568	Crown
Zultepec	Oaxaca	253	Marcos de Paredes
Zumpahuacán	México	219	Alonso de la Serna
Zumpamanique	Colima		Crown
Zumpango del Río	Guerrero	221	Cecilia Lucero
Zumpango	México	237	Alonso de Avila Alvarado
Zuyutepec	Oaxaca (Mixteca)		Juan de Tello de Medina

APPENDIX III

Numerical Index to Sketch Map

(Note: Map follows page 242. Where two or more places are included under the same number, they formed part of the same *encomienda* or *corregimiento*. They are listed separately in the Alphabetical List, Appendix II. Names of modern states in which communities lie are given in parentheses. Where an original Indian name has been changed, it is sometimes given also in parentheses.)

1. Atotonilco and Zacamal (Hid.).
2. Atlapulco (Méx.).
3. Axacuba (Hid.).
4. Apaxco (Méx.).
5. Yecapixtla, Pazulco, Atlamamulco, Tecajec, Zahuatlán, Xochitlán, Texcala, Achichipico (Mor.).
6. Amusgos (Oax.).
7. Acámbaro (Mich.).
8. Culhuacán (Méx.).
9. Chimalhuacán (Méx.).
10. Cuevas (Cuitlavaca) (Méx.).
11. Cuernavaca (Mor.).
12. Chiapa (Pueb.).
13. Calimaya (Méx.).
14. Zinacantepec (Méx.).
15. Zacatlán (Pueb.).
16. Zapotitlán, Calticán, Tequistepec (Pueb.).
17. Chilapa (Gro.).
18. Sirosto (Mich.).
19. Comanja and Naranja (Mich.).
20. Cuilapan (Oax.).
21. Chicomezuchil (Oax.).
22. Coatlán, Miahuatlán, Ejutla, Almolonga, Amatlán, Cuixtlán, Suchitepec (Oax.).
23. Sola (Oax.).
24. Epazoyuca (Hid.).
25. Eloxochitlán (Pueb.).

26. Etla (Oax.).
27. Huazalingo (Pueb.).
28. Cuatinchán (Pueb.).
29. Huaquechula (Pueb.).
30. Oaxaca (Oax.).
31. Ilamatlán and Atleucián (Hid.).
32. Igualtepec and Suchiquizala (Oax.).
33. Yanhuitlán (Oax.).
34. Metepec and Tepemachalco (Méx.).
35. Metztitlán, Tenango, Quezalatengo (Hid.).
36. Mixquic (Méx.).
37. Nextlalpan (Méx.).
38. Acolman (Méx.).
39. Oapan (Gro.).
40. Ocotlán (Oax.).
41. Papaloctipa and Tlacolultepec (Pueb.).
42. Teotihuacán (Méx.).
43. Tacuba (D. F.).
44. Tequixquiac (Méx.).
45. Toluca (Méx.).
46. Tlachichilpa and Malacatepec (Méx.).
47. Tlanchinol and Acuimantla (Hid.).
48. Tulancingo (Hid.).
49. Tlanalapa and Talistaca (Méx.).
50. Tepexpan (Méx.).
51. Tequisistlán and Totolcingo (Méx.).
52. Tianguistengo (Hid.).
53. Tenango del Valle (Méx.).
54. Tlacotepec (Méx.).
55. Texcatepec and Tuzantalpa (Hid.).
56. Tultitlán (Méx.).
57. Tutotepec and Nopala (Oax.).
58. Tuxtla (V. C.).
59. Tecamachalco (Pueb.).
60. Tlapa, Igualan, Tlachinola (Gro.).
61. Tlacozautitlán, Tulimán, Copalillo, Zacualpa, Mitlancingo, Temalacacingo, Oxtutla, Papalutla, Tenancingo, Mexquitlán (Gro.).
62. Tepeojuma (Pueb.).

Appendix III: Index to Sketch Map

63. Tepapayeca (Pueb.).
64. Tixtla (Gro.).
65. Tancítaro (Mich.).
66. Taximaroa (Mich.).
67. Tarímbaro (Mich.).
68. Tepetlolutla (Oax.).
69. Tamasulapa (Oax.).
70. Uruápam (Mich.).
71. Jasso (Xipacoya) (Hid.).
72. Xilotzingo (Méx.).
73. Xilotepec (Méx.).
74. Xiquipilco (Méx.).
75. Jojupango, Matlaque, Tonatico (Pueb.).
76. Jalapa (Oax.).
77. Cuitzeo, Huandacareo, Cupándaro, Uriparao, Xerveo (Mich.).
78. Atoyac (Jal.).
79. Sayula (Jal.).
80. Amacueca (Jal.).
81. Techalutla (Jal.).
82. Teocuitatlán (Jal.).
83. Zacualco (Jal.).
84. Cocula (Jal.).
85. Jocotepec (Jal.).
86. Chapala (Jal.).
87. Acaxuchitlán (Méx.).
88. Ayutla, Tultepec, Suchitonalá (Gro.).
89. Acultzingo (V. C.).
90. Apoala, Apasco, Jocotipac (Oax.).
91. Atoyaquillo (Oax.).
92. Zempoala (Hid.).
93. Tochimilco (Pueb.).
94. Chilcuautla (Hid.).
95. Coyoacán and Tacubaya (D. F.).
96. Sultepec (Tlax.).
97. Zacualpan and Tenancingo (Méx.).
98. Chapulco (Pueb.).
99. Chila (Pueb.).
100. Quecholac and Villanueva (Pueb.).
101. Zoquitlán (Pueb.).

102. Huatusco (V. C.).
103. Coyotepec (Oax.).
104. Coixtlavaca (Oax.).
105. Sosola and Tejotepec (Oax.).
106. Huachinango and Otzolotepec (Pueb.).
107. Chichiquila and Quimixtlán (Pueb.).
108. Huango (Mich.).
109. Huizuco and Utlatlán (Gro.).
110. Ixtapaluca (Méx.).
111. Huehuetlán (Pueb.).
112. La Rinconada (Ixcalpan) (Pueb.).
113. Indaparapeo (Mich.).
114. Ixtlán (Oax.).
115. Huacana (Mich.).
116. Michimaloya (Hid.).
117. Malinalco (Méx.).
118. Jocotlán (Jal.).
119. Churubusco (D. F.).
120. Ozolotepec (Oax.).
121. Pachuca (Hid.).
122. Tlamaco (Hid.).
123. Tepexi (Hid.) and Utlaspa (Méx.).
124. Tlacotepec, Temoac, Zacualco, Huazulco (Mor.).
125. Tolcayuca and Tizayuca (Hid.).
126. Acapulco, Zazapotla, Jaltianguis, Coyuca, Maxcaltepec, Atlala, Acamalutla, Yacapal, Naguala (Gro.).
127. Tepetlaoxtoc (Méx.).
128. Tlacuilotepec (Pueb.).
129. Texcaltitlán, Temascaltepec, Texupilco (Méx.).
130. Tezontepec (Hid.).
131. Tenampulco (Pueb.).
132. Tecámbaro (Mich.).
133. Tlaxiaco, Chicahuaxtla, Atoyac (Oax.).
134. Jicayán and Atoyac (Oax.).
135. Totolapan (Oax.).
136. Etlatongo and Huautla (Oax.).
137. Piaxtla (Pueb.).
138. Ometepec, Igualapa, Xochistlavaca (Gro.).
139. Xiutetelco–San Juan (Pueb.).

Appendix III: Index to Sketch Map 223

140. Jicayán (Oax).
141. Cacalotepec (Oax.).
142. Yautepec and Tepoztlán (Mor.).
143. Tamazunchale (S. L. P.).
144. Ocotepec (Oax.).
145. Ocotepec (Oax.).
146. Coyuca (Mich.).
147. Peribán and Tepehuacán (Mich.).
148. Turicato (Mich.).
149. Pahuatlán and Acaxuchitlán (Pueb.).
150. Ayacaxtepec (Oax.).
151. Metlaltoyuca (Pueb.).
152. Acayuca (Hid.).
153. Zoquitlán, Azuntepec, Ixpuchtepec, Necotepec, Olintepec, Tepexistepec (Oax.).
154. Achiutla, Chicome, Aguatepec, Mitla, Tecomaxtlavaca, Justlavaca (Oax.).
155. Astata (Oax.).
156. Actopan (Hid.).
157. Atotonilco el Grande (Hid.).
158. Atzcapotzalco (D. F.).
159. Autlán (Jal.).
160. Calpa, Tamalol, Chila (V. C.).
161. Acamixtlavaca (Gro.).
162. Chichilintla (V. C.).
163. Amatepec (Oax.).
164. Atlacomulco (Méx.).
165. Ixtapa (Méx.).
166. Cuautitlán (Méx.).
167. Axapuxco and Zacualpan (Méx.).
168. Coyuquilla (Gro.).
169. Coeneo and Carandacho (Mich.).
170. Coyotepec (Oax.).
171. Chapantongo (Hid.).
172. Cutzamala (Gro.).
173. Tlacotepec, Xochicuautla, Quezala (Méx.).
174. Chila and Mecatlán (V. C.).
175. Chucándiro (Mich.).
176. Cinamacatitlán and Cholo (Col.).

177. Huautla, Nanatiquipac, Ixcatlán (Oax.).
178. Epatlán (Pueb.).
179. Hueypoxtla (Méx.).
180. Suchitepec (Oax.).
181. Ixcatlán and Nopala (Oax.).
182. Ixcatoya (Oax.).
183. Ixmiquilpan and Tlacintla (Hid.).
184. Tiltepec and Jaltepetongo (Oax.).
185. Mixtepec (Oax.).
186. Metatepec and Tantoyuca (V. C.).
187. Cotaxtla (V. C.).
188. Mitlantongo (Oax.).
189. Malinaltepec (Gro.).
190. Ocuilan (Méx.).
191. Olinalá and Papalutla (Gro.).
192. Orizaba and Jalapa (V. C.).
193. Noxtepe (Gro.).
194. Papantla and Tuxpan (V. C.).
195. Pomucuarán (Mich.).
196. Puctla (Oax.).
197. Pungarabato (Mich.).
198. Xaltocán (Méx.).
199. Cocula (Gro.).
200. Tamazola, Amatlán, Axomulco, Cacaotepec, Suchitepec (Oax.).
201. Taymeo (Mich.).
202. Calpulalpan (Oax.).
203. Castilblanco (Ixcamoxtitlán) (Pueb.).
204. Achiotepec (Hid.).
205. Tecali (Pueb.).
206. Tecoloapan and Calcoyuca (Méx.).
207. Tlacamama (Oax.).
208. Texaquique (Méx.).
209. Tehuacán (Pueb.).
210. Tehuantepec (Oax.).
211. Tornacuxtla (Hid.).
212. Tempoal (V. C.).
213. Tepecuacuilco (Gro.).
214. Zacapu and Tescalco (Mich.).
215. Tetela del Río (Gro.).

Appendix III: Index to Sketch Map 225

216. Teotlalco and Centayuca (Pueb.).
217. Coatepec (Oax.).
218. Totimehuacán (Pueb.).
219. Zumpahuacán and Soacango (Méx.).
220. Xocotitlán (Méx.).
221. Zumpango (Gro.).
222. Cuapan (Pueb.).
223. Oaxaca Viejo (Oax.).
224. Macuiltianguis and Cusmiquila (Oax.).
225. Tlaxmalac and Mayanala (Gro.).
226. Tetipac (Gro.).
227. Ostuma and Alahuixtlán (Gro.).
228. Oaxtepec (Mor.).
229. Huayacocotla (V. C.).
230. Mizquiahuala (Hid.).
231. Jumiltepec (Mor.).
232. Tepetitlán (Hid.).
233. Ayucan, Capulhuac, Caquete, Huejuca, Tepexoxuca (Méx.).
234. Juchitlán (Gro.).
235. Tetela (Pueb.).
236. Macuixóchitl (Hid.).
237. Zumpango (Méx.).
238. Chichatlán, Talchicua, Utlapicula (Hid.).
239. Xalatlaco (Méx.).
240. Tlanocopán–Santa María (Hid.).
241. Soyanaquilpan (Méx.).
242. Cacahuatepec (Gro.).
243. Jololpan (Pueb.).
244. Teopantlán (Pueb.).
245. Tututepec (Hid.).
246. Chachoapan (Oax.).
247. Mazatlán (Oax.).
248. Otlatitlán (V. C.).
249. Teozatlán (Oax.).
250. Huaynamota (Nay.).
251. Tulantongo (Oax.).
252. Xaltepec (Oax.).
253. Zultepec (Oax.).
254. Chinameca-Mixteca (V. C.).

255. Chilapa, Monzapa, Mazatlam, Calcuautla (V. C.).
256. Jaltipán, Olutla, Acayuca, Chacalapa, Tequistepec, Tiquiquipa, Zayultepec (V. C.).
257. Tecociapa, Ahuatitlán, Mecatixpam (Col.).
258. Petatlán (Col.).
259. Acaguapixca (Gro.).
260. Atenchancaleca and Zapotitlán (Gro.).
261. Chipila (Gro.).
262. Huitlalotla and Coahuayutla (Gro.).
263. Huiztlán (Gro.).
264. Tanquián (S. L. P.).
265. Mezaa (Mich.).
266. Mila (Gro.).
267. Puchutlán (Gro.).
268. Tolimán (Gro.).
269. Japutica (Gro.).
270. Ajijic (Jal.).
271. Axochitlán (Pueb.).
272. Atengo (Hid.).
273. Acatlán (Hid.).
274. Ayutla (Oax.).
275. Atlimaxacingo del Río (Gro.).
276. Azoyú (Gro.).
277. Atlixtac (Gro.).
278. Atlahuaca (Oax.).
279. Zacatepec (Oax.).
280. Chayuco (Oax.).
281. Moloacán (V. C.).
282. Coatzingo (Pueb.).
283. Chiconamel (V. C.).
284. Acapuzalco (Gro.).
285. Cutzco (Mich.).
286. Comalá (Col.).
287. Cuitlapa (Gro.).
288. Oxtotipac (Méx.).
289. Huautla (Hid.).
290. Puruándiro (Mich.).
291. Erongarícuaro, Uricho, Huiramángaro, Pichátoro (Mich.).
292. Xichu (Gto.). [*Not corrected on map*]

293. Tlaquilpa (Hid.).
294. Texhuacán (V. C.).
295. Atempa (Gro.).
296. Macatlán (S. L. P.).
297. Marabatío (Mich.).
298. Nexpa and Tlacolula (Gro.).
299. Otzolotepec, Mimiapan, Xilotzingo (Méx.).
300. Petlacala (Oax.).
301. Huamuxtitlán (Gro.).
302. Zirándaro (Gro.).
303. Tecama (Méx.).
304. Tuzapan (Pueb.).
305. Tlapanaloyan (Méx.).
306. Tiripitío (Mich.).
307. Tarecuato (Mich.).
308. Totomixtlahuacan (Gro.).
309. Tenango-Tepexi (Gro.).
310. Teotalcingo and Etlagón (Oax.).
311. Tequixistlán (Oax.).
312. Mixtepec (Oax.).
313. Temascaltepec (Oax.).
314. Jamiltepec (Oax.).
315. Zongolica (V. C.).
316. Huatulco and Suchitepec (Oax.).
317. Tetepec (Oax.).
318. Teozacualco (Oax.).
319. Tlacotepec (Oax.).
320. Yahualica (Jal.).
321. Contla (Jal.).
322. Chichicastepec (Oax.).
323. Chicahuaxtla (Oax.).
324. Zenzontepec (Oax.).
325. Ixtepexi (Oax.).
326. Mexcalcingo (Pueb.).
327. Mexticacán (Jal.).
328. Jalpa (Zac.).
329. Moyahua, Mezquituta, Tracache (Zac.).
330. Ocotlán (Jal.).
331. Ocotic (Jal.).

228 Population of Central Mexico

332. Pátzcuaro, Cúzaro, Huanimeo, Purenxícuaro, Serandaguacho (Mich.).
333. Juchitlán (Jal.).
334. Juchipila (Zac.).
335. Teacalco (Méx.).
336. Tezontepec (Hid.).
337. Pantepec (Pueb.).
338. Tepec (Jal.).
339. Tenamaxtlán, Tecolotlán, Vistique (Jal.).
340. Tlacochahuaya (Oax.).
341. Tlacoloaxtla (Col.).
342. Totolmoloya (Col.).
343. Tecuxuacán (Col.).
344. Tecociapa (Col.).
345. Temacatepan (Col.).
346. Chiapan, Tecocitlán, Coxiutlán (Col.); Amatlán (Mich.); Tezontlán (Jal.).
347. Tecolapa (Col.).
348. Tepehuacán (Col.).
349. Teponahuasco (Jal.).
350. Teul (Zac.).
351. Tlaltenango, Cicacalco, Totatiche, Momax, Huejúcar (Zac.).
352. Tepechitlán (Zac.).
353. Tepatitlán and Tepehuacán (Nay.).
354. Tequepespan and Camotlán (Nay.).
355. Tetitlán (Nay.).
356. Tepuzhuacán (Nay.).
357. Tepetlauaca (Nay.).
358. Tomatlán (Jal.).
359. Tala and Tezula (Jal.).
360. Tesixtán (Jal.).
361. Tequepaca (Jal.).
362. Tlacotán (Jal.).
363. Jalapa (Oax.).
364. Jalpan (Qto.).
365. Tancoyol (Qto.).
366. Tampamolón (S. L. P.).
367. Temapache (S. L. P.).
368. Tancuayalab (S. L. P.).

Appendix III: Index to Sketch Map

369. Ozuluama and Moyutla (V. C.).
370. Tiltepec (Oax.).
371. Tepanzacualco (Oax.).
372. Totolapilla (Oax.).
373. Tequixtepec (Oax.).
374. Tenango (Oax.).
375. Zapotán (Nay.).
376. Ciutlán (Jal.).
377. Zanatlán (Nay.).
378. Chiepetlán (Gro.).
379. Caltitlán (Oax.).
380. Apetatuca (Nay.).
381. Ahuacatlán and Suchipil (Nay.).
382. Amajaque (Nay.).
383. Amatlán (Nay.).
384. Atengoychán (Jal.).
385. Apozol (Zac.).
386. Acaponeta (Nay.).
387. Atiztac (Jal.).
388. Zacualpan (Nay.).
389. Chacala (Nay.).
390. Ixtapa (Nay.).
391. Ixcatán (Jal.).
392. Ixcuintepec (Oax.).
393. Ahuacapan, Mixtlán, Tecomatlán (Jal.).
394. Nexpa and Tauzán (Hid.).
395. Tamiahua (V. C.).
396. Jalisco (Nay.).
397. Jalcocotlán and Mecatlán (Nay.).
398. Jaltempa (Nay.).
399. Jala (Nay.).
400. Utlaspa–San Jerónimo (Méx.).
401. Acatlán (Pueb.).
402. Atitlaquia and Tlacustepec (Hid.).
403. Ameca (Jal.).
404. Atempan (Pueb.).
405. Ahuatlán (Pueb.).
406. Araro (Mich.).
407. Amatepec (Méx.).

408. Atemajac (Jal.).
409. Atenango (Gro.).
410. Colucan (Pueb.).
411. Chietla (Pueb.).
412. Cholula (Pueb.).
413. Zapotlán (Hid.).
414. Coxcatlán (Pueb.).
415. Zinapécuaro and Araro (Mich.).
416. Chilchota (Mich.).
417. Cuzalapa (Jal.).
418. Copala (Jal.).
419. Zapotitlán (Jal.).
420. Sihuatlán (Jal.).
421. Zimatlán and Tepezimatlán (Oax.).
422. Cosamaloapan (V. C.).
423. Chalco, Amecameca, Tlamanalco, Tenango, Chimalhuacán (Méx.).
424. Chiautla, Cohetzala, Ixcamilpa, Chila, Ocotlán, Xicotlán, Huehuetlán, Yetoixtlahuaca (Pueb.).
425. Chiconautla (Méx.).
426. Huatlavaca (Pueb.).
427. Xilitla (S. L. P.).
428. Huejutla (Hid.).
429. Huaniqueo (Mich.).
430. Huamelula and Tlacolula (Oax.).
431. Huajolotitlán (Oax.).
432. Izúcar and Tonalá (Pueb.).
433. Istlahuaca (Méx.).
434. Yautepec (Oax.).
435. Ixtepec (Oax.).
436. Iguala (Gro.).
437. Molango (Hid.).
438. Nochistlán (Zac.).
439. Miahuatlán (Oax.).
440. Nochistlán (Oax.).
441. Nejapa (Oax.).
442. Ocotlán (Oax.).
443. Papalotepec and Tutepetongo (Oax.).
444. Quiotepec (Oax.).

Appendix III: Index to Sketch Map

445. Xochimilco (D. F.).
446. Tlacotepec (Gro.).
447. Tecomavaca (Oax.).
448. Teotitlán del Camino and Justepec (Oax.).
449. Tequila (V. C.).
450. Tejaluca (Pueb.).
451. Tlatlauquitepec (Pueb.).
452. Tepeaca (Pueb.).
453. Tilapa (Pueb.).
454. Teloloapan (Gro.).
455. Totoltepec (Gro.).
456. Tetepango and Yetecomac (Hid.).
457. Tlacotlapilco (Hid.).
458. Tuxpan (Jal.).
459. Tamazula (Jal.).
460. Tlahuelilpa (Hid.).
461. Tetela de Ocampo (Pueb.).
462. Tlacolula (Oax.).
463. Teococuilco, Atepec, Jaltianguis, Zoquiapan (Oax.).
464. Teposcolula (Oax.).
465. Tejupan (Oax.).
466. Tlazazalca (Mich.).
467. Tingüindín and Tacuázcaro (Mich.).
468. Taxco, Atzala, Tamacasapa (Gro.).
469. Tonaguia and Tupetongo (Oax.).
470. Tuxtepec (Oax.).
471. Teotlaxco (Oax.).
472. Mixtepec, Tepexi, Tlacotepec (Oax.).
473. Teutila (Oax.).
474. Tula (Hid.).
475. Texcoco (Méx.).
576. Huitzilapan (Méx.).
477. Ucareo, Aguándero, Irechato (Mich.).
478. Usila (Oax.).
479. Jilotlán (Jal.).
480. Jalapa and Acatlán (Gro.).
481. Jacona, Cuarachán, Chicarapo, Tamandagapeo, Zanguayo (Mich.).
482. Jiquilpan (Mich.).

483. Jaltepec (Oax.).
484. Zoyatitlanapa (Pueb.).
485. Jonotla (Pueb.).
486. Necoxtla (Pueb.).
487. Atzalán (V. C.).
488. Matatlán (Jal.).
489. Zapotlán (Jal.).
490. Soyaltepec and Tonaltepec (Oax.).
491. Ajuchitlán (Gro.).
492. Malila (Hid.).
493. Chiquimitío (Mich.).
494. Capula (Mich.).
495. Cuyutlán (Jal.).
496. Zalatitlán (Jal.).
497. Poncitlán and Cuitzeo (Jal.).
498. Choapan (Oax.).
499. Cacalotepec (Oax.).
500. Comaltepec (Oax.).
501. Cuicatlán (Oax.).
502. Sayula (Hid.).
503. Ario and Iztaro (Mich.).
504. Macuilxóchitl and Teotitlán del Valle (Oax.).
505. Maltrata (V. C.).
506. Ocuituco (Mor.).
507. Pajacuarán (Mich.).
508. Pómaro (Mich.).
509. Quezalapa (Col.).
510. Coalcomán (Mich.).
511. Pochutla (Oax.).
512. Ixtacamaxtitlán (Pueb.).
513. Xochicoatlán (Hid.).
514. Tepatepec and Tepeitic (Hid.).
515. Tenango (Gro.).
516. Teutlán (Jal.).
517. Tuxcacuesco (Jal.).
518. Tequepa (Col.).
519. Tepetitango (Col.).
520. Tecomán (Col.).
521. Tampico (V. C.).

Appendix III: Index to Sketch Map   233

522. Copala and Juchitlán (Gro.).
523. Teozapotlán (Oax.).
524. Tepic (Nay.).
525. Matatlán (Jal.).
526. Tamuín (S. L. P.).
527. Talea (Oax.).
528. Tenayuca (D. F.).
529. Huapanapa (Oax.).
530. Tepeucila (Oax.).
531. Jicotepec (Pueb.).
532. Xochitepec, Pochotitlán, Xocutla (Gro.).
533. Chazumba (Oax.).
534. Sentispac (Nay.).
535. Amula (Jal.).
536. Aquila (Mich.).
537. Ixhuatlán (V. C.).
538. Yuriria, Guaríscaro, San Miguel, Tepécuaro (Gto.).
539. Charapaco (Mich.).
540. Chilpopotlán (Hid.).
541. Ahuatipán (Hid.).
542. Titicapa (Oax.).
543. Chichicapa (Oax.).
544. Talistaca (Oax.).
545. Tisupan (Mich.).
546. Coatitlán, Acaluacán, Ecatepec (Méx.).
547. Tepanco (Pueb.).
548. Jicalán (Mich.).
549. Tenixtepec (V. C.).
550. Ojitipa (S. L. P.).
551. Juchitlán (Gro.).
552. Alpatlahuac (Pueb.).
553. Chilpopocatlán (Hid.).
554. Acatzingo (Pueb.).
555. Huixtac (Gro.).
556. Ixtayutla (Oax.).
557. Ixcateopan (Gro.).
558. Ojitlán (Oax.).
559. Oconahua (Jal.).
560. Pinotepa (Oax.).

561. Lacoaba (Mich.).
562. Nexpa (Mich.).
563. Topetina (Mich.).
564. Chacala (Mich.).
565. Cihuatlán (Mich.).
566. Tepexi (Pueb.).
567. Borona (Mich.).
568. Zoyotlán (Mich.).
569. Atlán (Mich.).
570. Cuacuatlán (Mich.).
571. Mexcaloacán (Mich.).
572. Ciutlán (Mich.).
573. Pantla (Gro.).
574. Ixtapa (Gro.).
575. Tecomatlán (Gro.).
576. Ixtapa (Mich.).
577. Piquitla (Mich.).
578. Metlapan (Mich.).
579. Pichique (Gro.).
580. Ayutla (Gro.).
581. Pustlán (Gro.).
582. Zacatula (Gro.).
583. Acalpica (Gro.).
584. Camutla and Hueytlán (Gro.).
585. Temalhuacán (Gro.).
586. Paxalo (Gro.).
587. Zihuatanejo (Gro.).
588. Xihuacán (Gro.).
589. Petatlán (Gro.).
590. Ximalcota (Gro.).
591. Juluchuga (Gro.).
592. Nuxco (Gro.).
593. Cihuatlán (Gro.).
594. Pamutla (Gro.).
595. Tecpan (Gro.).
596. Zacalutla (Gro.).
597. Cayaco (Gro.).
598. Ixtayucan (Pueb.).
599. Huejotzingo (Pueb.).

Appendix III: Index to Sketch Map 235

600. Tlaxcala (Tlax.).
601. México (D. F.).
602. Tonatico (Pueb.).
603. Tlapotongo (Pueb.).
604. Colima (Col.).
605. Coatepec (Méx.).
606. Tlapaxala (Pueb.).
607. Atlatlauca and Xochiac (Méx.).
608. Zitlaltepec (Méx.).
609. Chinantla (Pueb.).
610. Hueytlalpa, Conzozotla, Esamayeco (Pueb.).
611. Huixquilucan (Méx.).
612. Ixcuinquitlapilco (Hid.).
613. Mexicalcingo (D. F.).
614. Mezquitlán (Gro.).
615. Otumba (Méx.).
616. Tepalcatepec (Mich.).
617. Tepotzotlán (Méx.).
618. Tequixtepec (Oax.).
619. Tliztaca (Gro.).
620. Tututepec (Gro.).
621. Totolapan (Mor.).
622. Tuzantla (Gro.).
623. Jalacingo (V. C.).
624. Cozoaltepec, Amatlán (Oax.).
625. Ixtepec (V. C.).
626. Misantla (V. C.).
627. Naolingo, Almería, Colipa, Malinalcingo, Tapacoya, Tamomolo (V. C.).
628. Tlacotalpan (V. C.).
629. Yahualica (Hid.).
630. Ayautla, Tepeapa, Putlancingo, Zinacamostoc (Oax.).
631. Soyaltepec and Zoyatlán (Oax.).
632. Peñoles (Oax.).
633. Ixtapa (Col.).
634. Xiquitlán (Jal.).
635. Tamala (Col.).
636. Xocotlán (Mich.).
637. Tlacavanas (Mich.).

638. Petlayuneca (Col.).
639. Acatlán (Col.).
640. Malacatlán (Col.).
641. Coatlán (Col.).
642. Xonacatlán (Jal.).
643. Xicotlán (Col.).
644. Xiloteupa (Col.).
645. Juluapan (Col.).
646. Cuzcatlán (Col.).
647. Moxuma, Achiotla, Ambuma, Salipa, Zacatitlán, Tequepila, Xuma, Penjema (Jal.).
648. Mazatlán (Jal.).
649. Miahuatlán (Jal.).
650. Maloastla (Col.).
651. Ahuacatlán (Jal.).
652. Tepeapulco (Hid.).
653. Jerécuaro (Gto.).
654. Teziutlán (Pueb.).
655. Tatetla (Pueb.).
656. Teremendo and Jasso (Mich.).
657. Tlaquepaque (Jal.).
658. Tonalá (Jal.).
659. Tetlán (Jal.).
660. Tlajomulco (Jal.).
661. Ahualulco (Jal.).
662. Etzatlán (Jal.).
663. Huehuetlán (S. L. P.).
664. Bocaneo (Mich.).
665. Ixtlahuacán (Col.).
666. Tlalnepantla (Méx.).
667. Jonacatepec (Mor.).
668. Mitla (Oax.).
669. Tonalá (Oax.).
670. Uchichila (Tzintzuntzan) (Mich.).
671. Jantetelco (Mor.).
672. Tepaltzingo (Mor.).
673. Amayuca (Mor.).
674. Telistac (Mor.).
675. Tepexco (Pueb.).

Appendix III: Index to Sketch Map 237

676. Amacuitlapilco (Mor.).
677. Atotonilco (Mor.).
678. Xalostoc (Mor.).
679. Tlayecac (Mor.).
680. Chalcacingo (Mor.).
681. Tetela (Mor.).
682. Atlacahualoya (Mor.).
683. Coatzacoalcos (V. C.).
684. Culiacán (Sin.).
685. Ixcuintepec and Elotepec (Oax.).
686. Ixtayuca (Pueb.).
687. Maninaltepec (Oax.).
688. Minzapa (V. C.).
689. Mitepec (Pueb.).
690. Nopalucan (Pueb.).
691. Pánuco (V. C.).
692. Tlaxco (Pueb.).
693. Puebla (Pueb.).
694. Indameo (Mich.).
695. [*Corrected*]
696. Huichapan (Hid.).
697. Huexotla (Méx.).
698. El Seco–San Salvador and Telitlazingo (Pueb.).
699. Ixtapalapa (D. F.).
700. Chalchicomula (Pueb.).
701. Chichicaxtla (Hid.).
702. Chapa de Mota (Méx.).
703. Valles (S. L. P.).
704. Coxcotlán (S. L. P.).
705. Apam (Hid.).
706. Calpulalpan (Tlax.).
707. Cuetzala (Gro.).
708. Milpa Alta (D. F.).
709. Tlacuiltenango (Mor.).
710. Aljojuca (Pueb.).
711. Amatlán (V. C.).
712. Tlaliscoyán (V. C.).
713. Silacayoapán (V. C.).
714. Calihuala (Oax.).

715. Tlacolula (V. C.).
716. Tepetlán (V. C.).
717. Miahuatlán (V. C.).
718. Almolonga (V. C.).
719. Actopan (V. C.).
720. Acatlán (V. C.).
721. Chalma (Pueb.).
722. Calmeca (Pueb.).
723. Coatepec (Pueb.).
724. Igualtepec (Oax.).
725. Huajuapan (Oax.).
726. Estetla and Totomachapa (Oax.).
727. Cuyotepexi (Oax.).
728. Ixcatlán (Oax.).
729. Tutepetongo (Oax.).
730. Chalcatongo (Oax.).
731. Yolotepec (Oax.).
732. Ayotzinapa (Gro.).
733. Río Hondo (Oax.).
734. Lapaguía and Pilcintepec (Oax.).
735. Ixcatlán–San Miguel el Grande (Oax.).
736. Ocotepec–Santo Tomás (Oax.).
737. Tutla (Oax.).
738. Coatlán–Santa María (Oax.).
739. Villa Alta–San Ildefonso (Oax.).
740. Moctún (Oax.).
741. Tlahuilotepec (Oax.).
742. Alotepec (Oax.).
743. Metlaltepec (Oax.).
744. Chisme (Oax.).
745. Tepitongo (Oax.).
746. Yaviche (Oax.).
747. Temascalapa (Oax.).
748. Yagoni (Oax.).
749. Jalahui (Oax.).
750. Yalalag (Oax.).
751. Ayoquezco (Oax.).
752. Sevina (Mich.).
753. Jalpan (Pueb.).

Appendix III: Index to Sketch Map 239

754. Ameluca (Pueb.).
755. Huitzila and Caxitlantongo (Pueb.).
756. Chicontepec (V. C.).
757. Zacapoaxtla and Nauzontla (Pueb.).
758. Jilotepec (V. C.).
759. Coacoazintla and Chapultepec (V. C.).
760. San Juan de Ulúa (V. C.).
761. Tlacotepec (Pueb.).
762. Huatusco, Coscomaltepec, Alpatlahuaya (V. C.).
763. Tepetlaxco, Ixhuatlán (V. C.).
764. Chocamán (V. C.).
765. Atzitzintla (V. C.).
766. Petlalcingo (Pueb.).
767. Mochtitlán (Gro.).
768. Temaxcalapa (Méx.).
769. Huitziltepec (Gro.).
770. Coatepec de las Beatas (Méx.).
771. Pizcaya (Gro.).
772. Coatlán and Acuitlapan (Gro.).
773. Xoquicingo (Méx.).
774. Ziotepec (Méx.).
775. Tilcuautla (Hid.).
776. Huehuetoca (Méx.).
777. Coyotepec (Méx.).
778. Teoloyucan (Méx.).
779. Yucuxaco (Oax.).
780. Tataltepec (Oax.).
781. Yococui (Oax.).
782. Huajolotitlán (Oax.).
783. Huiltepec (Oax.).
784. Cuquila (Oax.).
785. Tenexpa (Oax.).
786. Acaltepec (Oax.).
787. Topiltepec (Oax.).
788. Tlacuatzintepec, Quezalapa, Tecomaltepec (Oax.).
789. Yoloxnoquilla (Oax.).
790. Maquili (Mich.).
791. Tequila (Jal.).
792. Hostotipaquillo (Jal.).

793. Chimaltitlán (Jal.).
794. Compostela (Nay.).
795. Mascota (Jal.).
796. Huachinango (Jal.).
797. Teocaltiche (Jal.).
798. Mitic (Jal.).
799. Tecualtitlán (Jal.).
800. San Pedro (S. L. P.).
801. Alcececa (V. C.).
802. Pánuco (Villa) (V. C.).
803. Tancanhuitz (S. L. P.).
804. Axtla (S. L. P.).
805. Analco (Jal.).
806. Tlayacapan (Mor.).
807. Zinguilucan (Hid.).
808. Aquilpa (Gro.).
809. Alpoyeca (Gro.).
810. Atlimaxacingo del Monte (Gro.).
811. Zimapan (Hid.).
812. Axochiapan (Mor.).
813. Temoac (Mor.).
814. Texmelucan (Pueb.).
815. Atzala (Pueb.).
816. Cahuitlán (Oax.).
817. El Verde–San Salvador (Pueb.).
818. Huauclilla (Oax.).
819. Ostula (Mich.).
820. Tonaltepec (Oax.).
821. Cotahuixtla (Oax.).
822. Alcozaue and Mixtanejo (Col.).
823. Matalcingo (Mich.).
824. Alima (Col.).
825. Chiametla (Col.).
826. Totolapa (Gro.).
827. Lachichivia (Oax.).
828. Xuquila (Oax.).
829. Teitipac and Cetusco (Oax.).
830. Teitipac (Oax.).
831. Tepuxtepec (Oax.).

Appendix III: Index to Sketch Map

832. Huitepec (Oax.).
833. Yoveo (Oax.).
834. Camotlán (Oax.).
835. Camotlán (Oax.).
836. Zochila (Oax.).
837. Lalopa (Oax.).
838. Tagni and Lazagaya (Oax.).
839. Yacochi (Oax.).
840. Jalcomulco (V. C.).
841. Coatepec (V. C.).
842. El Chico (Xicochinilco) (V. C.).
843. Huitzizilapan (Méx.).
844. Jalapa (V. C.).
845. Tlaxcoapan (Pueb.).
846. Teotlalcingo (Pueb.).
847. Tlapancingo (Oax.).
848. Tlacotepec and Tepeji (Oax.).
849. Amoltepec (Oax.).
850. Sahuayo (Mich.).
851. Guaracha (Mich.).
852. Ixtlán (Mich.).
853. Tangamandapio (Mich.).